With this impressive genealogy of the thinking that underwrites current interest in epigenetics, Meloni provides us with a much-needed frame for one of the most compelling ideas in contemporary bioscience. This book should be required reading for anyone curious about the ways that we, as living beings, carry the past both with and within us.

Ed Cohen, Professor of Women's and Gender Studies, Rutgers University, author of *A Body Worth Defending*

Impressionable Biologies, a tour de force, engages with a concept of inherent bodily plasticity recognized as one form of another from classical humoralism to present day epigenetic effects due to the increasingly toxic environments in which we now live.

Margaret Lock, PhD, author of *The Alzheimer Conundrum: Entanglements of Aging and Dementia*

Impressionable Biologies

During the twentieth century, genes were considered the controlling force of life processes, and the transfer of DNA was the definitive explanation for biological heredity. Such views shaped the politics of human heredity: in the eugenic era, controlling heredity meant intervening in the distribution of "good" and "bad" genes. However, since the turn of the twenty-first century, this centrality of genes has been challenged by a number of "postgenomic" disciplines. The rise of epigenetics in particular signals a shift from notions of biological fixedness to ideas of plasticity and "impressionability" of biological material.

This book investigates the long history of beliefs about the plasticity of human biology, starting with ancient medicine, and analyses the biopolitical techniques required to govern such permeability. It looks at the emergence of the modern body of biomedicine as a displacement or possibly reconfiguration of earlier plastic views. Finally, it analyses the return of plasticity to contemporary postgenomic views and argues that postgenomic plasticity is neither a modernistic plasticity of instrumental management of the body nor a postmodernist celebration of potentialities. It is instead a plasticity that disrupts clear boundaries between openness and determination, individual and community, with important implications for notions of risk, responsibility and intervention.

Maurizio Meloni is a social theorist and a science and technology studies scholar. He is the author of *Political Biology* (Palgrave 2016), co-editor of *Biosocial Matters* (Wiley 2016) and chief editor of the *Palgrave Handbook of Biology and Society* (2018). He is Associate Professor of Sociology at Deakin University, Australia.

Impressionable Biologies

From the Archaeology of Plasticity to the Sociology of Epigenetics

MAURIZIO MELONI

NEW YORK AND LONDON

First published 2019
by Routledge
52 Vanderbilt Avenue, New York, NY 10017

and by Routledge
2 Park Square, Milton Park, Abingdon, Oxon, OX14 4RN

Routledge is an imprint of the Taylor & Francis Group, an informa business

Library of Congress Cataloging-in-Publication Data
A catalog record for this title has been requested

ISBN: 978-1-138-04940-6 (hbk)
ISBN: 978-1-138-04941-3 (pbk)
ISBN: 978-1-315-16958-3 (ebk)

Typeset in Avenir and Dante
by Out of House Publishing

Contents

Contents

Preface and acknowledgements

Problematizing the turn to plasticity

Since the turn of the twenty-first century, human biology has become seemingly more sensitive and perhaps vulnerable to exposure to biophysical environments and sociocultural experiences. Scientific claims about the openness of the brain, the body, genome expression and even biological heredity to history, biography and culture have become increasingly visible over the last two decades. Paralleling a similar process in the neurosciences, the powerful rise of epigenetics and the consolidation of developmental origins of health and disease (DOHaD) since 2000 signals a shift away from notions of biological fixedness and toward ideas of "impressionability" of biological material – ideas that seemed forgotten during most of the twentieth century at the peak of genetic explanations. Rather than being hardwired, gene expression, brain structures and biological bodies are rewritten as alterable and capable of modifying themselves in response to pressures from inside and outside the body itself. In a word, they are described as *plastic*. Arguments about "biosocial research" and "biosocial entanglement" also reflect this awareness of a multi-causal and multi-level co-determination of social and biological matter, of what lies beyond and within the skin. Alongside these epistemic shifts, a whole new landscape of ethical and sociological quandaries is rapidly unfolding. In this landscape, some of the conventional dichotomies forged during the last century are rapidly becoming obsolete: that biological heredity is not environment and environment is not heredity; that cultural factors are above the skin and not in the gut, the bones, or the genes; that genes are either the bases of behaviours or are irrelevant to them; that if race is a social construction, it is not a biological reality; that biological explanations are individualistic and erase social factors, while sociocultural explanations omit biological embedding; that heredity stops at birth and is only contributed to by biological parents; that plasticity is counter to biological determinism and racialism, and taking the side of nurture is more progressive than endorsing the stability of traits in developmental debates.

Rather than examining these claims about plasticity directly in a prescriptive fashion, this book takes a longer genealogical perspective to suggest a more complicated state of affairs about the self-proclaimed revolutionary nature of these ideas. This *longue durée* history focuses on the widespread ancient and early modern belief in the plasticity of biological matter, its permeability to surroundings, the link between environment, food and health, and the biopolitical techniques required to govern a porous body. Rather than simply the latest episode in a history of innovation, it sees the present challenge to biological fixedness as encompassing the notions of multiple historical times and perturbingly resonating with older and non-Western epistemologies of the body.

The book problematizes the ubiquitous claim that epigenetics and related ideas of plasticity are "a break from past thinking" about heredity (Bonduriansky and Day, 2018). It reminds the reader that past thinking about heredity (i.e. genetics) was in itself a huge (revolutionary) break with traditional views of heredity and generation.[1] These older views displayed some of the characteristics (including a belief in parental and ancestral influences on heredity, especially maternal) that are resurfacing today in the molecular language of twenty-first-century biology (see Zimmer, 2018: 542–545). If plasticity means an ongoing interaction with the surrounding environment, and biological matter is always nurtured and situated, corporeal plasticity seems the standard, not the revolutionary, view in a global history of body–world configurations; at least, that is, before the rise of the modern biomedical body in Europe after the second half of the nineteenth century. Rather than an explanation of plasticity, the underlying question emerging from this book is the opposite: how did biological fixity (to a certain degree) and abstract universality of the body come into being? How did nineteenth-century European biology come to suggest an idea of relative insulation of the body, heredity and internal milieu as a condition for independence, freedom and individuality (Bernard, 1878; Weismann, 1891)? How did such views later come to dominate the twentieth century and steer competing paradigms?

By "conjugating" (Anderson, 2009) knowledge and ethical visions of the body generated by the latest advancements in molecular biology with a range of discourses about biological matter preceding this nineteenth-century modernistic break, this book raises questions about the temporality, novelty, direction and pace of change in historical knowledge. It points to a deeper genealogical tree for the epigenetic body that is well beyond the controversial "return of Lamarckism", given that I situate Lamarckism within a much older history of plasticity of organisms to their surroundings. When William James claims that pre-Darwinians "thought only of adaptation" and "made organisms plastic to environment" (1988), I take this notion seriously and look at it as an intellectual thread to cover periods well before modern evolutionary debates.

To offer an intellectual map beyond twentieth-century biology–society debates, *Impressionable Biologies* follows three axes of analysis: science, knowledge and power.

1) The scientific axis addresses a growing obsolescence of modernistic views of the body, biology and heredity based on notions of a secure and unique individual core, a relative separateness from environmental factors, and the skin as a well-defined boundary between inner and outer, the biological and the social. At the scientific level, this obsolescence is mostly driven by the awareness of a growing number of anomalies in the long-held "normal" views of genetic functioning that were forged during the twentieth century. Hype and uncertainties are far from rare in contemporary challenges to genetic determinism, and many emerging findings in epigenetics or microbiomics still await validation in what is called the "postgenomic era". However, a facile critique that points its finger at sensationalistic findings would obscure the impressive growth of research and integration between emerging programs, which genuinely challenges and even violates long-held views in biology. Often the emphasis of these novel findings is about bringing the environment into the genome. And yet, one of the most intriguing aspects of epigenetic research is not the addition of the environment to an already existing genome, but the entire reconfiguration of the ontology of the genome. The gene is no longer experimented on and represented as an informational medium, but as a very material and impressionable body that brings back to actuality ancient metaphors of plasticity as marking and imprinting. This embodied nature of the genome may be used to challenge the flatness of the digital language of molecular biology.

2) The knowledge axis extends my previous argument (2016) about a return of the repressed in contemporary epigenetic research, or that scientific time future may be – in some cases at least – "contained in time past"

(Gissis, 2017). However, here, the "repressed" is not just nineteenth-century soft heredity but ancient, early modern and non-Western body–world configurations based on ideas and practices of bodily fluidity. Notions like the maternal imprint, the specific connection between body and place, the environment as a bioactive force, the blurring of the boundary between food and drug, the porosity of heredity to ancestral events, and even the inheritance of acquired behaviours, pangenesis and telegony (notions which have been recently evoked in molecular forms in epigenetics[2]) have always been well known in ancient, early modern and non-Western medical doctrines. It is this molecular resurfacing of past tropes implied by epigenetics that offers a unique opportunity to question polarities between "traditional" and "modern" knowledge. By focusing on how bodies are rewritten as plastic and vulnerable in epigenetics, the book may contribute not only to challenging the congratulatory rhetoric of innovation in contemporary life sciences but also to focusing on forms of epistemic hybridity where past and present, centre and periphery, global and situated exist in a deeply entangled way (Raj, 2013; Anderson, 2014). This means, genealogically, the possibility of a reappraisal of counter-traditions of the body as genuine sites of knowledge production. Where one sees the accumulation of pacified knowledge, genealogy reveals bellicose relationships.

3) The power axis highlights the complex coproduction of the political and the biological in the history of the body and the legacy of the politics of plasticity, at both the individual and the collective level. By focusing on the government of malleable bodies – always porous to environmental influences – the book sheds light on an alternative form of biopolitics and challenges views of an inherently liberating potential of biological plasticity. Building on the longer history, it dissects the contemporary implications of corporeal and genomic plasticity and (re-)emerging connections of environment and disease for notions of risk, responsibility and intervention. If the body is rewritten as permeable to its genomic core, it is also vulnerable to new risks and amenable to new forms of intervention, particularly in special windows of biological sensitivity. During these peaks of plasticity, prevention and other policy initiatives are described as more effective, but the lasting impacts of negative experiences are also deemed more significant and difficult to correct.

Finally, the book addresses the impact of epigenetics on existing notions of plasticity in the life sciences. Epigenetic research does not exhaust plasticity, a complex term that encompasses multiple research programs in biology, often with competing meanings. However, epigenetics is rapidly becoming a key mechanism in several iterations of plasticity, especially in neuroscience and gene expression. Epigenetics, I argue, contributes in this way to shifting the overall inflection of the term across the biosciences. It brings to the fore a more complex meaning of plasticity that is less about potential for reorganization and optimization and more about absorption of environmental disruptions, inertia and viscosity of long-term effects. This is somehow a bleaker and certainly more sobering inflection of plasticity, which is far from being the opposite of stability or even fixity (Bateson and Gluckman, 2011). It is a plasticity of enfoldment in ancestral histories and entanglement in places that challenges both modernistic and postmodernistic appropriation of the term as, respectively, a property securely in the possession of the sovereign consumer or a symbol for infinite freedom and fluidity of identity.

Acknowledgements

Portions of Chapters 2 and 5 have appeared in "A Postgenomic Body: History, Genealogies and Politics", *Body and Society*, 24(3), 3–38. An earlier version of Chapter 3 was published as "Disentangling Life: Darwin, Selectionism, and the Postgenomic Return of the Environment", *Studies in History and Philosophy of Science Part C: Studies in History and Philosophy of Biological and Biomedical Sciences* (2017) 62, pp. 10–19.

My gratitude and recognition go to a number of people with whom I have shared thoughts and hypotheses about the research and arguments of this book. In a time of liquid academic life, they have been like an invisible department from which I have extensively benefitted through stimulating exchanges and profound intellectual discussions. They include a number of persons with whom I have organized exciting panels at various international conferences where some of the ideas behind this book were presented: Stephanie Lloyd (Université Laval), for the panel on *Plasticity: Encountering Biosocial Models of Creation, Adaptation, and Destruction from Genomics to Epigenetics* at the 2015 American Anthropology Association conference in Denver, CO and for a number of conversations around the world on the specific nature of epigenetic plasticity; Deborah Bolnick (University of Texas), for the panel on *Race in Postgenomic Times* at the 2016 American Anthropological Association conference in Minneapolis, MN; Aryn Martin (York University) and Megan Warin (University of Adelaide), for the *Track on Biosocial Futures* at the 2016 Society for Social Studies of Science (4S)/European Association for the Study of Science and Technology (EASST) conference in Barcelona; Becky

Mansfield (Ohio State University) and Martine Lappé (Columbia University), for the panel on *Plasticity, Postgenomics, and the Politics of Possibility: Critical Reflections on the Environmental Turn in the Life Sciences* at the 2017 Annual Meeting of 4S in Boston, MA; Jan Baedke (Ruhr-Universität Bochum) and Eva Jablonka (Tel Aviv University), for a double special panel on *Conceptual and Political Challenges in Postgenomics* at the 2017 International Society for the History, Philosophy and Social Studies of Biology meeting in Sao Paulo; Becky Mansfield and Ariel Rawson (Ohio State University), for the panel entitled *From the Anthropocene to Postgenomics: New Configurations of Body–World* at the 2018 American Association of Geographers conference in New Orleans, LA; and Megan Warin, Michelle Pentecost (Kings College) and Fiona Ross (University of Cape Town), for the *Track on Political Transformations of Developmental Origins of Health and Disease and Epigenetics in the Global South* at the 2018 Meeting of 4S in Sydney.

A number of people have been part of an ongoing discussion on these topics. They include Margaret Lock (McGill University), Samantha Frost (University of Illinois Urbana–Champaign), Deborah Youdell (University of Birmingham), Jörg Niewöhner (Humboldt-Universität Berlin), Sarah Richardson (Harvard University), Giuseppe Testa (University of Milan), Ruth Muller and Michael Penkler (Munich Center for Technology in Society), Warwick Anderson (The University of Sydney), Jack Reynolds (Deakin University), Luca Chiapperino and Francesco Panese (University of Lausanne), Maria Damjanovicova (previously at the European Institute of Oncology (IEO) Milan), Isabelle Mansuy (University of Zurich), Liz Roberts (University of Michigan), Kim Hendrickx and Ine Van Hoyweghen (KU Leuven), Hannah Landecker (University of California Los Angeles), Caroline Arni (Universität Basel), Chikako Takeshita (University of California Riverside), Courtney Addison (Victoria University, Wellington), Erik Peterson (University of Alabama), Tatjana Buklijas (The University of Auckland), Snait Gissis (Tel Aviv University), Chris Renwick (York University), Gregory Radick (University of Leeds), Paolo Vineis (Imperial College London), Steve Fuller (University of Warwick), Paul Martin (University of Sheffield), Sue White (University of Sheffield), Andrew Bartlett (York University and University of Sheffield) and Dave Wastell (University of Nottingham). Special thanks to all the participants in the *Biopolitics of Epigenetics Symposium* at the University of Sydney, June 2017 (and Melinda Cooper as discussant of my paper), organized by Sonja van Wichelen. Special thanks also to Vincent Cunliffe (University of Sheffield) for help in clarifying the role of chromatin and for several debates on the mechanisms of epigenetics (although he has no responsibility for any possible mistake made here). The research behind this book was initially supported by a Leverhulme Trust grant in the Department of Sociological Studies (principal investigator Paul Martin) at the University of Sheffield, my former academic affiliation. My new academic home, the Alfred Deakin Institute for Citizenship and Globalisation at Deakin University in Melbourne (Australia), and its emerging Science and Society Network, led by Emma Kowal and Eben Kirksey, have provided fantastic infrastructural help since I joined in March 2018. Conversations at Deakin with Jeff Craig and Evie Kendal have also been highly stimulating. Thanks finally to Simon Waxman (Boston), Jenny Lucy, Sarah Webb, Will Cox and Claire Kennedy (all in Melbourne) for assisting with copyediting.

This book is for my sweet, smart and gorgeous daughters Eva and Rebecca, the result of a unique biosocial combination of change and stability, acquired and innate.

Melbourne (Australia), June 2018

References

Anderson W (2009) From subjugated knowledge to conjugated subjects: Science and globalisation, or postcolonial studies of science? *Postcolonial Studies* 12(4): 389–400.

Anderson W (2014) Racial conceptions in the Global South. *Isis* 105(4): 782–792.

Bateson P and Gluckman P (2011) *Plasticity, Robustness, Development and Evolution.* Cambridge, UK: Cambridge University Press.

Bernard C (1878) *Leçons sur les phénomènes de la vie communs aux animaux et aux végétaux.* Paris: J. B. Baillière et fils.

Bohacek J and Mansuy I (2015) Molecular insights into transgenerational non-genetic inheritance of acquired behaviours. *Nature Reviews Genetics* 16(11): 641.

Bondurianksy R and Day T (2018) *Extended Heredity: A New Understanding of Inheritance and Evolution.* Princeton: Princeton University Press.

Cossetti C, Lugini L, Astrologo L, et al. (2014) Soma-to-germline transmission of RNA in mice xenografted with human tumour cells: Possible transport by exosomes. *PloS ONE* 9(7): e101629.

Crean A, Kopps A and Bondurianksy R (2014) Revisiting telegony: Offspring inherit an acquired characteristic of their mother's previous mate. *Ecology Letters* 17(12): 1545–1552.

Gissis S (2017) Is time future contained in time past? *Studies in History and Philosophy of Biological and Biomedical Sciences* 62: 51–55.

James W (1988) *Manuscript Lectures.* Cambridge: Harvard University Press.

Meloni M (2016) *Political Biology: Science and Social Values in Human Heredity from Eugenics to Epigenetics.* London: Palgrave.

Raj K (2013) Beyond postcolonialism … and postpositivism: Circulation and the global history of science. *Isis* 104(2): 337–347.

Sharma A (2017) Transgenerational epigenetics: Integrating soma to germline communication with gametic inheritance. *Mechanisms of Ageing and Development* 163: 15–22.

Weismann A (1891) *Essays upon Heredity and Kindred Problems*, Vol. 1. E Schoenland and A Shipley (eds.). Oxford: Oxford University Press.

Zimmer C (2018) *She Has Her Mother's Laugh: The Powers, Perversions, and Potential of Heredity*. New York: Dutton.

Notes

1 In politics, the term "counter-revolution" is often used to describe a break that removes and overturns the conditions of a previous revolutionary break; however, to think of the current challenges to the modernistic body of biomedicine (and its views of heredity, reproduction and relationships to the environment) in these terms would render too simplistic the argument here advanced about the coexistence of multiple temporalities in the history of science.

2 For molecular versions of inheritance of acquired behaviours, see Bohacek and Mansuy (2015). For pangenesis (direct communication between somatic and germ cells) in which exosomes potentially play the role of Darwin's gemmules, see Zimmer's comment (2018: 545) to Cossetti et al. (2014), and Sharma (2017). For molecular versions of telegony (how a *previous* mate's features are passed to offspring), see Crean et al. (2014).

An archaeology of plasticity

1

Living in postgenomic times: Of imprinting and plasticity

Claims of a new entanglement of bodies and the environment are increasingly relevant in postgenomic models:[1] "the life sciences are generating a transformative view of the biological body not as fixed and innate but as permeable to its environment and, therefore, plastic" (Mansfield, 2017: 355). Since the early 1990s there has been much emphasis on the brain's synapses and gross organization as sculpted by social and cultural influences, even in adult life (Clark, 1998; Glannon, 2002; Park and Huang, 2010; Overgaard and Jensen 2012; Rees, 2016). Now, fields like *environmental epigenetics, developmental origins of health and disease* (DOHaD) and *microbiomics* lead even wider arguments about the dynamism of biological matter (Charney, 2012; Majnik and Lane, 2015; Moore, 2015). These fields have shown how the human body is permeable to environmental effects (e.g. toxins, food and socioeconomic status) to its genomic core, entangled inseparably "with environmental forces (macro and micro) from the moment of conception on throughout life" (Lock, 2015: 151).

A wealth of evidence has accumulated since the early 2000s that not only is the human brain plastic, and hence changeable at the structural and functional level (Rubin, 2009; Rose and Abi-Rached, 2013), but also the microbiota and epigenome are moulded by the impact of food, lifestyle, toxins, chemicals, stressors and socioeconomic factors. Environmental or social epigenetics is the most well-known example of this emerging interest in the biological embedding of social experience and the appreciation of *the power of the environment* in explaining health trajectories, development and biological identity. By showing how various material instantiations of social life become literally embodied in the epigenome, epigenetics is said to illustrate how *the environment gets inside the body* and makes "the boundary of the skin of little significance" (Landecker and Panofsky, 2013: 339, referring to Michael Meaney's work). Chiselled by the incessant workings of external forces, postgenomic bodies are described nowadays as fully absorbed in their surroundings (Solomon, 2016): the boundaries between the body and the outside world become uncertain. This is not quite the same as saying that genes and environment "interact", as we have known for the whole of the twentieth century (Hogben, 1933; Tabery, 2014). In postgenomics the environment is no longer a mere *container* for gene expression (Stallins et al., 2016); it is increasingly seen as a productive, bioactive force (Landecker, 2011), an inducer and generator of phenotypes (West-Eberhard, 2003). Even in terms of biological capitalism, postgenomics introduces a different logic that makes not just DNA sequences alone but the "whole spatial and temporal contexts and circumstances surrounding DNA" a new potential source of biovalue (Stallins et al., 2016).

Changes in evolutionary thinking are also significant: the formative power of the environment is wielded not only via indirect selective pressures, as in the classical neo-Darwinian account; the emerging logic of epigenetics now implies that the environment directly instructs the organism (Jablonka and Lamb, 2014). This reconceptualization has an impact on the way in which bodies are rewritten: not just as "reacting to" or "withstanding" the environment but as "composed of transduced representations" of it (Landecker, 2016: 87). Since external conditions are understood as *reflecting directly*, at the molecular level, in the body's "internal biological changes", a model of *imprint* replaces one of random genetic mutation (Lappé and Landecker, 2015). Metaphors of writing, marking, coating and labelling, as well as notions of memory, scars and erasures, have nowadays become widespread in the epigenetic landscape.

If imprint is a key metaphor for conveying the notion that the environment leaves a durable mark on the genome, *plasticity* is probably the word that best captures the spirit of postgenomic times. Plasticity, which the Oxford English Dictionary defines as "the ability to be easily moulded or to undergo a permanent change in shape", is a very complex notion. It is too often confused with its antonym,[2] *elasticity*. The difference between plasticity and elasticity is obvious in the science of matter. While elasticity is the capacity to regain an original form after the deforming pressure has ceased, plasticity is about undergoing a permanent change:

If a coiled spring is pulled *beyond the limits of elasticity*, it will be *permanently elongated*. Provided that the spring does not break, the change is *plastic*.

(Bateson and Gluckman, 2011: 31)

However, this distinction is more blurred in biology, where plasticity often flirts with elasticity or even *polymorphism* (the possibility to assume a nearly infinite number of forms), and is too often taken as equivalent to "change", "malleability", "reversibility" or "tractability". Its multifarious history reveals, however, a more complex polysemy, and an association with ideas of stabilization and retaining of forms after a perturbation. This connotation of plasticity as continuous with stabilization (Bateson and Gluckman, 2011), which had been neglected in modern writings, is coming powerfully back to the fore nowadays. As I will argue in this book, this is mostly an effect of emerging claims in epigenetics and related programs such as DOHaD, which explains health trajectory as the durable result of *in utero* effects.

Contemporary plasticity

Plasticity is today a trendy catchall term "encompassing multiple processes regulated in a variety of different ways" (Bateson and Gluckman, 2011: 5). In contemporary life science, plasticity appears in many guises: synaptic, morphological, immunological, not to mention psychic, behavioural and mental. Plasticity spans a number of cutting-edge research programs, including cloning and stem cells (plasticity as reprogramming of cell fate), immunology (producing antibodies to pathogens not encountered before), neuroscience (plasticity as rewiring of synaptic connections, even in the adult brain), and epigenetics (malleability of genomic expression). Due to their impact on notions of corporeal plasticity, phenotypic and developmental plasticity are the two areas of major interest in this book. *Phenotypic plasticity* is "the ability of individual genotypes to produce different phenotypes when exposed to different environmental conditions" (Pigliucci et al., 2006; Nicoglou, 2015, 2018); *developmental plasticity* (which looks at the same phenomenon from a developmental angle and is often used as a synonym) is usually defined as the capacity of an organism or the body to react to an environmental input "with a change in form, state, movement, or rate of activity" (West-Eberhard, 2003: 34). Reference to these notions brings to the forefront the capacity of humans to adjust quickly and flexibly in "heterogeneous environments" (Gabriel et al., 2005; Kuzawa and Bragg, 2012), relying less on forms of "genetic commitment" (Wells, 2012: S470).

Given this multifaceted situation, the semantic "unity" of the term is by itself questionable. As scholars in Science and Technology Studies (STS) know, it is best in this case to understand scientific terms as the result of a complex negotiation across multiple scientific communities shaped by different "research questions, [and] practices of scientific measurement" (Pitts-Taylor, 2016: 36). Plasticity, therefore, ultimately comes in the plural, and genealogy is exactly what is needed to diffract this polysemy of the term into its multiple instantiations.

The flourishing status of plasticity in several scientific research programs and social science writings shows a significant discontinuity with last-century debates. One visible case is evolutionary biology. For a large part of the twentieth century, with few pioneering exceptions, the term was considered a simple "nuisance" (Forsman, 2015: 276; see alternatives in Weber and Depew, 2003; Morange, 2009; Nicoglou, 2018). A key text of twentieth-century neo-Darwinism, Ernst Mayr's 800-page *Growth of Biological Thought* (1982), features the word "plastic" just twice, firstly to be criticized as an antiquated view and secondly in the sense of modern surgery. The contemporary scenario is very different. Plasticity research "has grown tremendously from ten papers published per year before 1983 to nearly 1300 papers in 2013" (Forsman, 2015: 282). This increase is paralleled only by that of epigenetics, which has escalated in the last decade by comparable figures (Meloni and Testa, 2014; Skinner, 2015). The two areas support each other and in several cases even overlap, with epigenetics offering a plausible molecular but non-genetic mechanism for biological plasticity and rapid adaptation to changing environments (Kuzawa and Bragg, 2012). In terms of its social translation, "plasticity" is currently used to describe the openness of the body and the brain to complex environmental interactions throughout life, and particularly in specific critical periods of heightened sensitivity (especially early-life experiences). It is invoked to mark a shift from premillennial notions of biological fixedness and genetic hardwiring. It is used as a powerful rhetorical platform drenched in hope to suggest that brains can reprogram and repair themselves and bodies are always open to forms of intervention to optimize biological fitness, enhance therapeutic potential and even correct past injustice (Duffau, 2006; Moller, 2006; Rubin, 2009; Rose and Abi-Rached, 2013; Lloyd, 2018; Lloyd and Raikhel, 2018).

Plasticity, especially in social science quarters, has a strong allure, and is very often captured into a discourse of *social progress*. Boas famously played the card of the "instability or plasticity" of human racial types (Boas, 1912: 557) against typological racists and American eugenists, inaugurating a long tradition of liberal anthropology based on plasticity *against* biological fixedness. The post-Boasian tradition further reinforced this association of values, neatly aligning a discourse of fixity with one of exclusion and a discourse of plasticity with one of emancipation. This polarized strategy was probably favoured by the specific research design that American anthropology privileged (Hulse, 1981): physical changes (such as increase in stature) in the descendants of poor or rural migrants moving to the USA (Shapiro and Hulse, 1939; Goldstein, 1943; see also Lasker, 1952, 1954). In her review, Bernice Kaplan (1954) discusses twenty-five studies on human plasticity, of which only a few referred overtly to its negative effects, one written by a non-American author (Ivanovsky, 1923, on the effects of inanition in Russia). This debate is so value-laden that nowadays, one century later, attacking Boas' study (Sparks and Jantz, 2003) still has deep political implications.

However, this one-sidedly emancipatory use of the term "plasticity" is one of the most important obstacles to an appreciation of its plurality of meaning. Plasticity is an inherently dualistic term, caught between *openness* and *determination, agency* and *vulnerability* (Paillard, 1976; Malabou, 2005; Pitts-Taylor, 2016). Analogous to the Greek *phármakon*, which can cure and poison at the same time (Derrida, 1981), plasticity in emerging styles of epigenetic reasoning is the domain of a profound indecision compatible with conflicting social and ethical scenarios (Lloyd, 2018; Lloyd and Raikhel, 2018). This fundamental ambiguity of the concept of plasticity between creation, reception and annihilation of forms (Malabou, 2005; see also 2009, 2010) will be turned in this book into a heuristic for unpacking its rich polysemy across various epochs. A *longue durée* and non-linear history of the plastic body shows how each of its conceptual facets may have become prevalent in certain historical moments, at the expense of others. Its ambiguity becomes here the very source of its productiveness (Rheinberger, 2003).

Plasticity, etymology and history

Even a quick look at the etymology and recent history of the term aptly demonstrates some of the traps connected with it. As for its etymology, plasticity comes from the Greek *plassein*, which means to mould, shape or form, and by extension, to fabricate, forge, sculpt and train someone; hence the adjective *plastikos*, a thing to which a form can be assigned, but also all the arts and techniques by which a form can be produced:

> "Plastic" as an adjective has two meanings. On the one hand, it means "to be susceptible to changes of form" or "to be malleable." Clay, in this sense, would be "plastic." On the other hand, it means "having the power to bestow form," as in the expression "plastic surgeon" or "plastic art" understood as "the art of modelling" in the arts of sculpture or ceramics. Plasticity describes the nature of that which is plastic, being at once capable of receiving and of giving form.
>
> (Malabou, 2005: 65)

A similar polarity arises when observing the nature of plastic matter. In his *Meteorology*, Aristotle highlights the singular nature of plasticity as located between two poles: a hardness that resists all modifications, and a softness or fluidity that does not retain any. Notably, this definition came many centuries before William James' often cited and, in fact, derivative definition of plasticity as "semi-inertness" – "the possession of a structure *weak enough* to yield to an influence, but *strong enough* not to yield all at once" (1890: 105; my italics).[3] Aristotle writes:

> Some things, e.g. copper and wax, are impressible, others, e.g. pottery and water, are not. [...] Those impressibles that retain the shape impressed on them and are easily moulded by the hand are called "plastic"; those that are not easily moulded, such as stone or wood, or are easily moulded but do not retain the shape impressed, like wool or a sponge, are not plastic. The last group are said to be "squeezable".
>
> (Book IV, part 9: Webster, 1923)

In another work, *On Memory and Reminiscence*, Aristotle offers the example of "running water", on which no form could be implanted, as a case of a material too fluid to be considered "plastic" (2014).

Plasticity belongs, therefore, in this intermediate space between ability to change and capacity to retain a shape, "between the opposing moments of total immobility and vacuity", fixedness and dissolution (Malabou, 2005: 12). It often overlaps with the apparently opposite notion of *robustness* (insensitivity to environmental changes), which is part of the same gradual continuum (Bateson and Gluckman, 2011). These semantic tensions, as we shall see, are inherent in the definition of plasticity and have not gone away in contemporary debates.

The modern historical trajectory of the term also presents a number of traps. From Aristotle's definition to Herder's eighteenth-century book *Plastik* (on plastic arts like sculpture) (1778 [2002]), plasticity belongs to the realm of inanimate matter, not living organisms. I will explore in the next pages a rare exception to this, in Renaissance embryological debates around the Neoplatonic notion of a *vis plastica* (plastic power: Smith, 2006; Hirai, 2007a). However, albeit not exclusive, the non-biological sense of plasticity remained predominant until Herder's time, when the term started to significantly increase in all the many European languages.[4] Besides reelaborating some of the Greek themes about giving and receiving forms, Herder's book adds a further twist to the meanings associated with plasticity. He uses the term in a strong polemic against the modern primacy of sight versus touch, painting versus sculpture. While sight has a destructive function, to transform everything "into planes and surfaces", plastic arts like sculpture create an experience of the in-depth, of a three-dimensional body (1778 [2002]). Plastic is here the opposite not of fixed, but of flat, superficial, two-dimensional. So far, plasticity is not associated with modernistic ideas of continuous change, regeneration, tractability, improvement, or optimization.[5]

This is, instead, the meaning that plasticity would gradually acquire when it was imported since the nineteenth century into the biological and medical sciences. Here it was used to convey the idea of adaptability to environmental changes and, in medicine and neuroscience, renewal of tissues, memory formation, creation of new brain structures and potentiation of synaptic strengths (Stahnisch, 2003; Berlucchi and Buchtel, 2008; Overgaard and Jensen, 2012).

At the turn of the twentieth century, in the evolutionary writings of James Mark Baldwin, plasticity became a principle above natural selection to explain the evolution of intelligence and learning (Baldwin, 1902; Weber and Depew, 2003). Baldwin made plasticity a keystone of advancement toward higher stages of life (Spencer, a generation before, actually did the same, often with a racialist tinge). He posited that a correlation between

> increasing plasticity of the nervous system and increasing mental endowment holds as we ascend from a lower to a higher stage [in the scale of life].
>
> (1902: 36)

This association of plasticity with progress is even clearer in the work of another psychologist, Pavlov. In his 1930s neurological writings, Pavlov described the higher nervous system as plastic, because of its "immense possibilities" and endless capacity to change. In plasticity, he claimed,

> nothing remains stationary, unyielding and everything could always be attained, all could be changed for the better, were only the appropriate conditions realized.
>
> (1932: 127, cited in Weidman, 2006: 79; see Todes, 2014: 524)

It is this utopian sense that we still find today in claims of "irreducible openness" of the plastic brain (Rees, 2016). What we can here notice is that, from this point onwards, the new plasticity of modern biology left behind the original meaning of plasticity in the sciences of matter. This latter implied a process of irreversible loss of possibility and inability to recover an initial form (Malabou, 2005: 34). In sculpture, plastic art *par excellence*, the immense potentialities of a block of marble or a piece of wood are irrevocably transformed into a statue: once the material has been shaped and carved, and of all the possible figures only one has been crystallized into its final form, there is no way back. The statue can be destroyed, but it cannot be undone, un-formed and restored to its original state.

There is nothing wrong or surprising in the fact that a scientific term accumulates a number of often opposing meanings along its trajectory through different vocabularies and paradigms (Canguilhem, 1955). But it is sociologically significant to highlight the crystallization of values between plasticity, potential for change, educability and progress during the course of the twentieth century. It is significant because it blinds us to the reality that emerging models of biological life may represent a departure from this one-sided view of plasticity, pointing instead to a less teleological and more complex, if not darker, meaning.

The dialectic of plasticity in contemporary social life

Outside of the life sciences, human plasticity has often remained the province of biological anthropologists, very far from sociological radars. However, things may be rapidly changing, given the widespread usage of the term to describe both processes of corporeal modification and biological embedding of social exposures that often come in socially stratified ways (Pitts-Taylor, 2016). It is enough to quickly scan a number of popular science books to realize that the social circulation of claims about the plasticity of the brain and the body becomes more visible by the day. These stories, however, are not neutral or homogeneous. They are often divided into two very different strands that nicely capture the subtle paradoxes of plasticity. When it comes to the possibility of successfully manipulating our brain, genome, or microbiota to become a better us (better mood, better health and better mind), plasticity is mostly sold to a global middle class as a rosy message of individual control and optimization of function. It highlights how we can "train" and regenerate our brain and now our genomic expression through meditation, healthy diet, or exercise (Doidge, 2008; Shenk, 2010; Reynolds, 2014; Douglas, 2015; Le Doux, 2015). It builds on and expands an ideology of individual consumption and personal freedom deployed in the service of neoliberal and marketized models of health. Its popular versions emphasize choice, control and reversibility. It is possible today, we are told, to stimulate "new brain cells and networks where and when we need them" as well as to turn "genes off and on at will to repair brain damage, restore function, and optimize performance" (Horstman 2010: 8). In other popular accounts, epigenetics is described as offering hope that everyone can become a genius (Shenk, 2010), challenging the hard truth of a genetic basis for IQ as in past sociobiological accounts. This is the perfect version of biological plasticity for a culture where "care of the self is always about self-improvement, enhancement, and becoming something better" (Jones, 2008; Berkowitz, 2017: 33).

However, this is not the only phenomenology of plasticity that exists, though it is the one that has been most studied by sociologists (Papadopoulos, 2011; Rose and Abi-Rached, 2013; Pitts-Taylor, 2016; Berkowitz, 2017). A different, darker and more viscous plasticity, one that highlights irreversibility and loss of control, relates not to individual consumers but to vulnerable populations in Euro-America and increasingly more the Global South.[6] If plasticity lies in a paradoxical mid-way between the power to shape and the susceptibility to receive forms, it is vulnerable human groups, rather than individual consumers, that take upon them this second meaning: the *burden of plasticity*, that is, being sculpted by overwhelming social forces *beyond their control*. This is where plasticity should sound familiar to sociologists: it describes not only a faculty available to an individual agent (a habit that is a "possession" or a "disposition," as in the Latin and Greek etymology) but a power of transmission of social structures through embodied dispositions and practices. This is closer to ideas of modes of reproduction, inheritance and habitus in Bourdieu's term, something that cuts across a dualism of structure and agency, community and individual body (Bourdieu and Passeron, 1979; Bourdieu, 1986; Crossley, 2013). Its contemporary rephrasing as *biohabitus* (Warin et al., 2015) is probably even more pertinent to describe the entanglement of biological and social environments that is at stake with emerging models of biosocial life.

Contemporary analyses of biosocial plasticity are very close to this socio-logical insight about a non-individualistic reproduction of social life. They don't see a chasm between individual and social bodies, and don't under-stand biological factors as operating within the skin of the individual, as fixed at birth, or as socially insensitive to the effects of social structures. Quite the opposite. Even Bourdieu's notion of capital is explicitly mobilized and expanded to cover new areas (for instance "maternal capital") in an effort to "facilitate integration" between sociological and biological explanations (Wells, 2010).

However, these models of human plasticity understand the reproduction of biosocial life in a specific way. Whether it is the lasting legacy of child abuse (Cecil et al., 2016), racial violence or antenatal depression in post-apartheid South Africa (Redinger et al., 2017), the incidence of diabetes in urban India (Gluckman and Hanson, 2012), the Aboriginal health gap and transgenerational trauma in Australia (Berger et al., 2017), the everyday effects of racism (Kuzawa and Sweet, 2009), or the long-term ones of slavery for Black Americans (Jasienska, 2009), environmental effects deemed to make a visible impression on bodies and brains are seen mostly in nega-tive terms: pollutants, malnutrition or overnutrition, violence and trauma. Sometimes these effects are even seen to travel across generations. A biology sculpted by environmental events appears mostly in its pathological dimen-sion. This is probably the most visible contrast with earlier studies of human plasticity that referred (mostly) to the positive effects of favourable environ-ments on the bodies of immigrants.

The connection between plasticity and progress seems less visible in emerging biosocial models. These are not just some gloomy findings on the powerful effects of environmental insults, though. With the understanding of this special porosity of human biology and its susceptibility to possible damage from the environment, an *anxious vigilance emerges*. If our bodies are permeable to their genomic core, should we not monitor people's lifestyles more carefully than ever (Wastell and White, 2017)? And which people in par-ticular? Not all bodies are considered equally permeable. If it is in the womb that many epigenetic effects are "programmed", should intensified attention and obligations be placed on pregnant women (Warin, 2012; Richardson et al., 2014; Mansfield, 2017)? Should they be monitored even before concep-tion (for a wider reading of pre-pregnancy care: Waggoner, 2017)?

Consider the theory of the developmental origins of health and disease (DOHaD) or "foetal programming" (Gluckman and Hanson, 2005). DOHaD originates from the work of British physician David Barker, who brought to attention the long-term health effects (cardiovascular disease, diabetes) of events occurring in critical moments of fetal development. The notion was far from new, but Barker was an enthusiastic propagator and a catalyst for the idea (the "Barker Hypothesis") that many chronic diseases in adult life have intra-uterine roots (Almond and Currie, 2011; Warin et al., 2015). Initial fetal programming studies focused on epidemiological statistical correlations between "conditions of early-life and later-life health in historical cohorts in British public records and turned them into clinical and experimental physio-logical problems" (Buklijas, 2018: 180; Adair and Prentice, 2004). These studies, originally labelled "foetal origins of adult disease" (Hales and Barker, 1992; Barker, 1995; Paul, 2010), mostly focus on the negative effects of *in utero* events (pollutants, stress, over or under nutrition, smoking) in increasing the risk of non-communicable disease later in life.

Interestingly, with their findings translated in related campaigns such as *The First 1,000 Days* (Pentecost, 2018), DOHaD studies in the Global South are making their way to the forefront of works in developmental plasticity. Since its founding meeting in Mumbai in 1990, DOHaD has always had a Southern focus (Pentecost, 2018), but this has become more visible in the last years. It is the case of economically emerging regions (such as India or China) that are undergoing dramatic nutrition transition (adoption of Western diet) and are characterized by cyclical patterns of intergenerational metabolic and coronary disease (Yajnik, 2001; Adair and Prentice, 2004; Watson et al., 2017). India, in particular, is home of the Pune Maternal Nutritional Study, which has gained international status as an explanatory model for long-term developmental effects of maternal undernutrition on diabetes epidemics in several Southern countries (Krishnaveni and Yajnik, 2017). The so-called "thin–fat" Indian baby syndrome – how Indian babies are "thin morphologic-ally but metabolically obese according to [their] impaired insulin sensitivity and elevated levels of lipids" (Solomon, 2016: 22; Yajnik, 2004) – has come to popularly represent the notions of an epigenetic (developmental) origin, as opposed to a genetic origin.

Not only is the importation of Western diet at stake in these emer-ging studies in the Global South. It is also the case of poorer areas where DOHaD-related studies investigate the lasting effects of war, genocide and famine in hindering social and economic growth: studies have investigated the transgenerational transmission of stress via epigenetic mechanisms in women exposed during pregnancy to the Tutsi genocide or the long-term effects of nutrient restriction on offspring growth in rural Gambia (Perroud et al., 2014; Norris and Richter, 2016; Dasgupta, 2017; Eriksen et al., 2017).

Economists are also coming to use these developmental studies of shocks in human populations. Awareness of the long-term effects of plasticity has inspired recent macro-economic analyses of the "developing world" that recommend investments during critical windows of plasticity (pregnancy and early childhood) in an effort to foster economic growth and improve human capital. An emerging body of literature in health economics, which includes also influential economists like Nobel Prize winner James Heckman (2012), asks: "what if the nine months *in utero* are one of the most critical periods in a person's life, shaping future abilities and health trajectories – and thereby the likely path of earnings?" (Almond and Currie, 2011: 1; Almond et al., 2012). In this new operationalization of plasticity, "economics goes into the womb not only under the skin" (Wastell and White, 2017) – particularly the wombs of those living in "developing regions" (Currie and Vogl, 2013), or exposed to systematic stressors in "developed" ones. Drawing on plasticity rather than genetic fixedness, a new biopolitical management of vulnerable populations is emerging.

A genealogy of plastic power

In order to understand the polysemic meaning of plasticity as referring to both control and loss of control, capacity to remake oneself at will and realizing one's vulnerability to overwhelming forces in the near past and the present, reversibility and irreversibility, I suggest in this book an exercise in genealogical thought. Rather than address directly emerging forms of biopower and governmentality based on plasticity and related epigenetic notions, I prefer to take a longer genealogical perspective and show the complexity of the sociological discourses associated with the government of corporeal plasticity in ancient and early modern times.

In the specific meaning conferred on it first by Nietzsche and later by Foucault, a genealogical analysis connects "untimely" histories (Nietzsche, 1873/1997) to reveal complex filiations and struggles among competing epistemic paradigms (Foucault, 2003; Koopman, 2013).

Genealogy is an eminently sociological task (Rose, 1996; Greco, 1998; Diedrich, 2005) for showing the social and interactive nature of what is often taken for granted in narrow presentist interpretations (Aspers, 2007). It is a form of history of the present that examines the conditions under which certain powers and practices come into being. As such, it contributes to a problematization of historical sedimentations that obscure the contingency of the present social and intellectual order (Dean, 2003), and may build stimulating bridges with various areas of sociological research, including historical sociology. This disclosing task of genealogy is well summed up by social theorist Ed Cohen:

> Genealogy's basic premise holds that the world is much more virtual and much more mutable than it presents itself. In genealogy we disclose contingencies secreted within phenomena which propose themselves to us as the essential dimensions of our world. Through this disclosure, genealogy hopes to glimpse instabilities where we often see inevitabilities, to imagine possibilities where we resign ourselves to necessities, and thus to learn to think and live otherwise than we supposed imaginable heretofore.
>
> (2009: 23)

My genealogical approach to contemporary plasticity builds on Foucauldian archaeology. Archaeology aims at describing discursive practices and epistemic formations while abandoning neat normative distinctions between subjected and authorized knowledge (Chimisso, 2003). Albeit it is often believed that genealogy replaces archaeology, it is more correct to say that, in Foucault, genealogy supplements archaeology. Foucault's endeavour can therefore be properly described as an "archaeological-and-genealogical inquiry into the emergence into being of related vectors of knowledge, power, and ethics" (Koopman, 2013: 44).

In this book, I follow a Foucauldian strategy to challenge the naïve and Eurocentric notion that plasticity has, until today, been silenced, pacified and marginalized in favour of a biology of fixedness; that fixedness has prevailed for centuries with its neat distinction between the interior of the body and the outer environment, and hence between nature and nurture; that plasticity is somehow a late gift of modernity, the effect of incremental scientific advance that has overthrown a centuries-long metaphysics of fixedness; and that only under a fixed view of biology do racism, eugenics and biological determinism became possible, with all of their enormous political consequences. Many of these assumptions do not withstand further examination. Perhaps more importantly, genealogy helps displace the notion that plasticity is a unitary phenomenon, coming in the abstract. It helps illuminate the unequal distribution of different forms of plasticities across social, gender and ethnic groups – inequality that alters the risks individuals face, the responsibilities imputed to them, and the interventions to which they may be subject. Genealogy serves as a healthy reminder that histories of corporeal plasticity have always been highly gendered, racialized and classed, mapping and reproducing hierarchies through physiological distinctions (Paster, 1993). Rather than being inherently liberating, as many think, plasticity is ambiguously situated between making and unmaking essentialist notions of class, gender and race. It can be used to promote post-racial views that get rid of racial essences or arguments that once again lock people to place, time and the burden of experience. Racialization in science is not a matter of choosing plastic over fixed biology, epigenetics over genetics.

Plasticity and its troubled history: When we were plastic and how we forgot it

The possibility of a genealogy of plasticity seems to fly in the face of what many disciplinary chronologies in the life sciences tell us: that biological plasticity is a recent invention based on the discovery of some properties in our cells or neurons that were previously overlooked by constructions that emphasized stability and permanency. We are led to believe that an original metaphysics of fixedness in Western views of the body has been followed by a perception of plasticity driven by recent innovative research programs. Certainly, this narrative is mostly valid for various local branches of the life sciences (cell differentiation and culture: Landecker, 2007, see also Kraft and Rubin, 2016; neuroplasticity: Berlucchi and Buchtel, 2008; Rose and Abi-Rached, 2013; Rees, 2016; and plant biology: Baranski and Peirson, 2015). However, it does not hold true when we think of whole-body plasticity and notions like race or heredity. When extended to these wider aspects of human biology, it would be more correct to say that *generalized plasticity preceded fixedness*. If we define plasticity as above – the capacity of an organism to change in response to an environmental change (West-Eberhard, 2003) – the experience of plasticity is literally everywhere in ancient, early modern and non-Western understandings of the body.[7] As any historian of medicine knows, the belief in malleability of traits, and a continuous capacity to adjust the human body to a change in place, winds or food, was largely predominant before the rise of the modern biomedical body. This plasticity of traits may still be today the signature of a certain Southern understanding of human biology (Anderson, 2014).

It is particularly through humoralism and its global ramifications that the biopolitical problem of how to live with a permeable body became pervasive in premodern times. Humoralism, the doctrine that the body is composed of elementary fluids (humours) whose balance was altered by changes in the surrounding environment, implies a view of the body as radically embedded in places (Rosenberg, 2012). Bodies are "characterized by a constant exchange between inside and outside, by fluxes and flows" (Nash, 2006: 32); they are, to paraphrase Deleuze, "made of contracted water, earth, light and air" (1994: 73). A fluid body, however, is also one that requires intense vigilance and control. Moreover, humoralist authors applied this basic instability of bodily traits to wider biological phenomena, including reproduction and what we call today heredity. Even the notion of the inheritance of acquired characteristics, and the interplay of nurture and nature in shaping heredity, attributed to Lamarck, is actually clearly part of the humoralist imagination, for instance in the Hippocratic *On Airs, Waters, and Places*, a key text of Greek humoralism (Chapter 2).

Ancient plasticity is not exhausted by humoralism, however. It is more accurate to say that in the premodern world, humoralism worked as a catalyst for a vast number of tropes about corporeal and racial plasticity that went well beyond its language and were widespread from the Greek to the Arabic and Indian world. Humoralism was just one among many possible views of corporeal plasticity and biological impressionability in medicine, philosophy and geography. Take, for instance, the notion that racial traits were directly shaped by environmental factors, the sun or cold, food or stars. Theories of racial malleability were used to explain ethnic diversity in the ancient world. Often combined with a strong moralistic flavour (Livingstone, 1991), they condemned whole human groups to inferiority because of the unfavourable environment they were shaped by or, more subtly, by claiming that their placement in particularly unfavourable places was a sign of their subordinate nature. In the pseudo-Aristotelian *Problemata*, after a connection is made between the excesses of climate and brutality of character, we read that "the Ethiopians and the Egyptians" are "bandy-legged", possibly because "their bodies become distorted by heat, like logs of wood when they become dry". "The condition of their hair", the author claims, in an obvious moralistic use of geography, "supports this theory; for it is curlier than that of other nations, and curliness is as it were crookedness of the hair" (book IV: "Problems connected with the effect of locality on temperament"; see Foster, 1927: 902). Other notions were less moralistic but not less important. Take, for instance, the role of the moon in shaping the morphology and inner nature of earthly bodies. Soranus of Ephesus, the author of the most important gynaecological treatise of the second century CE, notes the shrinking of a mouse's liver lobes with the waning of the moon; the Roman writer Pliny the Elder (CE 23–79), in his encyclopaedic *Historia Naturalis*, highlights the growth of shellfish with its waxing. Pliny writes that "it is certain also, that the Bodies of Oysters, Mussels, Cockles, and all Shell-fishes, grow and waste by the Power of the Moon". He also states that "in the small liver of the mouse the number of lobes corresponds to the day of the moon" (Pliny, 1991: book I, 41 and book II, 76; cfr. Barton, 1994). Although many considered Pliny's treatise the source of naïve beliefs in ancient times,[8] Pliny, in fact, can be seen as part of a centuries-long tradition of belief in lunar effects. These views were still recognized as true in the mid-seventeenth century by the English royal physician Walter Charleton,

> who in 1654 explained that shellfish grew larger at full moon, perhaps because of the "Moon's great Humidity" developed from the lunar seas, "as the most and best of our Modern Astronomers have believed".
>
> (Schaffer, 2010: 159; see also Harrison, 2000)

A few years later, the German (or Dutch) anatomist Dirk Kerckring noted in his influential *Spicilegium anatomicum* (1670) the story of

> a young gentlewoman whose beauty depended upon the lunar force, insomuch that at full moon she was plump and very handsome, but in the decrease of the planet so wan and ill-favoured that she was ashamed to go abroad.
>
> (cited in Schaffer, 2010: 159)

The power of the moon was extremely important in the ancient and early modern world. Generally speaking, the logic was that, as the queen of heaven, the moon ruled over the fluids in the sublunary world (the part of the cosmos opposed to heaven, according to Aristotelian cosmology). Below the heavens, whatever is of watery nature will be affected by the moon's movements. Several centuries after Pliny, Albert the Great (1200–1280) wrote that it was "especially the eyes, in whose composition water's nature abounds", that "receive the greatest alterations and increases and diminutions according to the moon" (Resnick and Albertus Magnus, 2010: 53). The opinion was shared by other key scholastic thinkers in Latin West. Robert Grosseteste (1175–1253), bishop of Lincoln, had explicitly linked lunar movements to brain alterations. Since we know

> "by experience that, of all the heavenly substances, the moon exercises the greatest control over moist and cold bodies" Grosseteste wrote, "certain people are called lunatics because, when the moon wanes, *they suffer a diminution of the cerebrum*, since the cerebrum is a cold and moist substance".
>
> (Dales and Grosseteste, 1966: 461, my emphasis; see also Laird, 1990).

The special influence of lunar and solar rays on health and disease was a key theme of Arabic medical astrology (iatromathematics) from the eighth century onward (Meyerhof, 1931; Klein-Franke, 1984; Siddiqui, 1996; Saif, 2017). It continued as a respectable medical theory in the West well into the eighteenth century, as seen, for instance, in Richard Mead's *Of the Power and Influence of the Sun and Moon on Humane Bodies* (1708) (Harrison, 2000; cfr. Roos, 2000) and even later with Erasmus Darwin's Zoonomia (1794–96).[9]

Plasticity before plasticity: A longer history

By assembling these disparate bodies of knowledge about "ancient plasticity", I do not mean to suggest that people have long understood its molecular mechanisms and evolutionary significance, or that Grosseteste's passage can be used to date back neuroplasticity to Latin scholasticism of the thirteenth century. I am not looking here for a theory of predecessors, and I do not want to reify past traditions and practices of the body as a finished package of ideas or a stable referent that can immediately speak to our present concerns. I agree that the current understanding of plasticity is indeed a product of recent discoveries in neuroscience and molecular biology, made possible once scientists began to discard late nineteenth- and early twentieth-century notions of stability and permanency. However, a deeper and more pluralistic history of how living organisms were understood demonstrates that corporeal plasticity is not an event enabled by the linear unfolding of scientific innovation. Rather, a range of discourses, practices and ethical visions have stubbornly persisted and resurface today in the hype, potential and anxiety surrounding plasticity. A fresh, de-ossified approach to past counter-traditions and even forms of disqualified knowledge and anti-science (Foucault, 2003) suggests that the present has not been reached teleologically. A chief aim of this book is to show that the past is never entirely displaced, thus complicating the supposedly clean points of rupture in historical epistemology (Rheinberger, 2010; Loison, 2016). The postgenomic moment with all its scientific controversies exemplifies the contingency and precariousness of perceived epistemic closure. It uncannily overlaps ancient and very modern statements on the permeability of bodies to surrounding conditions. It undermines and provincializes ideas of a supposedly monolithic Western thought based on notions of stability and insuperable human–nature dualism, a cherished mythology for postmodernist and posthumanist authors.

A different family album for the epigenetic body

This applies also to the case of epigenetics, which I will describe in detail in Chapters 4 and 5. Through my pre-history of the plastic body I aim to reframe the current rise of interest in epigenetics within a broader history of body–world configurations. Usually, the most common origin stories of epigenetics cite Conrad H. Waddington's causal analysis of cell differentiation during development as its starting point (Waddington, 1957, 1968; Peterson, 2017; Squier, 2017; Buklijas, 2018). In more radical cases, epigenetics can be dated back to the early nineteenth-century theories of Jean-Baptiste Lamarck (Gissis and Jablonka, 2011) or the experiments of interwar heretic biologist Paul Kammerer (Taschwer, 2016). These links are accurate accounts in terms of molecular mechanisms and evolutionary debates. However, sociologically speaking, there is more to the present resurgence of interest in epigenetics than just Waddington or Lamarck. If we look at epigenetics as a contemporary template for a certain plasticity of the body; if we think of an epigenetic body as continuously metabolizing its surroundings, penetrated by multiple influences; if we think of epigenetics as a proxy for a certain malleability of heredity that extends beyond birth; if we think of race not as a fixed essence but as the embodied accumulation of environmental exposures; if we look at developmental origins of health and disease (DOHaD) as resurrecting a view of pregnancy as no longer a passive biological state but a moment of acute permeability requiring a permanent regime of vigilance; then none of the above claims look new or exceptional, and epigenetic and related postgenomic views of plasticity have a much deeper history to excavate.

I recognize that connecting the genealogical tree of epigenetics to ancient and early modern views of the body, such as humoralism, rather than twentieth-century explorations in embryology or molecular biology, goes against the grain of mainstream views. However, I am persuaded that this longer reading, even at the cost of losing some of the fine-grained quality of other approaches, presents multiple advantages, especially for a historical sociology of the body. Firstly, it offers a strong corrective to the present over-identification "with the temporal economy of innovation", where the appropriation and resurfacing of past themes is simply forgotten or denied (Cooper, 2017). Each age has its intellectual opium, and in contemporary life, innovation seems to be the winning one. In the Middle Ages, it was a point of honour to believe that ancient knowledge could not be surpassed. We seem to have made quite a radical inversion of this position, but no less uncritical. We simply make it a point of honour to ignore our past and overstate the radicalism of our present so as to equate the innovatory with the valuable. In order to produce the current state of excitation and hype, the social imagination around biology must foreclose past histories of plasticity. In contemporary scholarship, active forgetting (Proctor and Schiebinger, 2008) and ignoring are the conditions of accumulating new intellectual capital.[10] Taking a longer view of the plastic body and looking at plasticity not as a riddle solved by contemporary Western science but as a ubiquitous belief in traditions predating and coexisting with modern medicine will help disabuse ourselves of the seeming radicalism of today's turn to permeability and the exceptionalism of Western findings. It will help us understand that we must look beyond segmented studies of history (the modernistic body) to recognize the long shadow cast over the present by the dispersed and complex roots of notions of corporeal plasticity.

Secondly, this genealogical approach helps conjoin twenty-first-century and earlier body–world configurations and epistemologies. It offers a unique opportunity to dislocate polarities between modernity and tradition, Western and Southern medicine, and hegemonic and subjugated bodies of knowledge, given the global ramifications of humoralism as a form of *plasticity before plasticity*. It does so by focusing not on the molecular mechanisms of plasticity, but on plasticity as a form of life, that is, a number of ethical questions and related *techniques of existence* about how to live with a permeable body and how to govern permeable populations with mutable racial traits. This allows us to problematize the utter separation between our modern science and body–world configurations based on ideas and practices of bodily fluidity particularly in the Global South (for India: Langford, 2002; South Africa: Dubow, 1995; Philippines: Anderson, 2006; Australia: Douglas and Ballard, 2008). This is a powerful antidote to the modernistic attitude of authors who "believe in epistemic ruptures so radical that nothing of that past survives in them" (Latour, 1993: 68). It is at the same time a key tool to problematize a "hypostasised" version of the West as absolutely other to "traditional cultures and histories" (Washbrook, 1997; Therborn, 2003). It is also important for developing a truly global study of science (Raj, 2013) that considers the non-Euro-American areas as site of knowledge production rather than of passive recipients of external expertise (Anderson, 2002). A global phenomenology of the body plastic before and aside the modernistic body of biomedicine can facilitate a more pluralistic study of science.

Thirdly, universalizing biological plasticity as a sort of default commitment contributes to *a provincialization* of biological fixity. This is of the utmost importance for a global sociology of the body. It enables us to raise questions about the specific construction of the modernistic body of biomedicine as an exceptional sociocultural endeavour. If bodies have always been impressionable, heavily engraved by the power of external factors, how did we come to think of biological identity, heredity and race as immured from the external world? How did we come to think of ourselves as fixed and hardwired in genes? Rather than a generalizable case, biological fixedness (i.e. the genetic view of heredity), to paraphrase Walter Mignolo, is "a spectacular case of a global design built upon a local history" (2000: 22). However, as with every case of extraordinary intellectual success and hegemony, this intellectual prodigy needs a serious intellectual engagement and sociologically aware explanation. The implicit question behind this book is therefore to address the emergence not so much of current beliefs in plasticity as of those in fixity and hardness of bodies, race and heredity. How did a certain number of white, northern European men, mostly of Protestant background, come to equate biology with stability and lack of porousness since the last decades of the nineteenth century? Some of these men – Francis Galton, August Weismann, Ernst Mayr and Francis Crick – contributed to an insulation of the biological from its milieu and ideas of a hard nature writing at key junctures of political developments: the making of colonies and empires; nation-state building; the defeat of totalitarianism; and Cold War deployment. As others have noted, these wider biopolitical projects have framed and saturated the modernistic understanding of the biological body (Martin, 1994; Haraway, 1999; Cohen, 2009). As children of the twentieth century, we tend to believe that modernistic ideas of the immured body and insulated germ-plasm still offer the natural choreography of the relationship between the biological and the social, the fixed and the changeable. I don't mean to make these men – Galton, Weismann or Crick – the scapegoats of a cheap denunciation against modernism or individualism in biological theory. Their displacement of ideas of plastic bodies, races and heredity had, in several cases, an unquestionably emancipatory function (Meloni, 2016a). By highlighting how they worked against the grain of long-established views, I want instead to understand biological individualism, or perhaps biological liberalism, as a very fragile conceptual construct that may be already on retreat today (Gilbert et al., 2012; Bapteste and Dupré, 2013). Rather than being the default position, the notion of autonomy of the individual and disentanglement from environmental forces was achieved with great efforts in biological theory. Going through this history again may be particularly significant today, with claims of a new absorption of biology in its milieus again on the rise. It may also help provincialize emphatic claims of a vitality of matter, or intense traffic of body and milieu, that some postmodernist authors – unaware of this deeper history and blinded by the belief in a monolithic ontology of fixedness that has never been there – hope to rescue in the interstices of a modernity that is more precarious than they can ever imagine.

An alternative genealogy of biopower

Genealogy is an essential tool in challenging universalizing narratives about plasticity (or lack thereof), as though there were a single and timeless human body. From a genealogical perspective, plasticity is less an ideal signification than the result of historically situated techniques for constructing and governing mutable and porous bodies. It is also the effect of some specific material phenomena and infrastructures, such as writing technologies, as I will claim later. Ancient and early modern plasticity was forged not in abstract philosophical discussions but in concrete biopolitical practices, medical investigations and classificatory techniques to hierarchically distinguish between sexes and among ethnic groups on the basis of their softness and vulnerability to the all-encompassing power of the environment. Through medical, philosophical and climatological cartographies, the differential plasticity of various populations was used to separate ruling from ruled groups, Europeans (Greeks and later Romans) from Asians, temperate countries from the tropics. This inaugurated a tradition that lasted well into nineteenth-century colonialism: plasticity of traits at the service of military conquest and imperial designs (Osborne, 2000), but also plasticity as fear of racial deterioration after migrations to the new colonies, and hence unknown food, stars and climates (Earle, 2012; cfr. Stoler, 1995; Anderson, 2016).

The ancient biopolitics of plasticity presents some recurring themes that are worth keeping in mind. One is the construction of Oriental populations as *softer, more delicate* and *unwarlike* because of the way they are shaped by the monotony or gentleness of their climate. This trope can be found, to different degrees, in Hippocrates' *On Airs, Waters and Places*, in Aristotle's *Politics* and in later Roman authors. The argument about Oriental lack of "manly courage (*andreion*)" was easily turned into a platform for imperial strategies (Kennedy, 2016) and theories of natural slavery (as in Aristotle's *Politics*, 7.7). In the Middle Ages, the influential historian Gerald of Wales (1147–1220) still relied on this delicacy of Eastern groups to suggest how to defeat them militarily (Irby, 2016). Noticeably, from the fifteenth century and the first global colonial invasions, a North–South axis based on *latitude* (Wey-Gómez, 2008) juxtaposed this predominant Orientalist construct to classify tropical populations as less capable of governing themselves and being free. Aristotle's *Politics* is a compendium of all these ideas, with people living in temperate (*mediocriter*) places presented as the most capable of producing the best political systems:

> The nations inhabiting the cold places and those of Europe are full of spirit but somewhat deficient in intelligence and skill, so that they continue comparatively free, but lacking in political organization and capacity to rule their neighbours. The peoples of Asia on the other hand are intelligent and skilful in temperament, but lack spirit, so that they are in continuous subjection and slavery. *But the Greek race participates in both characters, just as it occupies the middle position geographically, for it is both spirited and intelligent; hence it continues to be free* and to have very good political institutions, and to be capable of ruling all mankind if it attains constitutional unity.
>
> (Pol. 1.327b23–33, my italics)

Views of direct environmental influence and the porosity of bodies to these effects also entered the military machines of ancient empires, like that of the Romans. Officers, such as Vegetius (*De re militari*, I/2), suggested avoiding recruiting troops from cold climates as they had too much blood and, hence, inadequate intelligence. Instead, he argued, troops from temperate climates should be recruited, as they possess just the right amount of blood, ensuring their fitness for camp discipline (Irby, 2016.). Delicate and effeminizing land was also to be abandoned as soon as possible, according to Manlius or Caesar (ibid.). Probably the most famous geopolitical dictum of antiquity reflects exactly this plastic power of places: "soft lands breed soft men", according to the claim that Herodotus attributed to Cyrus.

The strict relationship between geography and virtue is one of the most important biopolitical leitmotifs of ancient and early modern history, reaching scholastic philosophers such as Albert the Great and early modern political thinkers, including Bodin and Montesquieu. The moulding influence of geography produced various cartographies of racial and imperial domination based on soft, not hard, traits. While I will explore these and similar sites of ancient plasticity more systematically in the next chapter, my point here is that this oft-forgotten history matters to counter versions of biopower, colonial domination or racism as only being traceable to essentialist notions of fixity and innateness. This is a fundamental anachronism for ancient and early modern times. The supreme power of environmental effects was a key biopolitical dispositive of past and early modern authors. Environmental tropes of corporeal and racial plasticity were rarely used in a benign way. This is why we need to take a critical distance from the exquisitely twentieth-century notion of environmental effects as "more imaginative, more rational and more humane" (Toynbee, 1934) than other forms of biopolitics and racism.

However, is it appropriate to speak of biopolitics regarding these wide-spread environmentalist tropes? Is this an anachronism? It is undoubtedly an anachronism, but so is the usage of the word in Foucault for eighteenth-century police science (Ojakangas, 2016a). It is not my ambition to challenge directly the Foucauldian idea that a true biopower starts from early modern absolutism, and is only partly anticipated by forms of Christian pastorate (Foucault, 2003), but indirectly, I think I offer good evidence to problematize this claim. In the light of the subtle complexity of managing physiological functions under a humoralist framework, I find it hard to claim, as Foucault does, that biological life has entered into "history" and the spheres of "political techniques" only "millennia" after the Greeks, at the threshold of modernity (1978: 141–142). I aim to complicate another claim in the light of humoralist techniques of the body (Chapter 2): that of a purportedly hard separation between bare and qualified life, *zoe* and *bios* (Agamben, 1998), according to which one can claim either that there was no contamination between cor-poreal processes and the political realm in ancient times (Arendt, 1958), or that an originally separated bare life was excluded in order to be assumed within the paradigm of power (Agamben, 1998). These (quite problematic) views of ancient life have been used to support the notion either that there is only one overarching paradigm in the history of biopower (Agamben, 1998)[11] or that there was no biopolitics or even politicization of biological matter in the Greek world (Foucault, 1978). In recent years, Mika Ojakangas has argued against this latter thesis and in favour of the legitimacy of the category of ancient biopolitics. He has claimed that notions of power in the Greek polis are connected to vital processes:

> Ancient Greek political thought does not revolve around laws, juridical persons, free wills, contracts, and obligations, but around the technolo-gies of power over natural life whereby, to paraphrase Foucault, the basic biological features of the human species become the object of political strategy.
>
> (2016a: 141; see also 2016b)

I am sympathetic to this idea that there is a strange blindness in Foucault's reading of biopower in the Greek and Hellenistic world. However, unlike Ojakangas, my claim is that this story of ancient biopolitics is only partially captured by the writings of Plato and Aristotle. It is even less understand-able by projecting onto Plato or Aristotle the traits of the authoritarian pedagogy of early twentieth-century selectionist eugenics (Roper, 1913; Günther, 1928; see Forti, 2006). This version of biopower is not the one I aim to find with my analysis of the ancient and early modern body. Firstly, neither Plato nor Aristotle shared the view of racial purity or heredity of mainstream early twentieth-century selectionists (see Klosko, 1991). Both of them thought in a very different framework: open to the influence of nourishment upon heredity (Aristotle, *Pol.* 7.1336a3–5) or even to the inheritance of acquired characters (Plato, *Laws* 6.775d). They were definitely proto-racialist (Isaac, 2006), but in a sense quite different from our post-nineteenth-century view of race. However, besides the philological readings of Aristotle and Plato, I take issue with Ojakangas' interpretation because in focusing only on ancient philosophers, physiological bodies become conspicuously absent. Authors like Agamben and Ojakangas who support notions of ancient biopower miss the everyday physiological governance of bodies that can be found in sources like Hippocrates or early modern moral treatises on *the art of living* based on humoralist tropes. Here one can find more clearly the traits of an ancient governmentality of the body (individual but also collective) based on ideas of corporeal malleability, environmental influences and biosocial effects. This is a different, more horizontal form of biopolitics that impregnated day-to-day practices constructing ideas of personhood, corporeal management, and recognition of the body's vulnerability to its surroundings. Interestingly, this older history of a soft biopolitics may have some resonances with contemporary forms of neoliberal governmentality and the somatic individual (Rose, 2007). In particular, one of its key features stands out: the tension between targeting individual behaviours and making collective identities and hierarchies among human groups. Ancient and early modern views of the body, particularly but not only via humoralism, gave rise to initial forms of biopolitics at the level of both the political anatomy of the individual body and forms of government of populations. The former side has been highlighted particularly by Michael Schoenfeldt (1997): the porous humoralist body became the site for a quite specific art of self-fashioning, in which prudence, to cite Foucault, vigilance and a "constant and detailed problematization of the environment" were constantly reclaimed (Foucault, 1990: 101). Especially in the doctrine of the six non-naturals (Chapter 2), humoralism pushed people to enter into a certain relationship of self-governance and self-examination with their own body. It was, for this reason, easily incorporated into liberal and even bourgeois doctrines of individual health later in the eighteenth century

(Coleman, 1974). This was not an abstract view of the legal individual but a truly biosocial view in which shaping and controlling bodily fluids, vital processes, pores and metabolism with the external world was of the utmost importance. However, and this seems a blind spot in Foucault's analysis of ancient ethics, there was more than just individual techniques of the self in ancient bodies, more than just self-reflexivization. Humoralist, physiological and wider environmentalist tropes became the platform for vast technologies of power by which different groups and sexes were classified, and ultimately governed, on the bases of their specific physiology, permeability and corporeal fragility (Paster, 1993). Perhaps these strategies were not centralized, as in the eighteenth-century police science analyzed by Foucault. Nonetheless, they displayed that "double process" of subjectivation and objectivation by which the production of individual bodies "could also be described from the external perspective as a relationship of power" (Detel, 2005: 34). This silent shift away from individualization to the making up of biosocial collectives (racialized, gendered) appears very profound in the history of corporeal plasticity and may serve as a guiding thread to an alternative and longer history of biopower.

Importantly, this *longue durée* perspective may also contribute to a sociological history of the "civilizing process" that aims to explain the making of *homo clausus* (the separate, contained individual of modernity) not as a starting point but as the culmination of a long and conflicted historical process (Elias, 2000). Unlike Elias, however, a focus on humoralism disconnects the emergence of practices of the self (exclusively) from the making of the absolutist state in sixteenth-century Europe. It also challenges the Eliasian notions that these disciplinary techniques were mostly based on a repression of bodily fluids and evacuations. Humoralism gave rise to a more complex and sophisticated body–world configuration than this repressive hypothesis would have (Paster, 1993).

Embedding plasticity in a material history: Plasticity and sexual difference

If we think of corporeal plasticity as a last-minute invention without recognizing the complex filiation of contemporary notions and practices, we risk missing its present ambiguity and silencing its inherently political moment. We may overlook the idea that contemporary plasticity enables, at the collective level, forms of gender and racial domination that go well beyond depoliticized individual consumerism. The contemporary sociology and anthropology of plasticity very often avoid this historical depth and genealogical awareness. Plasticity is either celebrated as an ethical epiphany where a "whole new figure of the neurological human emerged" (Rees, 2016: 278) or dismissed as a trick of "neoliberal pressures of self-care, personal responsibility, and constant flexibility" (Pitts-Taylor, 2010: 640). Both these alternatives are unsatisfactory. They are modernistic assumptions (from the Latin *modo*, "just now"; see Cohen, 2009) that ignore the sedimented histories that precede and inform current body–world configurations, which may unfold again. The biopolitical shadow of past usages of plasticity is elided, in all its complexity and subtlety, and with that the material dispositive in which ancient plasticity was devised and conceived.

The exception to this modernistic understanding of plasticity is Catherine Malabou's work (particularly 2005). Uniquely among contemporary social commentators, Malabou has written important pages that trace plasticity back to its original Greek moment. She has particularly highlighted Aristotle's key text *De Anima* as a source (via Hegel) of modern debates on plasticity and its influence on anthropology. In *De Anima*, Malabou claims, the notion of "noetic plasticity" emerges as a profoundly duplex notion: "the originary unity of *acting* and *being acted upon*, of spontaneity and receptivity" (2005: 186). Following Malabou's analysis is very helpful: we are still very much caught in this oscillation between agency and vulnerability, making and undergoing that, according to Malabou, exemplifies the Greek experience of plasticity (ibid.,: 40). However, Malabou's reading reflects an idealized view of plasticity that remains unsatisfactory from a genealogical viewpoint. It obscures the embedment of Aristotle's work in a number of highly gendered metaphors from which plasticity emerges in sublimated terms. This is where a historical sociology of plasticity, which looks at its socio-material infrastructures, may work as a corrective to idealized philosophical readings.

The Aristotelian *De Anima* is, as commentators have observed, as much a philosophical treatise as a biological one (Shiffman, 2011). If one reads the notion of noetic plasticity against the wider background of the Aristotelian corpus, and particularly his patriarchal view of sexual reproduction, it will appear very clearly that the dual economy of plasticity – the interplay of *moulding* and *being moulded* – is embedded in a profoundly gendered imagination. Famously, in another work, the *Generation of Animals*, Aristotle establishes his masculinist view of embryogenesis based on the fundamental opposition between the male "as the active producer [*poiĕtikon*] and mover" and the female "as passive [*pathĕtikon*] and moved" (*Generation of Animals*, I.21 729b15–18; cited from Bianchi, 2014: 54). In this patriarchal view of biological growth and sexual difference, male and female are distinguished by the fact that the former possesses a certain power/capacity to give form that the woman lacks. This reflects the basic idea for Aristotle that

> the semen of the male differs from the corresponding secretion of the female in that it *contains a principle* within itself of such a kind as to set up movements also in the embryo and to concoct thoroughly the ultimate nourishment, whereas the secretion of the female contains material alone.
>
> (*Generation of Animals*, IV.1, my italics)

This principle (or the "efficient cause of generation") is in fact originally a formative force: the vital heat (*pneuma*) possessed by the male semen that has the power (*dynamis*) to shape forms during generation. The menstrual blood of the female (*menses* or *catamenia*) is instead cold and, hence, deprived of formative power. "The menses are seed but not pure seed", Aristotle writes, "for it lacks one thing only, the source of the soul". Menses contains the inert material of generation and can only receive forms (*Generation of Animals*, books II and IV, in particular 768 b15–27).[12] Aristotle's *Generation of Animals*, as philosopher Emanuela Bianchi writes, is "the hidden and therefore never adequately studied foundational book of Western patriarchal metaphysics" (2014: 3).

Plasticity's inherent dualism of both "to fashion and to be fashioned" (Malabou, 2005: 40) looks much less mysterious if one places Aristotle upon his biological and sociological feet, in the context of ancient forms of gender domination. The two sides of plasticity, the power to shape and the vulnerability to receive forms, can be allocated to the paternal and the maternal causes, respectively, in embryogenetic processes. The father will historically take the first side of plasticity: an active power that is the generator of forms, a "maker". Interestingly, Aristotle makes an explicit analogy between the male semen and a sculpting power, as something that can puts things into form, as in a "work of art" (GA II. 4). The female embodies the second sense of plasticity: a passive substrate upon which formative power is exerted. This second sense of plasticity is nicely captured by Joseph Needham's comment on Aristotle's embryogenesis, when he writes that the "male dynamic element [...] gives a shape to the *plastic* female element" (1959: 43). Female plasticity is no longer the power to generate but just to absorb alien forms. That this embryological background is one of the keys to a genealogy of plasticity finds further confirmation in the trajectory of the notion of "plastic power" or *vis plastica*, which became very influential in Renaissance debates (Hunter, 1950; Hirai, 2005 and 2016; Smith, 2006). *Vis plastica* can be traced back to embryological debates (mostly in Galen) where the active power of the paternal semen (hotter than the female semen) is said to contain a special moulding faculty: *dunamis diaplastike*, plastic power, because it moulds the inert female matter. This faculty, via the work of Arab commentators like Avicenna, will transit to the Renaissance, becoming a "divine formative power" (Fernel, 1548) or a "plastic", spermatic logos, as in Schegk's *On the Plastic Faculty of the Seed* (*De plastica seminis facultate*, 1580). Cambridge Platonists in the seventeenth century will then turn this idea into a notion of "plastick might" in the sense of a transcendent intellect pervading and shaping all physical processes, not just foetal development (Hirai, 2005; 2007a and b; 2017). This is the only visible 'biological' usage of the term "plasticity" before modernity. Its history betrays a very masculinist origin in the radical asymmetry between the formative power of the male seminal liquid and the maternal receptive matter.

The political materiality of plasticity: Impressionable biologies

This is just one possible example of the way in which a genealogical approach may help not only trace forgotten filiations of ancient plasticity but also re-embed its vocabulary into a very material history of gender and race domination. There is a second genealogical route to diffract ancient plasticity through the prism of its very material origin. This genealogical route inspires the title of this book and my whole project of defining biological matter as deeply imbued with social meanings, not just "malleable" but durably "impressionable". It comes directly from writing techniques in classical times: incising marks on wax tablets using a small pointed metal tool (*stilus*) or sealing a block of wax with a metal stamp to make official signatures in relief. This infrastructural aspect offered a key metaphorical repertoire by which Plato and Aristotle conveyed the idea of marking a receiving surface. Importantly, this process of imprinting is often rendered with the Latin term *impressio* [from *imprĭmo, in-* + *premō*: to press in]. It is through this metaphor, as we saw above, that Aristotle defines plastic matter as an "impressible" matter in his *Meteorology*. The process of making an impression, Aristotle says,

> is the sinking of a part of the surface of a thing in response to pressure or a blow, in general to contact. Such bodies are either soft, like wax, where part of the surface is depressed while the rest remains, or hard, like copper. Non-impressible bodies are either hard, like pottery (its surface does not give way and sink in), or liquid, like water (for though water does give way it is not in a part of it, for there is a reciprocal change of place of all its parts).

(Book IV, part 9)

However, from this physics of plasticity, metaphors of impression are extended to much more complex models. Consider, for instance, two key passages in Plato and Aristotle, both translated by scholastic Latins with *impressio*. In the first, Plato famously compares the soul to "a block of wax" and the mechanism of memory to making "impressions from seal rings" upon it (*Theaetetus*, 191, c–e). In the second, Aristotle advances his influential theory of signification by comparing sense perception to "the way in which a piece of wax takes on the impress of a signet-ring without the iron or gold" (*De Anima*, II, XII). Here the Latin word *impressio* translates the Greek *sēmeion*, sign. One could extend these examples to the whole of antiquity, where metaphors of the soul or the body as written or impressed upon were common currency. However, the word *impressio* often took a stronger and cruder meaning beyond the description of a writing or sealing process. It overlaps with notions of *impetus, physical violence, assault, irruption, military attack*. This more violent sense is well retained in the Latin version of the Hippocratic treatise *On Head Wounds* (1999). Here, the text uses "impression" to refer to "the weapon which struck against the bone leaves its impression on the part which it struck" (part 7). Even more interestingly, at the intersection of writing mechanisms and physical pressures, *impressio* became, in the Scholastic tradition, a template for any form of "environmental" influences from heavenly bodies (*corpora caelestia*) onto inferior sublunary matter, including the Earth. This is, for instance, the sense in which it is used by Dante in his *Divine Comedy* when, describing the sun, he gives voice to Saint Thomas:

> Lo ministro maggior de la natura,
> che del valor del ciel lo mondo *imprenta*
> e col suo lume il tempo ne misura.
>
> *Commedia* III X 28–30 (my emphasis)[13]

Dante is simply reflecting here a widespread usage of metaphors of imprinting in scholastic times, from Albert the Great to Robert Grosseteste. This latter wrote in 1220 a treatise called *De Impressionibus Elementorum*, that is, *The Impressions of the Elements*. Thomas Aquinas (1225–1274) himself used the metaphor repeatedly. For instance, in his *Summa Theologica*, in an attempt to rescue free will from a too materialistic view of the imprinting powers of celestial bodies, he claims that "it is impossible for heavenly bodies *to make a direct impression* on the intellect and will". In so doing, however, he must concede that celestial bodies can "be a dispositive cause of an inclination to those operations *in so far as they make an impression* on the human body" (*Summa Theol.* II, II, 95 a 5; my emphasis). It is at this level that the widespread belief in astrology in Latin scholasticism and early modernity can be understood as a part of a general theory of impression and bodily plasticity. Authors like Albertus the Great, or later Machiavelli and Ficino described via astrological themes (especially when it comes to electoral astrology, that is, the influence on the course of everyday actions, not what is fixed at birth) a particular malleability of either the individual or the body politic to celestial influences.[14]

Interestingly, this framework of a direct impression of the heavens on sublunary bodies is not gender neutral. Here we are brought back to the above point about plastic power and sexual difference. In Aristotle, several Arab commentators and the later scholastic tradition, the analogy between *celestial influences as a paternal power* and the *receptive sublunary matter as a female* is quite literal. Impressions, as plasticity, originate from a masculine power to shape female matter. As Justine Smith writes, citing the Dominican philosopher Antoine Goudin (1668):

> according to Aristotle and Saint Thomas, earth and water furnish to everything arising from the bowels of the earth their matter and bosom, as would a mother, while heaven and the stars fulfil the office of the father, who imparts the form. A "male" formative principle exercises its influence over the "maternal" matter of the earth and thereby gives rise to forms in earth that resemble living beings.
>
> (2013: 262)

The general impressionability of sublunary bodies is therefore an aspect of their feminine and susceptible nature. This recipient matter is shaped by the dispositions left "from the imprint of the active principle (*principii agentis*)", as medieval theologians used to say (Arens, 1984: 464).

It is finally worth noting that, besides this widely used sense of a celestial influence on the earth, impression is also the framework through which theories of corpuscular vision and hearing are explained by scholastic thinkers (Aquinas, 1951). Notions of impressions are used in epistemological debates (how truth impresses itself into concepts) and even Trinitarian theology (how the Holy Trinity impresses its triune character upon the angelic hierarchy in Bonaventure). More significantly for future debates on the impressionability of female matter, both sensory cognition and generation were often explained "in terms of the impression of the images on soft or subtle matter" (Park, 1998: 260). For this reason, they were seen "not only as cognate faculties but faculties whose operation was physiologically linked" (ibid: 260, 262); hence one of the sources of the pervasive beliefs in maternal impressions – the capacity of women to mark, imprint or deform the foetus through "imagination" – which will represent one of the key pathways of plasticity until early modernity.

Overview of the book

The notion of impressionable biologies aptly condenses the original non-modern intuition of a body constantly exposed to an immense number of external influences. This was an attentive and excitable body, but also a body constantly *under pressure*, at the mercy of the all-encompassing power of the environment, physical and social, with profound patriarchal and racialist resonances. This vulnerable biological matter will be explored in the next chapter mostly through its most visible ancient and early modern champion, the humoralist body (Chapter 2). I will then discuss how this original plasticity and explanatory models based on the appeal of direct environmental influences had to be challenged by key nineteenth century authors in order to align the biological body to some key tenets of modern liberalism: *autonomy*, *inviolability* and *boundedness* of the individual body. I will focus on the contribution of Darwin and Weismann and the emerging views of heredity in genetics as quintessentially modernist strategies to displace ancient plasticity. They all broke with the "Hippocratic imagination" (Cohen, 2009) of a body circumfused by place. Darwin (at least for his selectionist thesis, given that his view of heredity is deeply "Hippocratic", i.e. pangenesis, as I will argue below) and Weismann produced conceptual technologies to subtract or buffer the individual from environmental pressures. This move included the breaking of ancestral ties to establish that individuals were born free, or at least unburdened by the actions of their immediate ancestors. After the rise of selectionism and later genetics, the environment was disentangled from the individual body, taking shape as a well-defined field of forces that one could look at externally, that is, as alien to an authentic and irreducible self. The radical plasticity and ecological inspiration of humoralism, a body of flows and liquid forces (Paster, 1993), including its most sinister versions (racial degeneration as a consequence of colonial migrations or environmental exposures), started to look increasingly problematic for late nineteenth century authors (Chapter 3). Chapter 3 is somehow a self-standing unit in the context of the book, but helpful to identify the moral implications of the nurture first/nature first debate that are resurfacing today in epigenetics.

In the third and final part I will discuss how epigenetics may open once again the door to a view of the permeable body in the language and framework of twenty-first-century molecular biology. I read with interest and curiosity the emerging wave of epigenetic literature, and am sympathetic to many of its efforts to put this knowledge in the service of under-represented groups and communities (Chapter 4). My main concern, however, reflects the lesson I have learned from the history of the plastic body: *a body shaped from and traversed by outside matter is also a body vulnerable to a number of disciplinary practices and forces*, open, that is, to "governmental intensification" (Rose, 1996). Albeit it may seem old-fashioned to claim this nowadays, biological liberalism – with its art of separation and boundary-making (Walzer, 1984) – had kept these forces contained through a strong notion of individual autonomy and physiological insulation. This withdrawal of the individual body from the towering power of the external environment gained momentum in nineteenth-century biomedical thought also because it could be perceived as a technology of freedom. The question in the final chapter is therefore what happens in postgenomics as a post-liberal biological world in which the individual is submerged again by environmental forces at the molecular level. I focus in particular on the emergence of the complex figure of plasticity generated by epigenetics: a plasticity that is neither about modernistic control (that is, responding to the desire of an agent-master) nor about endless potentialities, as in postmodernist narratives of fluidity and decentering of the subject. Epigenetics' emerging plasticity is not explainable in the above terms; instead, it is closer to an *alter-modernistic* view that disrupts clear boundaries between openness and determination, individual and community. The resonance of this notion with older epistemologies of the body and non-Western ecological views may explain the growing interest and appeal of epigenetics in postcolonial areas beyond the mainstream scientific Global West, as I highlight in the final chapter (Chapter 5).

Notes

1 Postgenomics is usually taken as a temporal label, to reflect a period inaugurated with the completion of the human genome project in 2003. However, in my reading I will favour the notion that postgenomics is a different "style of reasoning" (Hacking, 2002) compared with genomics – one that emphasizes the permeability of the genome to material surroundings and the plasticity of its functioning. I will define the term and its history more extensively in Chapter 4.
2 Antonyms are not really "opposite". While opposition implies incompatibility (single/married), antonyms are gradable pairs whose meanings are oppositional along a continuum (such as dry/wet). Some authors in semantics take opposites also to be a kind of binary antonyms, so in this case plasticity and elasticity would be "gradable antonyms" (see Lyons, 1977).

3 James' innovation is in his applying this older concept to organic matter (particularly the nervous tissue) and human behaviours (habit), rather than inanimate materials.

4 However, the usage of the adjective "plastic" is documented in all main European languages well before what Malabou suggests (2005: footnotes 24 and 25). Beside the Greek and Latin usage, "plastick" (but not "plastic") already appears in English in the first half of the seventeenth century in the work of Henry More (in the Platonic sense explained on p. 31) and Ben Jonson, but also in France from 1553 at least in the translation of the work of Leon Battista Alberti (*L'architecture et art de bien bastir, divisée en dix livres*, a translation of *De re ædificatoria*, 1443–1452). The Spanish usage has also a few early attestations from the late sixteenth century. In Italian the first usage I could trace occurs in an astrological book (Cornelio Malvasia, 1647, *Discorso dell'anno astrologico*) probably influenced by the Platonic view of a plastic cosmic power. The German usage is late, at the time of Herder and more frequently after that. Goethe's 1832 *Promemoria on Plastic Anatomy* belongs to a different genre of material culture of plasticity in wax anatomic collections that is outside my focus here (see, for instance, Mazzolini, 2004; Hopwood, 2004 and 2007; Maerker, 2011).

5 One generation after Herder, Hegel's *Lectures on the Philosophy of History* (written between 1822 and 1830, published 1837) are perhaps a point of passage toward the modernistic meaning of plasticity as mobility, freedom and even escape from the weight of matter; see Malabou (2005: 200)

6 Global South is an increasingly common shorthand in social science to include postcolonial areas outside the globally dominant regions of Europe and North America (Connell, 2007; Comaroff and Comaroff, 2012; Anderson, 2016).

7 The use of the word "environment" in the context of my analysis of ancient biology is obviously an anachronism, given that the English word exists only from the nineteenth century (Pearce, 2010). I here use the term as a shortcut to wider notions of external influences and impressions guided by my specific research question.

8 Including the popular belief in postpartum maternal shaping of cubs (supposedly born formless) through maternal licking (book I, chap. 54).

9 Besides an overt connection between lunar phases and menstrual periods, we can read in Erasmus Darwin that: "The periodic returns of so many diseases coincide with the diurnal, monthly, and annual rounds of time; that any one, who would deny the influence of the sun and moon on the periods of quotidian, tertian, and quartan fevers, must deny their effect on the tides, and on the seasons." (1818: 427).

10 This process, and related forgetting of alternative traditions, is dramatically facilitated by the increasing monolingualism of the academic community (Gordin, 2015).

11 Agamben develops his notion of bare life from an ancient legal figure (Homo sacer), but then the term is no longer confined to this specific aspect and is freely used for all physiological private processes (life itself) that are excluded/included into sovereign power (1998).

12 For more feminist scholarship on Aristotle, see Deslauriers, 2009; Freeland, 2010; Tuana, 1988.

13 The greatest of the ministers of nature, Who with the power of heaven the world imprints, And measures with his light the time for us (translation Henry Wadsworth Longfellow, Pennsylvania State University: Longfellow (1886).

14 It goes beyond the scope of my book to treat in a wider way ideas of plastic bodies (at both the individual and collective level, the political body as in Machiavelli) connected to medical astrology. See, however, for Albertus: Zambelli, 1992; for Machiavelli: Parel, 1992; for Ficino: Christopoulos, 2010. Overview in Barton, 1994 and Zambelli, 2012. See also: Azzolini, 2013.

Plasticity before plasticity: The humoralist body

2

What were bodies before the Enlightenment? How were they investigated and understood? Inspired mostly by a Foucauldian analysis, a growing historiography has emerged over recent decades, which attempts to destabilize a continuist view of the body as an unchanging natural reality across different epochs (Laqueur, 1990; Duden, 1991; Feher et al., 1989a, 1989b, 1989c; Kuriyama, 1999; Corbin et al., 2005a, 2005b, 2006).

As the "governing paradigm of function" through which people perceived their own body until early modernity (Paster, 1993: 16), humoralism is an excellent point of entrance to further pursue this strategy. If the history of the body "is ultimately a history of ways of inhabiting the world" (Kuriyama, 1999: 237), an investigation of humoralism enables us to recover an ecology of the body and emotions prior and alien to post-Enlightenment modalities (Paster, 2004). It presents us with a challenge, not only to know its technicalities, practices and rituals but to grasp "the lived feel" of its phenomenological reality (Kuriyama, 2008: 419; see Kuriyama, 1999; Duden, 1991). This is an especially hard task for Western modern readers, now accustomed to the notion of an inviolable selfhood that finds its biological mirror in the idea of a unique and unchangeable genetic program. But the body of humoralism was very different. "Once upon a time", as Shigehisa Kuriyama writes, "all reflection on what we call the body was inseparable from inquiry into places and directions, seasons and winds" (1999: 262; Rosenberg, 2012).

Although some humoralist frameworks traded in notions of stability, especially when identified with typologies of personality traits (represented in sixteenth-century comedy of humours), the humoralist body was always marked by *a contextual dependency on time and place* that gave it the resources to undermine or consume this fixity (Paster, 2004). In this chapter I will analyse humoralism not so much as a system of medicine but as an ontology of the body, through which I will assess the impressionable nature of ancient and early modern biology. The permeable and malleable body of humoralism has both resemblances to and differences from the modernistic perception of corporeal plasticity. On one side, it is profoundly different due to its strong emphasis on the ecological embedding of the body in places and times. It is a plasticity of receiving forms from external forces. In a poetic image, the humoralist body can be compared to an iron magnet attracted by various external forces, a vibrating diapason, or a body-sponge (Donne). Sometimes it is described as a sea-wave that swells or retreats in response to lunar changes: "As the sea waves, so are the spirits and humours in our bodies, tossed with tempestuous windes and stormes" (Burton, 1621 [2000]:120). This is obviously very different from the stability of the modernistic body. However, the management of this ecological vulnerability produced techniques of the self which are not alien to our mentality of bodily control: plasticity as giving forms. It also gave rise to forms of hope about regeneration of the body (including the political body), as well as anxieties about poisoning and degeneration at the individual and collective level, again congruent with our modern understanding. Finally, it displayed two further characteristics that are significant for our present. It gave rise to highly "personalized" medical techniques centred on the uniqueness of each individual temperamental mixture (Nutton, 2004: 281); and it enabled a "somatic" view of habits and behaviours, rooted in the notion that the movements of humours literally made mental faculties. Before looking at the political subtlety of this ontology of the body, however, it is important to better situate humoralism in its complex historical and geographical context.

The great historical unity of corporeal plasticity

Humoralism is the century-long doctrine that the body is composed of elementary fluids (humours) whose proportion and balance depended on wider "environmental" influences (a broad notion that included waters and food, airs and the positions of stars). It is a medical doctrine aimed at obtaining and maintaining humoral balance through nutrition, exercise, evacuations and secretion (Paster, 1993). Humoralism was the most important, albeit certainly not the only, school of ancient and early modern medicine. It is also a truly flexible and complex historical label (Nutton, 2004; Horden and Hsu, 2013): its multifaceted epistemologies, practices and techniques crossed and coexisted with different cultures, political systems and religions for more than twenty centuries (Temkin, 1973; Sargent, 1982; Siraisi, 1990). In Europe, for instance, humoralism influenced, among other things, the ancient and medieval psychology of temperaments (Klibansky et al., 1964); Renaissance theories of geopolitical differences (or geohumoralism: Floyd-Wilson, 2003); and the link between atmosphere and health that characterized a neo-Hippocratic revival in eighteenth-century Britain (Golinski, 2010), such as in works like John Arbuthnot's *Essay concerning the Effects of Air on Human Bodies* (1733). In Germany, one of the last translations of Galen's work for practising physicians dates to the 1820s (Reiss, 2003). In nineteenth-century France, the great philologist Émile Littré was a passionate translator and commentator of Hippocratic texts, often with an eye on recent colonial developments (for example, on the connection of climate and health in the new colonies, see Osborne, 1996).

It is not only the temporal, but also the spatial boundaries of humoralism that are impressive and complex. With possible roots in the work of ancient Egyptian and Mesopotamian physicians (van Sertima, 1992: 18; Mones et al., 2013), humoralist ideas became systematized in Greece only after the sixth century BCE. In the flourishing philosophical landscape of the Hellades, they became a canonical – albeit highly heterogenous - set of teaching with the Hippocratic corpus: a collection of twenty-seven treatises written in the fifth and fourth centuries BCE (Lloyd, 1978). In this Greek soil, medical humoralism grew, nurtured by a number of themes from pre-Socratic cosmology that heavily influenced its understanding of the body. For instance, both Heraclitus' (544 to 484 BCE) monistic materialism and his radical processual ontology of impermanency and constant change (Barnes, 1982; Graham, 2015) and Empedocles' (ca. 450 BCE) view of four elementary components or "roots" (*rhizōmata*) at the foundation of all existing matter – earth, water, air and fire – became central tenets of humoralist thinking. Other themes, like the Pythagorean fascination with the number four, the microcosm–macrocosm analogy by which every external element "has its counterpart in the human body" (Glacken, 1967), and Homeric themes of a body "without skin" (Gavrylenko, 2012), may have contributed to the wider philosophical background of humoralism.

The Greek synthesis of philosophy and medicine was a singular product. It produced an ontology of the body that cut across any substantial inner/outer separation (Padel, 1992): stuff of the outside and stuff of the inside often overlapped. One case in point is the Greek notion of *pneuma*, which can mean both an aspect of the physical environment (air or wind) as well as the body's interior, spirit or breath, and often became a placeholder for passions (as in Antigone's chorus: Kuriyama, 1999). This materialist connection of cosmology and ontology implies a profound openness of the body. As Ruth Padel has written, all Greek medical theory is a theory of *poroi* (πόροι), a theory of the "infinitely penetrable body" (1992: 58). *Poroi* are literally the pores, channels or paths that enable a constant exchange between the interior of the body and its environment, placing not only the whole body on the verge of constant change but each part of the body potentially movable by changes in other parts. Albeit not exclusive to humoralist doctors, humoralism made intense usage of this notion:

> The Hippocratic uses *poroi* with zest. Sweating is caused by air in the body condensing when it hits particular pores, flowing through them to reach the *body's* outer surface. Dropsy occurs when breaths have dilated the poroi by passing through the flesh; moisture follows the breaths into the poroi, the *body* becomes sodden, the legs swell.
>
> (ibid.)

However, humoralism went well beyond Greek or European medical knowledge. It became a truly global phenomenon spreading over time to the whole *Oikoumenē*, the "historically interconnected totality" of the ancient world for the Greeks, stretching from the boundary of Gibraltar (the Pillars of Hercules) to India (see Kroeber, 1945). A key event in the global circulation of humoralism is its Islamic translation and incorporation. After the eighth century CE, humoralism seeped into Arabic and Muslim culture, mostly via Egypt and Persia (Arikha, 2007). Inspired by the philosophico-medical synthesis of authors like Al-Kindi, Ibn Sina (Avicenna) and Ibn Rushd (Averroes), this Greek-Perso-Arabic synthesis became known as *Unani* medicine (meaning from the Ionian sea, i.e. Greek), and was also based on the idea of four humours (*akhlaat*). Through the Arabs, it reached India and the Malay peninsula, where its influence continues today (Liebeskind, 2002; Ernst, 2002; Attewell, 2007). It is to the Arabic cultivation of humoralism that Western Medieval medicine owes its existence, mostly via the work of Latin scholars who travelled to the Arabic world from the twelfth century (Nutton, 2004). It is worth adding here that, besides the important role of direct geographical influences on the body, there is significant similarity[1] between humoralism and other non-Western medical traditions, such as traditional Chinese medicine (Helman, 1984; Kuriyama, 1999; Needham et al., 2000) or pre-Columbian Indigenous medicine (Foster, 1994). The analogies between the open body of humoralism and Ayurvedic physiology (based on three humours, or dosha) are also striking (Wujastyk, 2003). As in the humoralist framework, in Ayurveda the body is imagined in flux, as an open field in which one could discern "the flows of substances through channels, and the transformation of these substances into one another" (Trawick, 1992: 136). As in humoralism, patients are understood as deeply embedded in places, enclosing in their bodies a "social, climatic, or cosmic field" (Langford, 2002: 11). As in humoralism, cosmology and physiology almost overlap in Ayurveda: physiology is not only about bodily function but is also governed by "the circulation of fluids in the environment, including the saps in plants, the aromas in cooking different kinds of meat, and the interplay of humours within the human body" (Zimmermann, 1988: 197). These non-Western epistemologies, in which the body is represented and lived as a process or landscape, profoundly resonate with ancient and early modern European medical views based on humoralism. Before the rise of modern biomedicine, there was a great historical unity in the ontology of the body based on the fluidity of its processes and their ecological embedding. This synthesis was displaced only by the definitive breakdown of Hippocratism in nineteenth-century Europe. It is from this collapse that the enclosed body of modern biomedicine takes shape.

A processual ontology of the body

Humoralism's key premise is a constant flow between the body and its surroundings. Given the strict correspondence between bodily and cosmic matter (each humour corresponds to an external quality, a season, a time of the day, and vice versa), the body can be seen as a "system of intake and outgo", always in "dynamic interactions" with its milieu (Rosenberg, 1985: 40). This focus on patterns of modulatory influences (Paster, 2004) is not a metaphorical apparatus, as it often is in modern times, aimed to destabilize a prior and predominating perception of fixedness. It is, rather, an accurate description of physiology for a body that was often described as "Transpirable and Transfluxible, that is, so open to the ayre as that it may passe and repasse through them" (Crooke, 1615, cited in Paster, 1993: 9).

Humoral physiology well reflects this porous nature. According to Ibn Sina's (Avicenna's) classical compendium known as the *Canon of Medicine* (eleventh century), physiological issues are mostly about material substances entering "from without" and constantly pervading members and tissues. Take food, for instance: humours are ultimately "the soluble substances produced from food and drink by the various digestive processes in the mouth, stomach, intestines, blood, and organs" (Abu Asab et al., 2013: 22). The inner fabric of the body – the four humours, flesh and other tissues – is an end product or a "concoction" (the humoralist word for digestion or cooking) of ingested food (King, 1998). This is why Ibn Sina (as Hippocrates and Galen before him) goes to great lengths to distinguish carefully in his medical writings between different foods, their usage in different seasons and climates, and specific ways to cook them to favour the circulation of healthy humours and the discharge of morbid ones (Avicenna, 1999). In humoralism, the boundary between drugs and food, therapeutics and dietetics, is always tenuous (for Hippocrates: Lloyd, 1978: 69 and ff; for Galen, see Grant, 2000; see also Totelin, 2015).

The ontological continuum in humoralism is not only between food (or air, or any other "external" factors) and the body, however. It is also within the body, between passion and mental dispositions, psychology and physiology (Arikha, 2007: VI). As with the four humours, passions were "liquid forces of nature" (Paster, 2004: 4) that connected inwardness to material things. "Psychological" changes could be brought about by changes in a wide range of material factors: food, wine, wind and atmosphere; sleeping, taking baths and exercise;[2] ventilation of rooms, inhaling different odours and aromas, and drinking hard or soft waters (Kuriyama, 2008). Humours, some more than others (yellow or black bile, for instance, more than phlegm), were deemed "character-affecting (*êthopoios*)" (Bos, 2009: 35). They embodied "significance [and were] imbued with moral density and spiritual import" (Paster, 2004: 6). *Temperature* of the humours was *temperament*, or at least important enough to make people fall in love (Jacques Ferrand, 1610, *A Treatise on Lovesickness*; cfr. Totelin, 2005). "The Minds inclination follows the Bodies Temperature", noted the English jurist John Selden (1614: cited in Paster, 2004: 31). "When the humours by the Aire bee stirred, he goes in with them, exagitates our spirits, and vexeth our Soules", claimed English clergyman Robert Burton in his *Anatomy of Melancholy* (1621 [2000]), and so believed philosopher Edmund Burke (1757) (Golinski, 2010).

Humours themselves – blood, choler, black bile and phlegm, according to Galen's later systematization – were not immutable essences like the four bases of DNA nowadays. Although each one had its own distinctive effect on the body, each could easily turn into another (King, 1998). Lemnius Levinus (1505–1568), the influential Dutch doctor, complained that complexions were difficult to frame and were "*easelye one into an other transmuted*" (cited in Spiller, 2011: 28–9). Since the quantity and prevalence of humours in the body were defined by their relation to the external environment (food consumption, temperature, age, season, and even "intellectual" acts such as reading, hence, the physical dangers of its excesses), this provided ample opportunities to rebalance humours (Spiller, 2011). "Regardless of one's predominant temperament [...] humours shifted according to what one ate and drank, to where one lived, and to climate and season" (Arikha, 2007: VII). Eating warm foods generated more bile, cold foods more phlegm. Similar shifts occurred during what were perceived as warmer or colder life periods. "Each one's humoral relation to the outside world [was] expected to change daily and seasonally" as the humoralist body passed through life stages (in the context of Malay humoralism: Laderman, 1987). Individual complexion was shaped and altered by different "intake of food and condiments", each of which also had "its own complexion", so that both a person and a food (black pepper, for instance) could be considered choleric (Albala, 2002: 5). And, just like food, humours also could be transformed in the process of "cooking". Arab doctors in particular highlighted the ongoing transformations and mingling of humours: a series of concoctions could always change

> food into phlegm, black bile, yellow bile and blood in turn, and the higher could always degenerate to lower as blood by chilling, for example, or yellow bile by burning.
>
> (Reiss 2003: 40)

Besides metaphors of cooking, an important part of the humoralist repertoire was represented in ideas of liquidity and fluidity, and the associated risks of leaking. The fluidity of humours is connected to the same origin of the term, which comes from botanical observations: humour (*ikmas* or *chumos* in Greek) means literally *a juice* or life-giving *moisture* (King, 2013; see also Thomas, 2000), such as would nourish a plant in soil. This explains one of the most common analogies in the humoralist world: that between plants and humans (King, 2013: 25). It was both a mechanistic analogy that emphasized the similarities in human conception and plant growth (Lonie, 1981) and a developmental one that considered human characteristics, like those of plants, to be deeply affected by places. Given a change in the properties and nourishment from the soil, availability of sunlight and intensity of the wind, moving the plant, or planting the same species elsewhere, would produce different results. The same would happen with people, individually and at the group level. *Like plants, they would change with a change of place.* This was a common trope in ancient and early modern understandings of racial characteristics, from Bartolome de Las Casas' defence of Indigenous people based on ideas of malleability of racial characteristics (1542) to, later in the sixteenth century, authors like Bodin and Montaigne. Reflecting this metaphorical legacy, which owes its origin to humoralism, in the *Six livres de la République*, Bodin writes that "if men are transplanted from one country to another, although they do not react as quickly as plants which suck their nourishment from the very soil, nevertheless in time they also will change" (book

V, 1576 [1962]). Montaigne also claimed of people that, although there are significant factors of influence beyond places, "like plants, they will assume new characteristics when they migrate" (Glacken, 1967: 450).

These tropes of instability are characteristic of humoralist themes. Despite the importance of the notion of *individual complexio* (the Latin word for the temperament, i.e. balance of humours), the humoralist body was never a stable achievement or essence. Certainly, dominant humours and inborn qualities were investigated and systematized, especially after Galen, who classified nine types of temperaments (Paster, 1993). In the post-Galen tradition, these inborn qualities often constrained boundless change and mutability. However, it would be a serious misunderstanding to project onto them the stable core of identity of post-Enlightenment views of personhood (Reiss, 2003) and consider them essentialist rather than relational categories (Fend, 2015). A "phlegmatic", "sanguine" or "choleric" character was not a permanent constitution but subject to a complex process of balancing. Temperaments and "innate" factors were potentially always ready to metamorphose into something else "according to temperature, time, place, age and diet: for all humours arise and increase at every moment and season" (Montserrat, 1998; Grant, 2000: 15). Incidentally, the same misunderstanding exists in relation to astrology, which was often connected with humoralist tropes. The ancient and early modern understanding of medical astrology was less about fixed fate at birth than about navigating and manipulating the complexity of celestial (or occult) influences through everyday acts and decisions (Zambelli, 1992, 2012; Barton, 1994; Arikha, 2007; Azzolini, 2013; Floyd-Wilson, 2013; Siraisi, 2015).

Biological identity and stability are not the starting point for humoralism. They are dynamically achieved (often only briefly) through a complex micropolitical governance of the individual's relationship with its surroundings. As Noga Arikha writes:

> The humoural being's life, from conception to death, remained a balancing act. Sexuality, appetites, passions, and perceptions, all changes and crises, and all responses to the environment required a readjustment of the humours and of the body's secretions. Even spiritual life was sustained by physiology, and the line between illness and health was not necessarily clear.
>
> (2007: 99)

This is very similar to the techniques of the self described by Foucault for the fragile ancient body, in which all "elements of the milieu were perceived as having positive or negative effects on health" (Foucault, 1990: 100). This ancient ontology of the body seriously undermines the idealized division of ancient life into bare and qualified life, *zoe* and *bios*, which a philosophical tradition has often proposed, simply ignoring the centrality of ancient medical traditions. It also challenges Foucault's idea that only at the threshold of modernity does there occur an immediate reflection of "biological existence [...] in political existence" (1978: 142). If basic vital functions were not immediately political in ancient times, they were certainly deeply moralized by humoralist treatises on the art of living, which became widespread in Western and non-Western traditions of medicine. It is difficult to claim in the light of this legacy that "for millennia, man remained [...] a living animal with the additional capacity for a political existence" (Foucault, 1978: 143). Foucault himself came to recognize that this boundary is much more blurred, given how a "medical" perception of places and circumstances led to a necessary micropolitics of the self in everyday life, since Greek antiquity (1990).[3]

However, before addressing the importance of this specific politics of the humoralist body, it is important to free humoralism from a narrow focus on medical history.

More than a medical doctrine

If the phenomenological experience of humoralism, and thus the ancient body, is no longer accessible to us, it is in part because the theory is almost the exclusive province of traditional medical histories, which characterize it mostly as a disqualified precursor to later scientific views. This understanding is much too narrow, as a more recent historiography has shown. Humoralism was a medical practice, but it was also an "ethnography" and "sociology" of the ancient world (Thomas, 2000: 25 and ff.; Grant, 2000: 199, respectively). It was an attempt to come to terms with the kaleidoscopic experience of bodies and ways of inhabiting the world that were not only radically diverse from place to place but also subject to alteration because of a change in nutrition, the position of the stars or migration. Jacques Jouanna, leading expert on Hippocrates, writes that in the Hippocratic corpus we find the first "rational ethnography" that "extends the etiological method to the study of people, so that medicine develops into an ethnography" (Jouanna, 1999: 35).

This is particularly the case of Hippocrates' *On Airs, Waters and Places*. Written in the fifth century BCE as a medical guide for travelling doctors (Pappas et al., 2008), the treatise famously recommends a full knowledge of the physical landscape, its winds, the hardness of its waters, its variations in temperature and the exposures of its cities before the pronouncement of any diagnosis.

> "Whoever wishes to investigate medicine properly" the treatise starts "should proceed thus: in the first place to consider the seasons of the year, and what effects each of them produces for they are not at all alike, but differ much from themselves in regard to their changes. Then the winds, the hot and the cold, especially such as are common to all countries, and then such as are peculiar to each locality. We must also consider the qualities of the waters, for as they differ from one another in taste and weight, so also do they differ much in their qualities. In the same manner, when one comes into a city to which he is a stranger, he ought to consider its situation, how it lies as to the winds and the rising of the sun; for its influence is not the same whether it lies to the north or the south, to the rising or to the setting sun."
>
> (Lloyd, 1978: 148)

However, the text concerns not only the physical environment. When Hippocrates investigates the acquisition of a hereditary trait, the elongated head, among a mythical population called Macrocephali (long-headed), he is not only clearly implying a "Lamarckian" understanding of heredity but also addressing, for the first time in Greek writings, the articulation of *nomos* (laws and costumes) and *physis* (nature), corresponding roughly to our culture/nature distinction (Jouanna, 1999: 43). For Hippocrates, the unusually elongated skull of the Macrocephali was considered primarily the result of the effects of customs, their practice being to fashion it with bandages so to alter its original form for aesthetic reasons. However, after a certain number of generations, force becomes no longer necessary, and the acquired trait is transmitted naturally. It is worth citing the whole text:

> There is no other race of men which have heads in the least resembling theirs [the Macrocephali]. At first, usage was the principal cause of the length of their head, but now nature cooperates with usage. They think those the most noble who have the longest heads. It is thus with regard to the usage: immediately after the child is born, and while its head is still tender, they fashion it with their hands, and constrain it to assume a lengthened shape by applying bandages and other suitable contrivances whereby the spherical form of the head is destroyed, and it is made to increase in length. Thus, at first, usage operated, so that

this constitution was the result of force: but, in the course of time, it was formed naturally; so that usage had nothing to do with it; for the semen comes from all parts of the body, sound from the sound parts, and unhealthy from the unhealthy parts. If, then, children with bald heads are born to parents with bald heads; and children with blue eyes to parents who have blue eyes; and if the children of parents having distorted eyes squint also for the most part; and if the same may be said of other forms of the body, what is to prevent it from happening that a child with a long head should be produced by a parent having a long head? But now these things do not happen as they did formerly, for the custom no longer prevails owing to their intercourse with other men.

(*On Airs, Waters and Places*, part 14 in Lloyd, 1978: 161)

Beside the case of the Macrocephali, *On Airs, Waters and Places* also sketches a geopolitical classification of ancient populations. Asians are "more gentle and affectionate" and live in a land where everything grows "more beautifully", but are also more indolent, cowardly and mentally flabby. Europeans are exposed to greater seasonal changes and, in the case of the Greeks, are more "independent" and capable to "enjoy the fruits of their own labor". The Scythians, living on the steppes at the border of Europe and Asia, are small and weak like their vegetation, and all "very uniform" like their seasons (Lloyd, 1978). In making these general classifications, Hippocrates inaugurates a wider ethnographic tradition that will culminate in Renaissance geohumoralism (Floyd-Wilson, 2003, 2011). This is a "region-ally framed" version of humoralist ideas that connected geographical variations to changes in national characteristics, and represented "the dom-inant mode of ethnic distinctions in the late sixteenth and early seventeenth centuries" (Floyd-Wilson, 2003: 1; Feerick, 2010; Spiller, 2011). A mixture of fluidity and essentialism, geohumoralist tropes posited a strong causality of soil and seed. Given the lack of a vertical theory of hereditary transmis-sion, geohumoralism favoured "ethnic distinctions [that] were necessarily plastic" and pointed to the risk that "people could intentionally or acciden-tally estrange themselves from their native kind" (Floyd-Wilson, 2003: 54). This tendency is clearly manifested in anxieties about the degeneration of the body in cases of colonial migration. At the same time, however, it reflected an emerging modernist awareness that racial essence may exceed this frame-work of extreme mutability.

However, humoralist categories served not only ethnographic distinctions between races but also, in a few cases, sociological descriptions of class differences. Galen used humoralist categories, in his writings on food in particular, to offer a veritable window into the specific entanglement of bodies, places and social groups (Grant, 2000). Heir to a rich urban family, he views it as natural that "food flows from the countryside to the city as from [...] the intestines to the liver – along roads, which are like veins" (Mattern, 2013: 21). Peasants (*agroikoi*), upon whom this unequal arrangement fell, are often described as hardened and even disfigured in their bodies due to fatigue and poor or indigestible food (ibid.). As a consequence, their physiology appears as wholly different from that of the affluent urbanite: their food is different, and so are their symptoms. For Galen, "the adult, urban, Greek male, in the prime of life" is the standard against which other physiologies are measured as deviations (Mattern, 2008: 105). However, peasants are not just a medical challenge or an abnormality. While he respects their frugal lifestyle, Galen considers them a class apart, "almost another species" (Mattern, 2013: 23, 111), even "donkeys in their constitution" (Mattern, 2008: 105).

Humoralism from medicine to Rabelais

This intimate connection between bodies and places, and bodies and class, has been well preserved in literary studies rather than medical histories. Bakhtin's critique of the body of the classical canon is an obvious reference here. By analyzing plebeian celebrations, marginal cultural experiences, and bodies in the act of becoming, Bakhtin clearly perceived an alternative materialistic tradition of the ancient and early modern body. He explicitly refers to Hippocrates and Galen, among others, as the bearers of this non-classical and open view (Bakhtin, 1984: 28, footnote 10). In his seminal work on French Renaissance writer François Rabelais, Bakhtin understands the grotesque as an expression of the body's existence not as "a closed, completed unit" but as something "unfinished", that "outgrows itself, transgresses its own limits" and hence potentially liquefies in the external world (Bakhtin, 1984: 24; Holquist, 1990). The grotesque body emphasizes "apertures", "convexities" and "offshoots" through which the exchange with the outside world occurs: "the open mouth, the genital organs, the breasts, the phallus, the potbelly, the nose" (Bakhtin, 1984: 26). The analogies with the body of humoralism are not always visible but are nevertheless strong. Bakhtin himself recognizes several connections between the Hippocratic tradition and Rabelais. "Of all the literary sources of Rabelais' grotesque concept of the body", he writes, "[the Hippocratic] anthology is one of the most important" (1984: 361). Rabelais, who became a doctor after leaving the monastery, translated part of the Hippocratic corpus in Montpellier, one of the European centres of humoralism from the late thirteenth century. He was possibly also inspired by prodigious Indian tales of the body in the Ayurveda tradition (Langford, 2002: 146). The influence of humoralism is particularly explicit in Rabelais' descriptions of the physiology of laughter and joy (Bakhtin, 1984: 67–68). Another possible parallel with the somatic ethics of Hippocratic texts is the impact of food and wine on mental faculties, particularly the Hippocratic *On Winds*, where, during banquets and celebrations, "a sudden increase of blood" led to changes "in the soul and thoughts of men" inspiring hopes of a "happy future" – something clearly recognized by Bakhtin in Rabelais' "utopian nature of prandial speeches" (Bakhtin, 1984: 286).

Finally, the humoralist fear of an excessively transparent and penetrable body is radicalized and overturned in Rabelais when the determinist trope of bodies shaped by place is turned into places made of bodies (Broomhall, 1998; Smith, 2014: 80 and ff.). Panurge, one of the key figures in *Gargantua and Pantagruel*, comments, for instance, that because of the excessive sexual desire of local women, Paris is built of vaginas, which are "cheaper than stones" (Rabelais, 1991: 183; cfr. Broomhall, 1998). Similarly, through his urine, Pantagruel creates a number of hot springs as he moves through the countryside (Smith, 2014: 78). The Hippocratic shaping of mental faculties via the power of places is reversed into an anthropization of spaces in which any "duality between the creature and the place that contains it" is erased (Kappler, cited in Smith, 2014).

Governing the humoralist body

Governing a porous body was far from easy. On one side, the unstable physiology of humoralism demanded a constant vigilance in monitoring excretions, wastes, sweats, urine, vomits, stools and emission of sexual semen. The body was often understood as composed of "excretory ducts [that] were always smoking" (Corbin, 1986: 36; Paster, 1993). Humoralism displayed a rich phenomenology on secretions that goes well beyond our current understanding of things. One case in point is the vast number of types of sweat, and the recurring comparison between sweat and urine (Stolberg, 2012). Another aspect is the "forgotten fear of blocked pores", and particularly excrement (Kuriyama, 2008). This fear was evident in the importance of medical techniques such as bloodletting (phlebotomy), purges, blistering and cooling baths. These techniques have to be understood as part of the same continuum of "alternative" or "purgative" means aimed at favouring the discharge of unhealthy humours (Horden and Hsu, 2013), or "humores malos ó pecantes" in early modern Spanish humoralism (de Esteyneffer, 1719).

The opposite of the fear of blocked channels was the concern that pores were too easily opened and interpenetrable. This extreme transparency of the body was equally the source of a deep anxiety. It gave rise to a model of both intimacy and antagonism in the body's relationship with food, or any other external substance that could potentially disrupt its balance. As Kuriyama has pointed out, the above notion of "bad superfluities" (Meyerhof, 1931) to be eliminated reflects not only the perceived fragility of the humoralist body but also the otherness of food, which had to be "conquered" to be assimilated into the body (Kuriyama, 2008: 432). Hence, the key importance of dietetics goes well beyond sexuality, as Foucault pointed out (1990). Diet (regimen), from the Greek διαιτάω (di-aitao), implies both a sense of handling a life in the proper way and also a critical and scrupulous operation of "distinguishing, distributing, managing, maintaining, supporting" (Agerholm, 2013).

A number of complex factors and variables that needed to be governed in order to maintain the body's balance well exemplify this distinguishing activity. Particularly after Galen, efforts were focused on what were known as *the six non-naturals*. In contrast to *the seven naturals* (physiological aspects such as the four elements, qualities, humours, members and faculties) and the *three contra-naturals* (pathological aspects such as disease, its causes and sequels, which pertained to the doctor's competence) the *res non naturales* (non-naturals) were for the individual to take care of (Rather, 1968; Niebyl, 1970; Coleman, 1974; Emch-Deriaz, 1992).

The six *res non naturales* were all things that could shape humoral balance, factors one could not escape and therefore had to carefully govern. Depending on the various classifications, they included: a) passions, b) air or climate, c) food and its method of preparation, d) repletion and evacuation, e) sleeping and vigil, and f) exercise. The result was a micropolitics of self-moderation that characterized the many *regimen sanitatis* (or books of health management) that offered both *physical and moral* guidance and invited to temperance.

This moralistic side of humoralism is rather evident. If illness is defined as an imbalance or an excess, the notion easily conflates with a deviation from social norms. Equally, the effectiveness of humoralist therapies (such as bloodletting or purges), aimed at expelling excessive humours (an excess also known as "plethora") and carefully scrutinizing bodily boundaries, often can be explained simply in terms of a reinforcement of existing social and moral norms (Codell Carter, 2012). Particularly starting from the sixteenth and early seventeenth centuries, the porous ecological body of ancient times started to be rewritten as a dangerous battlefield (Kalff, 2012), always at risk of infiltration. Especially in northern European contexts, this moralistic literature found its way into a number of treatises that blurred medical and moral/religious obligations (Healy, 2001). Examples could include recommendations to moderate gluttony and other forms of intemperance, or simply to escape non-ventilated areas of the house. These treatises resonate with Codell Carter's argument (2012) that humoralism's long-term ideological effectiveness was mostly due to its strengthening existing social norms: "spirituality and morality intrude[d] increasingly heavily into the medical domain" and disease was at the same time both physical and symbolic (Healy, 2001: 35). In this literature, the humoralist body is frequently equated to a "castle" under siege, a fortified yet vulnerable and threatened enclosure. Out-of-control appetites and consumption menace its integrity and can lead to the damnation of the soul (Healy, 2001). The body is perceived as a fragile place which people had "to look after" and govern carefully (see also: Shildrick, 2001). It is "filled with insurrectionary forces, and in continual need of a monitoring from within and without". (Schoenfeldt, 1999: 39). Environmental descriptions also were highly moralized, often contrasting Edenic countryside scenes with polluted townscapes contaminated with corrupting air (Healy, 2001). In Protestant countries like England, this vernacular literature on body management and soul regeneration included *The Castell of Helth* (1536) by Thomas Elyot, and James Manning's *I Am for You all, Complexions Castle* (1604). In order to convey this perceived fragility of bodily boundaries, both relied heavily on the fortified castle metaphor, with its gates to defend and interior to be kept carefully clean (Healy, 2001). The bestselling *The Touchstone of Complexions* by the Dutch doctor Levinus Lemnius (originally published in 1561 in Antwerp as *De habitu et constitutione corporis*) was translated into English in 1576. As its long subtitle stated, it contained the "most easie rules & ready tokens" and "generallye applicable" and "profitable expedient" for all who were "desirous & carefull of their bodylye health". Equally significant in this literature was Tobias Venner's *Via Recta Ad Vitam Longam*, published in London in 1620, and described as: "A plaine philosophical discourse of the nature, faculties, and effects, of all such things, as by way of nourishments, and dieticall observations, make for the preservation of health with their iust applications unto every age, constitution of bodie, and time of yeare." Venner, an English doctor who championed bathing therapy in Bath and promoted tobacco for its digestive virtues, is considered one of the first authors to deal at length with obesity as a complex social disease (Gilman, 2008).

In Catholic contexts we can find books like *Examination of Men's Wits* (*Examen de Ingenios para las ciencias*, 1575, translated into English in 1594) by the Spanish Juan Huarte de San Juan (Hasson, 2009), and the later *Florilegio medicinal de todas las enfermedades* (1713) by Juan de Esteyneffer, a Jesuit working in Mexico (on its influence, Kay, 1977). From Italy, Luigi (Alvise) Cornaro's four-volume treatise *Discorsi della vita sobria* ("Discourses on the Temperate Life", posthumously published between 1585 and 1595 and reprinted numerous times) is a good example of longevity literature based on advice to avoid the accumulation of "humori soverchi, & maligni" (bad humoral residues). At a time when notions of a temperament fixed at birth by the stars (*complessione o calida, o frigida, o temperata*: hot, cold or temperate complexion) were increasingly circulating, Cornaro's text nicely shows how humoralist tropes always had the resource to overturn this deterministic language and take the body as a site for self-experimentation and change. As he writes, according to his long experience (he was in his seventies when he wrote the treatise, and died at 98):

> l'uomo savio domina le stelle. Io nacqui molto colerico, tal che non si poteva praticare meco; & me n'aviddi, & conobbi che un colerico era pazzo à tempo, quel tempo, dico; nelquale era dominato dalla colera; perche non haveva ragione in se, nè intelletto, e mi deliberai di liberarmi con ragione da tale colera; si che hora se ben son nato colerico, non però uso tal'atto, se non in parte: e quello che è nato di trista complessione, può similmente con il mezzo della ragione, & vita sobria, vivere sano, & lungamente, come ho fatto io, che nacqui di tristissima
>
> [a wise man rules the stars. I was born with a very choleric disposition, insomuch that there was no living with me; but I took notice of it, and considered, that a person swayed by his passion, must at certain times be no better than a madman; I mean at those times, when he suffers his passions to predominate, because he then renounces his reason and understanding. I, therefore, resolved to make my choleric disposition give way to reason; so that now, though born choleric, I never suffer anger entirely to overcome me. The man, who is naturally of a bad constitution, may, in like manner, by dint of reason, and a sober life, live to a great age and in good health, as I have done, who had naturally the worst.]
>
> (Cornaro, 1833: 98)

Through this humoralist conviction to overcome temperament we can better understand Michael Schoenfeldt's argument that humoralism, far from just promoting displacement of identity, was instrumental to the empowerment of modern subjectivity (Schoenfeldt 1997; 1999; see Paster, 1993). A body governed by humoral fluids became the ideal site for self-fashioning techniques. Rather than "immuring bodily fluids" or inhibiting their expression (as in an Eliasian view; see also Paster, 1993, 2004), humoralism offered a process of individualization via the careful manipulation of fluids (Schoenfeldt, 1999: 14). This argument resonates with Coleman's connection between the doctrine of the six non-naturals and the "full basic activism of Enlightenment rationalism" aimed at seizing possession of the self (Coleman, 1974). However, this view of humoralism, as with some contemporary readings of plasticity as an ideology of self-hood and consumerism, is too abstract and idealized. The genealogical critique here is that *not every body was equally malleable*, and plasticity was not a general predicament of the human condition before the emergence of the modern body. As various authors have noticed, the porous body was not just an individual physical self that could be adjusted in this way or that to one's benefit or detriment. Thinking in the abstract terms of a malleable body "of Renaissance Galenism simply ignores the realities of social and gender hierarchy everywhere" (Paster, 2004: 21).

A gendered plasticity

A genealogical approach helps illuminate how permeability was unequally distributed and affected groups of people differently. Gender and race rendered bodies differentially exposed, more or less at risk of leakage, and therefore subject to variously intensive regimes of regulation and surveillance, and arguments about degeneration. In ancient gynaecological treatises, as well as early modern midwifery textbooks, the female body was a point of particular anxiety. As philosopher Rebecca Kukla writes, "The unfixed boundaries of the female reproductive body have captured the medical imagination from the start" (2005: 5). Physiologically, it was widely assumed that women were of a softer, more permeable and less stable nature (Dean-Jones, 1994; King, 1998). In humoral medicine and beyond, women have been depicted as more liquid and transparent than men, subjects to passion, volatile and "leaky vessel[s]" (Paster, 1993; Shildrick, 2001). Well into early modernity, a woman's insides were perceived as fluid, porous and "a place of metamorphosis" (Duden 1991: 107).

This perceived impressionability of the female body emerged at the crossroads of several ancient physiological and philosophical traditions.

In Hippocratic texts, women are considered spongier, "with a capacity to absorb fluid which makes it directly analogous to wool or sheepskin" (King, 1998: 96). The inside of the female body was constructed around an open way (*hodos*, literally "road") going "from the orifices of the head to the vagina". The difference between women and men was epitomized by the need to discharge accumulated blood – one of the four humours – via menstruation (King, 1998). The uterus (*histera*) was understood not only as plastic in its contraction and expansion, but also as capable of "wandering throughout the female body, causing disease and distress as it travelled": hence the condition of hysteria, a sort of internal peregrination of the womb (Kukla, 2005: 5). It is noticeable, however, that in the Hippocratic tradition, both sexes contributed to reproduction, producing seed (*gonê*), which, after mixing, became "a living thing" (*to mellon zôon*, NC 14, L 7.492; Lonie, 1981: 7).

In an Aristotelian view, which would later be codified in medieval scholasticism, things were different: only men produced seed, while women contributed merely the raw material (menses). Women were not only seen to contribute mere passive matter; they were also considered to be of a more watery constitution (see also Paster, 1993). Following this Aristotelian line, Albert the Great and Thomas Aquinas thought that women would behave as any moist object would: that is, they would receive impressions more "easily but retain them poorly", as Aquinas claimed (2002: 68). In several works, Albert the Great instead made the claim that the mud-like impressionability of women could explain why "women are more inconstant and fickle than men" (Resnick and Albertus Magnus, 2010: 95). Their moister constitution made women more subject to lunar tides, too. The moon – as the "queen of heaven", which moves everything "from a distance, as a magnet moves iron" – "rules over the fluids [*umiditates*] of lower bodies" and has power over everything in which water abounds, Albert writes (ibid., 58 and 53). These and other tropes were instrumental in consolidating the image of women as more subject to passions and less shielded "against corrupting ingestions" (Kukla, 2005: 11). These ingestions included the power of imagination and the susceptibility to a number of social influences that we would nowadays call shocks or traumas.

Maternal impressions

Various physiological and cosmological reasons contributed to make women's bodies anxiously volatile and hence potentially subject to greater control, surveillance and obligation. Such understandings of women's permeability also lent support to the claim, pervasive in Western medical beliefs until the early twentieth century, of *maternal impression*. The theory was that a gestating mother's thoughts, her emotions, and even the contents of her sight – for instance, a wild animal or a scary event – could leave a permanent imprint on her unborn child (Fischer-Homberger, 1979; Roodenburg, 1988; Huet, 1993; Epstein, 1995; Kukla, 2005). Maternal impressions

> could be activated by such a wide range of objects – from portraits to animals to members of other races and onward – that almost no dimension of a pregnant woman's life was truly safe. Doctors could do little to control pregnant women's inner lives. All they could do was warn expectant parents about the obstetrical significance of women's character and ethical fiber and, when relevant use the deformed foetus as *ex post facto* testimony to her wayward or weak nature.
>
> (Kukla, 2005: 18)

In a sort of "pre-Freudian fetal psychology" in which the infant takes on "the literal shape of the trauma", the offspring deformity became the materialization of the morbid power of maternal appetites and passions (Stafford, 1991, cited in Shildrick, 2001: 42). As the above quote shows, the theory always oscillated between a pathologization of the pregnant womb and a recognition of some special female power to shape heredity that went beyond (male) doctors' capacity to control. The late displacement of this doctrine implied a reversal of both assumptions: pregnancy became a safer and less moralized period and the foetus more shielded from maternal influences, but women lost their formative power and were reduced mostly to passive carriers of the product of reproductive processes (Epstein, 1995).

The ancient world abounds with stories of maternal impressions as a result of observing paintings, objects and (particularly) people of other races. Soranus writes in *Gynecology* (125 ca CE):

> Some women, seeing monkeys during intercourse, have borne children resembling monkeys. The tyrant of the Cyprians who was misshapen, compelled his wife to look at beautiful statues during intercourse and became the father of well-shaped children; and horse-breeders, during covering, place noble horses before the mares. Thus, in order that the offspring may not be rendered misshapen, women must be sober during coitus because in drunkenness the soul becomes the victim of strange fantasies; this furthermore, because

the offspring bears some resemblance to the mother as well, not only in body but in soul.

(Temkin, 1956: 38)

In a racialized version of maternal impression that became widespread in the Renaissance (especially through the medical-teratological work of Ambroise Paré, *Des Monstres et Prodiges*, 1573; see Pallister, 1982), Hippocrates was said to have saved a white princess from the accusation of adultery when she mothered a child "black as a Moor". The father of medicine pronounced that a portrait of a Moor in the princess's bedroom was to blame for the case of dissimilarity in generation. Several cases of pregnant imagination are linked to race (see Doniger and Spinner, 1998). For instance, while Hippocrates saves the princess from the *accusation of having a black child*, in another famous story Galen *advises* a black couple how to "beget a white and beautifull childe, to set at his beds feete a faire picture, uppon which his wife might wistly looke in the time of her *conception*" (in Helkiah Crooke's 1615 *Mikrokosmographia* version cited in Iyengar, 2013: 35; but see Fissell, 2004: 207).

Strictly speaking, the impressionability of the female body went beyond these reproductive tropes and was invested also in female mysticism. One of the most famous examples is the early fourteenth-century case of Chiara [Claire] di Montefalco, an Augustinian abbess in Umbria, Italy. Having perceived the presence of Christ in her life, upon her death, Chiara's body was opened and found yielding "an unusual type of relic: religiously marked objects generated inside her internal organs". Clare's heart contained a crucifix, "together with other instruments of the passion (all made of flesh), while her gallbladder held three stones, which contemporary observers identified with the Trinity" (Park, 2002: 270; cfr Menestò, 1991).

It is worth noticing that cases of male impressionability were also reported (a man bitten by a dog containing canine images in his urine is sceptically reported in a correspondence by Descartes, letter to Meyssonier, 29 January 1640; see Smith, 2006), but they are certainly of little significance compared with the impact of the power of imagination on the female body.

This deep communication between imagination and bodily changes may seem superstitious or only metaphorical in the post-Enlightenment mindset, which neatly separates inwardness and external objects, but it was extremely literal and effective well until early modernity (Kirmayer, 2006). For the modern mind, the strength of dualism, as philosopher Charles Taylor has claimed, is revealed by the fact that "the onus of argument (....) falls to those who want to overcome dualism" (1989: 189; Paster, 1993). Up until the Middle Ages and early modernity, however, this supposition was far from being firmly established. Scholastic philosophers shared the notion that mental images could impress real forms into matter. Al-Kindi (ninth century CE), one of the fathers of Islamic philosophy and a translator of Aristotle, was attributed the notion that "Spiritualem substantiam ex sola imaginatione posse inducere veras formas" (the spiritual substance can induce true forms just through imagination) (Zambelli, 1992, Adamson, 2018). According to a persistent Scholastic and Renaissance tradition, humours and other bodily aspects could also be moved "spiritually" (*spiritaliter*) (Hirai, 2017). This cultural context, in which matter was shaped and excited by the internal sense of imagination (albeit in some authors in a more mediated way), can explain the pervasiveness of the doctrine of maternal imagination.

However, with early modern embryological debates the doctrine of maternal imagination broadened in scope. Once teleological views of embryonic development started to lose appeal in favour of purely mechanistic causes, imagination acted as a formative faculty to explain the acquisition of traits in emerging debates on heredity (Smith, 2006; Blank, 2010). With the fading of Aristotelian immaterial powers, the role of the imagination shifted from being predominantly negative, as a source of degeneration, monstrosity or defective births, to offering an explanation for the transmission of traits *tout court*.

> [While] up to the sixteenth century, the imagination theory was convenient, primarily in the explanation of aberrations; in the seventeenth century, deprived of formal and final causes in the account of organic growth, it was necessary in the explanation of the regular course of sexual reproduction.
>
> (Smith, 2006: 86)

Imagination was deemed to shape all hereditary traits, not just abnormalities or disruption, and for this reason was often resisted and criticized by scholars who highlighted the stability of natural processes and the reliability of resemblance among generations (De Renzi, 2007). The female imagination contributed to early theories of heredity in other ways; for instance, expanding on the notion of telegony. Telegony, or birth from distance, is the long-held belief that a *previous* mate's traits are transmittable from a mother to her offspring. In this case, it is the notion of a strong impression left by a prior partner on the maternal imagination that can "mechanistically" help to confirm the theory (Smith, 2006).

Whatever the shifting philosophical or embryological role of maternal imagination in the long history of heredity before genetics, the doctrine always came with specific prescriptions regarding maternal responsibility. The plastic and impressionable nature of female bodies was intimately connected to moral prescriptions about how women were supposed to conduct themselves in order to ensure the wellbeing of their offspring. Seventeenth- and eighteenth-century medical and midwifery texts, both technical and popular, offered harsh prescriptions lest women's attitudes poison their offspring's future. In Jane Sharp's *Midwives Book* (1671), imagination was said to promote "oftimes [...] Monstruous birth, when women look to much on strange objects". A woman, for instance, who saw "a boy with two thumbs on one hand, brought forth such another". Wombs were considered sensitive to the external world

> "as our senses are": since the "child takes part of the mothers life while he is in the womb, as the fruit doth of the tree, whatsoever moves the faculties of the mother souls may do like in the child".
>
> (1671: 87, 92)

Imagination was defined "as the strongest and most efficacious of all the senses" by John Maubray in his influential treatise *The Female Physician* (1724). When the soul is "elevated and inflamed with a fervent Imagination, it may not only affect its proper Body, but also that of Another". Therefore, pregnant women were encouraged to "suppress all Anger, Passion, and other Perturbations of Mind, and avoid entertaining too serious or melancholick Thoughts; since all such tend to impress a Depravity of Nature upon the Infant's Mind, and Deformity on its Body" (1724, cited in Shildrick, 2001: 42).

The moment of copulation was a particularly sensitive period for the power of maternal imagination: imagining her lover during coitus with the husband may lead to children resembling the adulterer.

The notion that pregnancy was "an active project requiring self-discipline and work on the part of expectant mothers" (Kukla, 2005: 21) became the natural counterpart of the logic of maternal imagination. However, the intensity and dangers associated with the power of the womb changed significantly with changing cultural contexts. For instance, the impact of the Protestant reformation in offering a pejorative view of the womb has been noticed by historians (Fissell, 2004). A significant rise in popular publications depicting the dangerous qualities of the womb, for example, took place in England from early 1600. Texts represented the womb increasingly as a source of possible damnation for the unborn child. Whereas the

> womb had been considered marvellous in a context in which women were taught to connect their own pregnancies with that of the Virgin Mary [...] when women were no longer encouraged to identify with

the Virgin, some of the miraculous connotations of conception and pregnancy faded [...] the womb moved from being very good to very bad.

(Fissell, 2004: 76)

Rather than a possible source of improvement, the womb became increasingly seen as the bearer of a potential misfortune for the foetus. As Kukla notes,

The wrong maternal passions could produce monsters, but there is no legacy, from this era, of thinking that the right maternal passions could improve the virtue, health, or form of the fetus beyond what it would attain if it merely remained uninfluenced and uncorrupted.

(Kukla, 2005: 22–23)

A long-term asymmetry between the prevalent negative effects of bodily permeability and scarce positive implications was consolidated. Emphasis on negative power also implied the notion of an infanticide "per imaginationem" (Fischer-Homberger, 1979).

The persistence and ubiquity of the belief in maternal imagination from the Renaissance to early modernity is striking. A large number of European intellectuals and doctors of this period held to it, from Ficino to Montaigne, Descartes to Gassendi (Hirai, 2017). Paracelsus claimed that "the woman is the artist and the child the canvas on which to raise the work" (cited in Pagel, 1982: 122); Montaigne that "we know by experience that women transmit marks of their fancies to the bodies of the children they carry in the womb" (cited in Huet, 1993: 13).

Interestingly, a critique of the maternal imagination emerged at a time when preformationist themes became significant in medical writings (Epstein, 1995; Wilson, 1999). As a doctrine that denied epigenesis-like effects on the developing form, it is logical but sociologically noticeable that preformationism, like genetics later, did not support but rather, undermined maternal impression. The English doctor James Blondel, for instance, in his *The Strength of Imagination in Pregnant Women Examined* (1729), challenged supporters of maternal imagination, such as his colleague Daniel Turner (*De morbis cutaneis*, 1714). Blondel claimed that "the wounds of the newborn, [...] are due to accidents and to poor obstetricians rather than to maternal phantasies" (cited in Fischer-Homberger, 1979). As the unfolding of a pre-existing plan, the embryo was buffered from maternal effects. Turner replied one year later in his *The Force of the Mother's Imagination upon her Foetus in Utero* (1730). He emphasized maternal power to shape the unborn and posited a deep physiological connection between mother and foetus. He claimed that imagination had the power "of producing such large and bleeding wounds on the body of the newborn as the mother had imagined" (cited in Fischer-Homberger, 1979).

This was a paradoxical situation: maternal imaginationists gave mothers a certain power, while preformationists ended up denying any significant role to gestating women "except as pack animals" (Epstein, 1995: 155). On the other hand, preformationists freed mothers from moral burdens, while imaginationists placed on them a heavy responsibility. Preformationists – those who believed that the embryo existed in miniature in the mother's egg – could easily discount the effect of maternal impressions. Epigenesists – who held that embryological development was gradual, or "evolutionary", in a pre-Darwinian sense – could easily accommodate the influence of strong maternal impressions on the baby (Ibid.).

In conclusion, it is worth noting that this complex debate anticipates a later one between classical hard-hereditarian eugenists (particularly geneticists) and supporters of the so-called "pre-natal culture" in the emerging field of foetal physiology, or antenatal pathology, from the late nineteenth century (Arni, 2015; 2016).

Stimulated by supporters of prenatal culture, the challenge that the maternal imagination presented to a genetic view of heredity is evidenced by an unsigned editorial in the *Journal of Heredity* in 1915. Even at so late a date, the editor of a flagship genetic (and eugenic) publication felt the need to correct "what is commonly called maternal impression, pre-natal culture, 'marking,' and so on". It is disconcerting, the editor claimed, that we still find nowadays in popular science publications superstitious claims that

> "The woman who frets brings forth a nervous child. The woman who rebels generally bears a morbid child"; Or that: "Selfcontrol, cheerfulness and love for the little life breathing in unison with your own will practically insure you a child of normal physique and nerves."
>
> (Editorial, 1915: 513)

The unsigned editorial had mainly two goals. One was scientific, with a direct moral implication, showing that

> most errors of development [...] are due to some cause within the embryo itself, and that most of them take place in the first two or three weeks, when *the mother is by no means likely to influence the course of*

embryological development by her mental attitude toward it, for the very good reason that *she knows nothing about it*.

(1915: 17; emphasis added)[4]

This meant that with their unscientific beliefs, maternal impressionists were "trying to place on" the pregnant mother "a responsibility which she need not bear". Beyond trying to keep herself in good health, the article continued,

> there is nothing the mother can do to influence the development of her child. There is not a shred of evidence to support the idea that a child's mental or physical character can be influenced in the slightest degree for better or for worse *in any definite way,* by the mental attitude of the mother before its birth.

(1915: 517–518)

However, there was also a more subtle and complex political aim in the text: to avoid distractions into the eugenic movements, to prevent any "shortcut to eugenics" (Editorial, 1915: 512). The prenatal school of thought that attributed to mothers not only the burden but also the power of shaping heredity was just a waste of energy in the light of a truly selectionist approach to eugenic matter. It is utterly meaningless to

> give a woman reason to think she might marry a man whose heredity was rotten, and yet, by pre-natal culture save her children from paying the inevitable penalty of this weak heritage.

(1915: 516)

Eugenics had to be just applied genetics without 'nurturist' detours (1915: 512). The text is still worth reading today as an interesting example that points to the dilemma presented in debates between moral assumptions and scientific claims, and the ambiguous positioning of notions of biological fixedness or plasticity in relation to gender and responsibility.

Ancient plasticity and the racialized body

The permeability of humoralist bodies meant not only that some bodies, such as women's, might be more or less subject to external influences (including the power of imagination), but also that any body could be presumed to be affected by place. The assumption that "every place had its own unique nature, that similar places gave way to similar natures, and that different places gave way to different natures" (Wey Gómez, 2008: 49) was dominant in ancient views and not exclusive to humoralism. It was shared by geographers such as Strabo and Ptolemy, historians like Herodotus, and philosophers such as Aristotle and Albert the Great (Tilmann, 1971). The power of places – "the power of containers that preserves or corrupts those things they contain" (Wey Gómez, 2008: 252, citing Albert the Great) – was a complex matter. Some places created virtues and nobility, and nurtured good customs and natural capacity to govern. Others were hostile, and condemned entire nations to inferiority and servitude. Even when no direct relationship between bad places and degenerate characters could be traced, another more subtle argument was used: that the placement of some human groups in particularly unfavourable places was an unequivocal sign of their subordinate and faulty nature (Livingstone, 1991).

The power of places was quite unequally distributed, and not always benign. Antiquity and the Middle Ages also saw other methods, disconnected from the power of geography (notions of pedigrees, divine curses on some specific groups), for explaining and constructing hierarchies between human groups (Goldenberg, 2003; Isaac, 2006; Bethencourt, 2013). However, the environmentalist modality that made people a mirror of the places where they lived was by far the most widespread and flexible intellectual device that asserted the superiority of certain human groups. It is this connection of *telos* and places, topography and character (Livingstone, 1991; Irby, 2016) that is at stake in ancient views of "proto-racial" identity (Isaac, 2006). Nations were fit or unfit to rule not because of heredity but because of the effects of climate on the body and mind (see for the Medieval period, Bartlett, 2001).[5] The geographical epicentre of climatico-moral superiority shifted over time, from Greece and Rome, and then to Northern Europe in early modernity (Floyd-Wilson, 2003). The axis of confrontation also changed over time. What was mostly a West–East axis for ancient writers like Hippocrates or Aristotle, who viewed Oriental populations as gentler and more effeminate due to their unchanging climate (see Chapter 1), became a North–South axis after the first colonial expansions.[6] In his pathbreaking work, historian Nicolás Wey Gómez shows the profoundly moral implications of the notion of *latitude* for Columbus' geopolitical cosmography. For Columbus, North–South, not East–West, determined the gradations of civilization. Torrid zones were home to degenerates, establishing the natural privilege of colonial rulers. Building on an ancient tradition, Pierre D'Ailly's tripartite geography (1410) of cold (North), temperate (middle: mostly Spain, Italy, Greece), and hot nations (South, tropical belt, Equator), offered a perfect conceptual resource "in the context of a nascent European colonialism in the second half of the fifteenth century". The tripartite model was a key inspiration for Columbus and theologians like de Sepúlveda to construe "Spain's Indians as the natural subjects or slaves whom Aristotle and his cohort had believed to be generated in the hot margins of the inhabited world" (Wey Gómez, 2008: 86, 56). Temperate countries produced temperate complexions that were naturally made to "govern themselves and others". As Columbus wrote, "The inhabitants of the North and the South are unfit for exercising power. In this respect, this [middle] region possesses both [i.e. spiritedness and intellect]" (ibid.: 100, 290).

The exact details of this geographico-political model would be revised amid later colonial expansions, readjusting its balance in favour of emerging northern European colonial powers, which were penalized in the above Mediterranean-centred paradigm (Floyd-Wilson, 2003). However, "moral climatology" persisted as a way of making ethnic distinctions well into the nineteenth century, often in conflict or continuity with the universalism of the body implied by the colonial endeavour (Livingstone, 1991; Harrison, 1999). More importantly, tropical and equatorial colonies remained the place for a specific plasticity: a certain vulnerability to environmental forces, whether due to the inclination of solar rays, or the unique power of the moon, in altering bodies and causing disease (see Mead, 1708; cfr. Harrison, 2000; Chakrabarti, 2004).

The existence of such views was not necessarily a product of humoralism but largely benefitted from the physiological underpinnings of humoralism, especially in its early modern versions in colonial places like Brazil or Mexico. While not exclusive in their support for proto-racial environmentalism, humoralist writings provided two important mechanisms whereby *people came to mirror* the places they inhabited. First, humoralists noted that local variations in temperature and humidity affected the opening or closure of pores. Naturally, this would regulate the circulation of humours between the body and the environment. Because the quantities of given humours affected temperamental characteristics (bravery, laziness or lustfulness), climate could determine the mental disposition of groups. Warm climates could relax bodies and make people torpid, lethargic or timid. Excessive humidity encouraged effeminacy. Cold climates could constrict veins and make people incautious or brisk (Irby, 2016). The theory was flexible (and inconsistent) enough to be open to any possible strategic interpretation. For example, the Franciscan missionary Diego de Valadés explained that the humidity of Spanish possessions left Amerindians morally and mentally debilitated: "stupid" because "they were born in thick air" (cited in Cañizares-Esguerra, 2006: 69). However, the theory was flexible. While fighting his intellectual battle for Indian rights, the Dominican Bartolomé de Las Casas made the converse argument: because of their exposure to an excellent climate and the right celestial influence, the Indians had the best possible constitution. The very temperate (*temperatísimas*) climate of these Indian regions yielded a very temperate complexion (*temperatísima complixión*) in their inhabitants (1992[1552]: 431).

Secondly, humoralists largely contributed to the widespread ancient belief that (in our language) environmentally conditioned traits were heritable. As many have noticed, this "Lamarckian" notion is in fact profoundly indebted to the centuries-long conviction about the plasticity of developmental mechanisms, largely shared in the ancient and early modern world (Zirkle, 1946; Isaac, 2006). Humoralism offered to this long-held belief a possible mechanistic foundation. It is the notion, known after Darwin as "pangenesis", that "semen comes from all parts of the body" (Hippocrates, *On Airs, Waters and Places*, part 14 in Lloyd, 1978: 161), which was universally imbued with humours.[7] This process of semen-making from the entire body is often understood by ancient authors in terms of cooking, distillation or, as said before, "concoction". If humours are the result of the cooking of food in the body, semen is a final stage of the cooking process. This is why the semen's borders with food and other residues were very blurred: hence advice about fully digesting food before sex (Laqueur, 1990).[8]

Beside the mechanism of pangenesis, what is important to highlight here is that it is the extreme porosity of the semen that makes it conducive to the effects of local habits. Places (mostly, but not only, via food) left direct marks on the bodies of human groups. Different foods shaped the semen differently and contributed to different progenies and "heredity". The power of place is magnified by such a mechanism. This was particularly visible at the time of the first colonial movements to the New World, which produced unprecedented anxiety among settlers about the stability of their bodily boundaries and the risk of racial reversibility. In *The Body of the Conquistador* (2012), historian Rebecca Earle describes Spanish dietary obsessions in the colonies. If humoralism – a key tenet of medical teaching at the newly founded *Universidad de México* – implied that the Spanish body would mutate in the New World (different food, but also stars and winds), then diet "more than any other factor" would separate Spanish from Amerindian bodies. Spaniards therefore paid attention to a very detailed micropolitics of food (importing bread, wine and oil, cultivating Spanish crops) for reasons that went well beyond "culinary nostalgia". An obsession with the integrity of old-world food was essential for the stability of the colonial body.

These concerns spoke directly to Spanish worries about the physical integrity of their bodies, and about the maintenance or dissolution of the most fundamental of colonial divisions: that between the bodies of the colonisers and the colonised.

(2012: 183)

This porosity of racial characteristics to nurtural aspects could support a variety of political agendas and moral dilemmas. Views of degeneration or regeneration, as well as politics of separation or friendship, could be equally applied to the plastic body of humoralism. Columbus, for instance, who was trained in medicine, supported the importance of Spanish food to protect the colonizer's body and restore health among settlers. He insisted on the importance of old world varieties in the New World, importing legumes and grapes, sugar cane and stock animals (Earle, 2014: 83). "Without the right foods Europeans would either die, as Columbus feared, or, equally alarmingly, they might turn into Amerindians." However, this discourse could easily be inverted and was, once again, in the service of Las Casas' optimistic understanding. In his defence of Amerindians, the Dominican friar claimed that any visible difference between settlers and colonized bodies was only due to different food traditions: "with the right foods ... Amerindians might perhaps come to acquire a European constitution" (2014: 2–3). Claims of a fundamental inferiority of native bodies were therefore unjustified.

As Earle's book shows, before turning into a fixed essence, race and racial differences were still mostly understood as the performative result of different "exercise regimes" (Earle, 2014: 32). The Latin American example of anxieties about degeneration because of the permeability of the colonizer's body is far from unique in colonial areas (cfr. Stoler, 1995; Anderson, 2006). Another instructive case of this instability and contestability of race, in the context of migration and settler colonialism, comes from the work of early modern historian Jean Feerick (2010: 21). In her *Strangers in Blood*, Feerick analyses how

early modern racial ideologies articulate with compelling force what modern racial ideologies seek to bury: the ever-present prospect of racial reversibility. If race denoted the noble markings that descended through a bloodline [...] early modern writers observed with increasing frequency that racial identity needed to be supported, that it required a range of prophylactics in order to maintain the mark of distinction it conferred.

(ibid.: 31).

Fears of degeneracy and debasement in the British long-term resettlement in Ireland after the Norman invasion are a possible example of this anxiety linked to the instability of the original bloodline in a new soil. However, the "lability of racial stocks" was always a double-edged sword in the language of "kind": settlers often used the early modern precariousness of race to celebrate their new settlement as a "wonderful" form of degeneration against their Old English counterparts (Feerick, 2010: 32). In light of my previous analyses on the botanical roots of humoralism, it is interesting to notice how here, too, organic metaphors appear to describe the potential and risk of "racial mutability". The unstable racial lexicon included terms such as "growing awry", "growing away" from a noble line, "decaying" and "altering". Other dynamic metaphors included *becoming* strangers (rather than being ones) because of the way in which settlers "dayly grew unto more and more alienation" (ibid.: 30). A similar metaphorical repertoire has been mapped in relation to French Huguenots' settlements in Florida in the second half of the sixteenth century, with overt metaphors of *planting* or *transplanting* a new race in a new soil (Hannaford, 1996). As Feerick again notes, in that context, settlers preferred the term "planting" to "colonizing" as a way to describe how "the inhabiting of another soil […] would affect not only themselves but their descendants". The idea was that the new colony could become the "place where these lowborn men could 're-race' themselves, ascending the social hierarchy armed only with discipline and hard work", regenerating their blood in a way that would not be possible in the homeland (Hannaford, 1996; Feerick, 2010: 19–20).

A final word on the complex impact of corporeal plasticity and humoralism on racial thought regards the idea of blood, a notion particularly unstable and far from being uniform in these early modern debates. At the intersection of the individual and the political body, the discourse of blood purity emerged as a key place in early modern European debates. It shifted the debate on national identity from a "multivariable" conception – based on "geography, culture, common history, beliefs, and caste as well as bodies" – to a taxonomic system based explicitly and essentially on biology and thus reducing difference to a single, immutable term." (Burk, 2010). But what was the role of humoralism in this transition? On one side, blood was the most important of the four humours, and humoralism was the key medical doctrine in places like early modern Spain where the notion of *limpieza de sangre* (blood purity) took shape. Certainly, the symbolic and religious value of blood well exceeded the importance of humoralism (Foucault, 1990; Camporesi, 1995), but it is possible to speculate on a potential filiation. As Earle, for instance, claims for Spanish America, "*sangre* was in part a metaphorical concept, but as a metaphor it derived its power from its base in the very real world of humours and flows" (2012: 207). On the other hand, humoralist tropes had an eroding impact on the notion of a pure racial identity determined by blood, as blood in a humoralist sense would always "absorb changes from new cultures and environments" (Feerick, 2010: 19). Humoralism is once again situated in a complex relationship with future modern debates. It mimicked, and at the same time, "contested notions of blood purity as a marker of racial difference and stable identity" (Burk, 2010). It made blood an even "more unstable signifier" (Feerick, 2010), creating a fundamental tension with essentialist discourses of race.[9] In early modern racial debates, humoralism was the platform for "a counter-discourse and a site of potential resistance" (Burk, 2010) to the more static qualities of racial identity. It both challenged essentialism and produced its own inherent racializing tropes. Once again, early modern corporeal plasticity was positioned ambiguously between the emergence of modern racialism, for which race is a fixed biological line, and the notion that race is the performative effects of shared social experiences.

Notes

1 See an overview of the debate for Latin America in Cueto and Palmer (2014: 15–16). See general disagreement on these analogies as just "fortuitous" coincidences in Nutton (2004).
2 Sometimes "passive" exercise, such as being transported in boats, as claimed by Renaissance doctor and mathematician Girolamo Cardano (1501–1576) (Siraisi, 2015).
3 Foucauldians might object that, unlike Christian forms of pastorate, the subtle ethics of the self generated by Greek antiquity was antithetical to producing normalizing effects. This straight dichotomy, however, and the argument that Greek techniques of the self were based not on the asymmetry of interpersonal relations but on a more innocent and free relationship to the self sound to me mysteriously weak. The supposed freedom of ancient ethics from the pervasiveness of power remains problematic at best (cfr. Detel, 2005).
4 It was instead a long-held Hippocratic notion that women could be aware of conception in the moment in which the uterus contracted around the semen.
5 It is doubtful that even the case of the so-called myth of autochthony (literally "sprung from the earth") of Athenian people, often interpreted in a modern racialist sense, meant anything more than the recognition of a specific intimacy between a certain genealogical group (*genos*) and a place, or even the power of a specific place to shape people's characteristics at birth (Kaplan, 2016; Kennedy, 2016; cfr. Rosivach, 1987).

6 This may explain the idealization of black people (from the south) in the Ancient literature as good and faraway barbarians (Romm, 1994), or being of a stronger constitution (Hippocrates) rather than a supposed lack of racism *tout court* in ancient thought (Snowden, 1983).

7 Aristotle and Lucretius were among the most famous skeptics of pangenesis.

8 Although the two notions are not necessarily related, pangenesis offers a strong mechanistic possibility for the inheritance of acquired traits: it is a way through which "each part of the body of each parent renders up some aspect of itself" to the next generation (Laqueur, 1990: 37). As Justin Smith claims, this solved a "fundamental problem in ancient thinking on generation concerning the resemblance of offspring to parent, for in a very literal, physical sense, the developing foetus begins from a number of chips off the old parental blocks" (Smith, 2006: 4). In pangenesis, a parent's body literally "manufactured the particles from which the body of its offspring will be constructed" (Bowler, 1989: 25). Bodies created bodies, one generation after the other, in an ongoing process of somatic communication. This model was so pervasive that Charles Darwin, to whom we owe the term, adhered to it (1875) and paid his debt to the Hippocratic legacy. While pangenesis had survived from Hippocrates to Darwin, it quickly capitulated after Galton, Weismann and the construction of hard heredity in genetics where there is, in principle, no communication between somatic and germ cells.

9 It is worth adding that it was not only blood and semen that were points of instability in early modern discourses on race. Breastmilk was also important, and with it came the persistent anxiety about the behaviours and social or racial origin of the wet nurse, who can shape the character and physical traits of the infant. Particularly, in a humoralist view, "to nurse from another's milk was essentially to imbibe their humours" (Earle, 2012: 50). From the Roman to the early modern world, the belief that breastmilk "had the power to make children resemble their nurses in mind and body" (Marwick, 1995) was widely held. Infiltration by racial and lower social classes was a feared problem in a context where the depth of the nursing relationship in shaping the child's features was considered of primary importance (Marwick, 1995; Stoler, 1995).

Taming plasticity: Darwin, selectionism, and modern agency

3

Fixing the humoralist body

The modern displacement of humoralism was a complex and often uneven process. At the end of the eighteenth century, the fluid and permeable humoralist body gave way to a new solid body that emerged from a different anatomical and clinical gaze (Canguilhem, 1966/2012; Foucault, 1973; Risse, 1997). Thinking about disease was differently spatialized and in a sense radically transformed: no longer dynamically revealed by changes in unstable fluids, or by the disturbance of a totalizing experience with nature (Canguilhem 1966/2012), pathology was now firmly localized and embodied in well-defined organs, fibres or tissues.

A different body came into view: "By the beginning of the Victorian era, the fluid-and-flux constitution, as formulated by traditional humoralism, had been completely replaced by the scientific classification of constitutional 'types'" (Ishizuka, 2012). While there is an abundance of detail on this transition in medical history, the biopolitical significance of this process remains less delineated. Two important stories have, thus far, been insufficiently connected: 1) the medical history of how humoralism was displaced by the bounded modernistic body of biomedicine; and 2) the consolidation of the liberal humanist subject, with its strong awareness of boundaries and a personhood relatively buffered from external influences. Humoralism stands in a complex relationship to this latter process. On one side, it promoted ideas of selfhood and techniques of body control that, on the whole, may have contributed to the rise of modern individualism. It even became incorporated in emerging bourgeois values of human educability and health mastery in eighteenth-century France. The humoralist doctrine of the six non-naturals strongly appealed to the educated public as a form of cultivation of the body. It presented a view of health hygiene that was "naturalistic, individualistic, and practicable" (Coleman, 1974: 421). On the other side, there were a number of incompatible aspects between humoralism and the defended body that came into place after the second half of the nineteenth century. An obvious one, from a medical viewpoint, is that humoralism could not keep up with the universal production of a fixed standard of health and disease "applicable to all men in all times" (ibid: 407). Bodies were too dependent on places to extract their singular experience into a generalized view of morbidity. It was the triad of naturalness of disease (rather than the effect of behavioural transgression) and necessity and universality of its causes (that is, of a specific aetiological agent, like a germ) that introduced a different vocabulary, with which humoralism could not keep up (Codell Carter, 2017). However, there is more than medical history here. As a form of human agency dispersed across bodies and landscapes (Nash, 2006), humoralism poorly served some of the emerging civic virtues of liberal humanism: autonomy, independency, inviolability of the body, and depth and uniqueness of the self. In humoralism, the notion of an inner core that is immutable, shielded from the pervasive power of environmental influences, always remained chimerical.

Following a number of authors in recent times, the argument that I want to explore in this chapter is that a different sort of body was required to underpin the modern fiction of a possessive body, a discrete individual subtracted from the overwhelming forces of nature and social relationships. Liberalism, understood as the application of an individualistic view to social relationships, is a very specific ontology and technology of the self (Dumont, 1986; Foucault, 2003). It is a moral outlook that apparently transcends any specific views of biological human nature (as well as physiology and heredity) when in fact it is consistent with only some of them. It is based on the highly idealized and normative view not only that human agency is secured through a stable inner self, but also that this inner core is entitled to a strong degree of independence from the "interference" of anyone else's activity (Berlin, 2002): a body (and a self) that is property to its own person and that no-one "has any Right to but himself", as Locke famously put it (1689/1967). Even though this self "reacts to acts and events coming to it from outside", these events are "quite apart from its internal essence [...] which has no history" (Reiss, 2003: 9). This is the view classically analysed (and criticized) by Macpherson in his book on *Possessive Individualism* in the British modern political tradition:

The human essence is freedom from any relations other than those a man enters with a view to his own interest. [...] The individual is proprietor of his own person, for which he owes nothing to society [...] Political society is a contractual device for the protection of proprietors and the orderly regulations of their relations.

(Macpherson, 1962: 269)

This can be seen as crude, but it is also part of a highly moralized view of a fundamental freedom from societal pressures, including social hierarchies. This moralizing line culminates in Kant's emblematic call for an autonomous modern subject that breaks with "his self-incurred minority [...] the inability to make use of one's own understanding *without direction from another*" (1784 [2013]: 17; my italics). The argument is once again aimed to *disentangle individual agency from external interferences*, including moral and social ones, and promote a strong notion of self-mastery and control. Political liberalism understands its "basic political task" mostly as "the protection of subjects from external impositions" (Bagg, 2018: 5).

The purpose in this chapter is to track how emerging discourses in biomedical disciplines in the second half of the nineteenth century incorporated and even underpinned some of these political values breaking with earlier connections of liberalism and sensibility.

Expanding Cohen's project

The most influential author in recent years to cover this dramatic convergence of the political and the biomedical is undoubtedly social theorist Ed Cohen (2009; Jamieson, 2016). Expanding on Foucault's programmatic analysis of the nexus of biopolitics and liberalism (2003), and works in science and technology studies on metaphors of the body and the political-economic system (Martin, 1994; Haraway, 1999), Cohen offers an enlightening analysis of how a "monadic modern body" took the stage in the second half of the nineteenth century. Cohen's theoretical task is to explore how "modern presumptions about personhood and collectivity" saturated biological views at the time of the transition to the body of modern biomedicine, and displaced "prevailing scientific theories [of the time] that apprehend living organisms as contiguous with, rather than fundamentally distinct from, their lifeworlds." "The modernized body", Cohen writes, "arises as an artefact of intense human interest and investment" (2009: 7) at the crossroads of experimental work, theoretical syntheses and wider biopolitical changes, including nation-state formations and the making of European imperialism. It did so firstly in Bernard's *physiology* and, subsequently, in *bacteriology* and the emerging science of *immunity*. While the complexity of these three fields prevents any simplistic link with emerging political formations, the way they deployed a number of military metaphors focused on boundary defence and favoured a neat demarcation between the inner and the outer, the proper and the alien, for individual bodies and populations was felt as particularly legitimate in the context of the emerging "Age of Empire" (Hobsbawm, 1995). As Cohen writes:

> Immunity strangely grafts or inoculates both military and political potentials into human biology as an entangled mode of explanation. In fact, immunity offers a peculiar hybrid of military, political, and biological thinking that "naturally" negates the distinctions among these realms. Rendering biological immunity as an organism's active process of defense, scientific medicine deftly fuses a bellicose ideology (which sees environmental challenge as a hostile attack) with a political notion of legal exception (which nevertheless affirms the law's universal applicability).

There is, however, another element of commonality in these three emerging disciplines: a break with the "Hippocratic imagination" (Cohen, 2009: 132), given how Hippocratic knowledge made problematic an isolation of the "proper" body from its outer/external forces. This anti-Hippocratic agenda was part and parcel of the novel artefact emerging in biomedicine. In the words of Claude Bernard, extensively commented on by Cohen:

> Ancient science was able to conceive only the outer environment (*milieu extérieur*); but to establish the science of experimental biology, we must also conceive an inner environment (*milieu intérieur*). I believe I was the first to express this idea clearly and to insist on it, the better to explain the application of experimentation to living beings.
>
> (Bernard, 1949: 76; see Holmes, 1986)

Bernard was not just aiming to find an ontological support for experimental science. He was also aiming at "a kind of independence of living beings in the cosmic environment". Bernard's point was that, to the extent that the organism becomes "more perfect", the "inner environment" becomes more and more specialized and isolated from cosmic forces (110). This is an utter reversal of the Hippocratic project.

Translated at the level of wider social values, what is at stake in this move is, among other things, a recognition of the incapacity of Hippocratism to protect not just the body but the whole individual agency from cosmic forces. As we saw previously, in ancient science these forces took different forms: geographic determinism; direct adjustability of the organism to its surroundings; and even the power of miasmatic forces (from marshy areas, vapours or other putrid influences) in producing disease, given how miasma theory was often seen in continuity with Hippocratic beliefs about direct atmospheric influences (Ackerknecht 1982; Golinski, 2010; Cueto and Palmer, 2014).

The modernized body analysed by Cohen is a complex immunitarian resource to regulate these overwhelming forces. It works partly by incorporating some of them (like the notion of milieu, now interiorized) and partly by disentangling the individual from cosmic influences:

> Instead of evoking the organism's essential connection to the world in which it lives, immunity refigures medicine as a powerful weapon in the body's necessary struggle to defend itself from its life-threatening context.
>
> (Cohen, 2009: 5).

Cohen's study is an indispensable guide not only to the process of delimitation of the modern sovereign body but to the making of a liberal-humanistic notion of free agency; however, his analysis could have been advanced further. Alongside Bernard's *physiology*, *bacteriology* and *immunology*, there are at least two other points of passage from which this repositioning of the relationship between body and milieu, organism and environment was developed in the second half of the nineteenth century: Darwin's notion of natural selection and Weismann's germ-plasm theory. Using selectionism to sever the deep imbrication of organism and milieu posited by the Hippocratic imagination, Darwin and Weismann came to offer a view of biology that could be highly compatible with the modernistic production of a buffered body, and related ideas of a private self and autonomous agency (Taylor, 1989). These five points of transition toward the making of a modernistic body in the second half of the nineteenth century – Bernard's physiology, the development of bacteriology, immunology as defence, Darwin and Weismann's selectionism, and Weismann's theory of heredity – are not to be taken as a caricatural denial of ideas of metabolic exchange, environmental effects or sensitivity to stressors that have well coexisted with later biomedical views. The physiological counterpart to the formation of the *homo clausus* (the encapsulated individual: Elias,

2000) has been definitely a precarious and contested process. They show, however, an overall repositioning of the relationship between body and surroundings and emerging notions of internal regulation, stability, control and individuality that were much less in view under a humoralist framework.

What Darwin and Weismann achieved: Selectionism and modernistic agency

Too facile sociological readings of Darwin's and Weismann's selectionism interpret them as the source of an unreflective biologism in which people are "prisoner[s] of heredity" (Kelly, 1981: 105), yet both crucially contributed to a liberal humanistic view of the sovereign body as endowed with a discrete individuality and disentangled *from the direct pressure* of cosmic forces. Darwin's notion of natural selection is key to a process of biopolitical individualization, because its focus on random variations reduced the direct causative power of "external conditions", enabling a separation between the organism and its surroundings (Lewontin, 1983). The case for Weismann is also cogent. In challenging the Lamarckian (and indeed much older) notion that a body's characteristics result from the deeds of a previous generation, Weismann aimed at a purification of heredity from any mundane influence. The doctrine of the continuity of the germ-plasm insulated the destiny of each generation from the actions of the previous one. The move was bold, and its political meaning not difficult to foresee. Weismann himself did not shy away from making in biological terms an argument that resonated quite clearly with political liberalism: "the hypothesis of the continuity of the germ-plasm", he wrote, "gives *an identical starting-point* to each successive generation" (1891: 168, my italics). This framework represents an excellent theoretical complement for what the liberal citizen is supposed to be, that is, a perfectly self-contained entity whose destiny starts from scratch each time: "every new generation comes into the world pure and uncontaminated, so far, by the surroundings and life history of parents", Benjamin Kidd commented after meeting with Weismann (quoted in Crook, 1994).[1]

While I have analyzed the social significance of Weismann's heredity for politics and sociology more widely in past publications (Meloni, 2016a, 2016b), I will focus in the following pages on the mechanisms of Darwinian evolution as technologies for the construction of a buffered individual, as required by modern liberalism. I will explore the corrosive impact of

Darwin's selectionism on the ancient belief in the direct formative power of the environment, of which humoralism was a key manifestation. The transition from externalist views of direct environmental effects on the biological organism to the more complex view of mediated environmental effects (via natural selection) posited by Darwinians is one of the most overlooked and misunderstood aspects of the sociological construction of the modernistic body. A buffering of the body could only occur through a distancing of organism and environment, and Darwin's natural selection was pivotal to reach this goal. In these last decades, Darwin has been helplessly turned into a precursor of evolutionary views of sociology and economics, someone who made it possible to generalize the "universal acid" of selectionism (Dennett, 1995) to all branches of knowledge. However, the real sociological contribution of Darwin lies elsewhere: in transforming the environment into a secular force that acts on the inborn quality of the organism not directly but only in mediated and random ways. William James well captured this shift when he read Darwinism as a displacement of the previously plastic view of evolution held by pre-Darwinians. Pre-Darwinians, James writes,

> thought only of adaptation. They made organisms plastic to environment. (....) [In Spencer's psychology for instance] The outer relations do all the work, the inner ones are plastic and without spontaneity.
>
> (1988: 136, 137)

Darwin's selectionism can be seen as a technology to strengthen the spontaneity of variations against an overly simplistic correspondence (plasticity) between the organism and the shaping power of outer causes.

I will then discuss the sociological implications of this paradigm shift in terms of moral topography, focusing in particular on the reactions of authors who, like Herbert Spencer, gave all credits to external relations over internal ones. Interestingly, as key a Darwinian as William James identified this latter position as emblematic of an ancient notion of plasticity in which all external relationships did the job of shaping internal identity. But the debate is more than epistemological. To assess the moral and sociological significance of the environmentalism–selectionism debate, I will focus on post-Darwinian controversies surrounding human agency and intellectual capacities, which had implications for notions of social change and racial differences. At stake within these debates is not so much the impressionability of bodies and biological matter as that of human agency: its capacity to withdraw from external influences and to construct an autonomous view of mental capacities less shaped by the power of outer relations. I consider this strengthening of inner psychological capacities a natural complement to the modernized artefact analysed by Cohen. Specifically, it highlights how the constructions of the modernized body focused on a stronger capacity for self-mastery and agency in contrast to the centuries-long environmentalist and humoralist tropes. This historical debate is important to keep in mind in the following two chapters, given the way I address the rise of epigenetics and the making of a postgenomic landscape as a revival of environmentalist and non-selectionist themes in defining biological identity.

The sociological significance of selectionism: Beyond stereotypes

We possess a well-defined picture of how Darwin's natural selection absorbed and projected some of the wider social values of his time onto nature, as well as many of the intellectual sources behind this transfer of values. Over the years, several authors have highlighted the multiple borrowings, direct and indirect, by Darwin from political economists and social scientists, including Smith, Ricardo, Comte, Quetelet and, more obviously and famously, Malthus (Young, 1969; Limoges, 1970; Schweber, 1977: 235, 1980; Schabas, 1990; Desmond and Moore, 1991). That Darwin "projected on organic life" economic ideas and sociological principles is not a new idea (Thomson, 1911: 72). This argument dates back to Marx's observation of the infiltration of Victorian capitalism into the Darwinian project (cited in Schmidt, 2013: 46). However, even if we are to take these analyses at face value, they remain limited in their understanding of the reverse relationship: the sociological impact of Darwinian selectionism on the wider social and intellectual values. Even if Darwin absorbed all the above social values into his project, it remains to be seen how, once they were refashioned by Darwin and catalysed by Darwinism, these values affected the wider social landscape. In this regard, bogeyman terms such as Social Darwinism and eugenics have historically hampered a balanced evaluation, in spite of the tenuous historical validity of the same notion of Social Darwinism (Bannister, 1988) and the less-than-direct relationship of Darwin to eugenics (Paul, 2009). Moreover, what is often overlooked is that natural selection played little role in the evolutionary racism of the late nineteenth century (Bowler, 1989), which was largely

Lamarckian. Selectionism remains mostly a bad word outside of biological circles, where the term is still associated with crude ideas of merciless competition, harsh militarism, extermination of "inferior races", or a sanction of the old argument that "might makes right". Darwin was horrified to read about such associations in the popular reception of his work (see Browne, 2002: 107). It is unquestionable that selectionism, anthropomorphized in various guises, especially in some countries, such as Germany, became a catalyst for militaristic and nationalistic energies (Kelly, 1981). The role of cultural context in these instances, however, was significant, as the Russian example shows (Todes, 1989). However, even in the case of Germany, Darwinism remained a vague and easily appropriated label at the disposal of nearly any sort of project (Kelly, 1981). In the following pages, I therefore attempt to delimit this debate to just one single aspect: the implications of the rise of selectionism for the "ancient doctrine" (Wallace, cited in James, 1880: 452) according to which external circumstances directly shape an organism's traits. This doctrine, which included mental and moral features in humans, was one of the theoretical pillars of the Hippocratic imagination, as we have seen in the previous chapters. In its ancient version, plasticity of the body is, after all, just the conceptual counterpart of the primacy of environmental forces in shaping an organism's traits. It implies a view of the environment as a direct and active producer of change, not a mere passive backdrop where various organismic forces can unfold their different "programs". From this view, there follows a larger malleability of organismic forms to life's conditions. This conceptual framework, which was based on a logic of imprint rather than selection, was a pillar of geography, medicine and historiography from Hippocratic writings to the geographical and political speculations of early modern theorists like Bodin. This is not to say that one can conflate all these different forms of environmental determination in a smooth continuum before the rise of modern biomedicine. Hippocratic themes in the ancient world were fairly different from their usage in eighteenth-century Britain (Golinski, 2010). The idea of the inheritance of acquired characteristics that was present in the ancient authors lacks the aspect of creative power that was later attributed to the organism by the Lamarckian authors. Yet, there is a degree of continuity in Hippocratic themes (Koller, 1918; Thomas, 1925; Spitzer, 1942; Glacken, 1967; Canguilhem, 2001) in terms of both the recurring tropes, often borrowed from ancient authors, and the wider biopolitical implications. This line of thought was attractive to a naturalist like Darwin. Both the century preceding Darwin's work and his own century were not short of such theories.

Eighteenth-century environmentalism: Montesquieu and Buffon

The eighteenth century is considered the pinnacle for theories positing a deep connection between humans and their environment, particularly climatic determinism (Glacken, 1967). What was an ancient humoralist trope, the power of weather and seasonal changes in shaping health and disease, was reconceived in naturalistic terms in the attempt to trace some of its regularities. It was "the climate of the Enlightenment" that often connected these meteorological and climatic considerations to wider debates on the fate and stages of different civilizations (Golinski, 2010). One key example is the work of Montesquieu. In his influential *Spirit of the Laws* (1748, particularly books XIV–XIX) "the empire of the climate" is vividly celebrated as a powerful force capable of producing temperamental, moral, cultural, political and institutional variations. The inextricable embedment of national institutions in local physical conditions is confirmed by the famous antagonism posited by Montesquieu between hot climates and despotism, on the one hand, and cold climates and liberty, on the other. Montesquieu also anticipates another trope apparent in later views: that once the environment has made a population, it cannot unmake them; for example, in the case of the Tartars, who, for Montesquieu, "carried into their deserts that servile spirit which they had acquired in the climate of slavery" (1748/1914: 353). Montesquieu's environmentalism was obviously not unchallenged, and a number of authors expressed scepticism about his sweeping claims (Voltaire). Others wanted to retain some of this framework, but make its generalizations subtler and more complex (Herder). Notwithstanding these challenges or remodulations, atmospheric and climatic themes were, overall, rather prevalent across Europe (for France: Glacken, 1967; for England: Golinski, 2010).

Buffon is a much more complex figure than Montesquieu in his analysis of the relationship between humans and the environment. The way in which he situates himself vis-à-vis this environmentalist debate is no less influential, however. Buffon enables the transition of eighteenth-century climatological theory to the more complex nineteenth-century environmentalism, on which Lamarck (Buffon's student) later capitalizes with his notion of the *circonstances influentes*. His emphasis on the power of the outer circumstances is less straightforward than in dogmatic externalism. Unlike other animals, for Buffon, humans can create humanized spaces where the direct influence of the climate is averted (Febvre, 1924: 8; Glacken, 1967: 503). At the same time, however, Buffon reinforces aspects of the enduring environmentalist narrative, making his rejection of geographic determinism "at best partial" (Sloan, 1973: 306). His theory of race formation, for instance, considers direct environmental influences the key to explaining racial variations, allowing him to save his professed monogenism (Sloan, 1973). According to Buffon, of the three causes (climate, food and customs) that directly produce racial variations ("degeneration"), climate is the most important. However, it is food, acting molecularly on the "internal mold", that is the channel through which the power of place enters and shapes the human body. Moreover, Buffon's theory of generation relies profoundly on an environmental model in which external influences are passed directly – again, mostly via nutrition – on to the semen, where they form the basis for the bodily organization of the new generation (Zirkle, 1946). More importantly, Buffon crucially links for the first time two different historical strands: the older anthropogeographic tradition of Hippocrates, Bodin and Montesquieu; and Newton's cosmology, from which the notion of milieu originates as a French translation for "fluid" (Canguilhem, 2001: 8–9).

Nineteenth-century imbrications of organism and milieu: The Lamarckian solution

The nineteenth century produced both a significant shift and a radicalization of this environmentalist legacy. On the one hand, the old natural theology with its broad physical and climatic terminology started to decline, giving way to a biological and evolutionary lexicon. On the other hand, some of the older physiotheological wisdom survived in views of biological adaptation as the result of a harmonious and pre-established correspondence between milieu and organism (Glacken, 1967; Ospovat, 1995). Importantly, the nineteenth century was the moment when the term "milieu" lost its technical connotation, gaining widespread and cross-disciplinary popularity. Its meaning shifted from referring to a plurality of circumstances to being a singular term that gathered together a number of different factors (climate, food) while concealing their differences (Pearce, 2010).

The impact of the term on the social sciences is profound. The sociology of Comte had largely depended on and expanded the notion of milieu (Koller, 1918; Braunstein, 1997; Petit, 1997). While the term in English was coined by Carlyle (1828), Comte's usage of milieu, via Martineau, went on to decisively influence the work of Spencer (Pearce, 2010). Later in the eighteenth century, French and Belgian sociologists Jacques Bertillon (1872) and Guillaume De Greef (1886–1889) introduced, separately, the notion of "mesologie" as an autonomous subfield of sociology aimed at studying the influence of different milieus on social groups. In wider society, novelists like Balzac and later Zola, and public intellectuals and historians such as Renan, Taine or, in England, Buckle, made the milieu into a veritable heuristic key to explain the laws and directions of historical developments. Nietzsche, always an excellent intellectual seismographer, noted sarcastically in 1885 how the "milieu-theory" was used recklessly in any possible field but with little explanatory gain (cited in Spitzer, 1942: 184). The complex terminological fate of the term "milieu" as it travelled from various disciplinary contexts and linguistic traditions has been carefully documented (Spitzer, 1942; Canguilhem, 2001; Pearce, 2010). In the context of my analysis, two things remain important to highlight, however. The first is the reification of the concept in the nineteenth century. What was originally a relational term to define in Newtonian physics a field of relationships between two bodies (Canguilhem, 2001: 8) gradually became a self-standing entity endowed with causal explanatory power. Secondly, the impersonal view of external natural forces, typical of eighteenth-century mechanism, took on a different connotation in nineteenth-century biology. The environment, the immediate or external circumstances, the conditions of existence, became a true "milieu createur", something elevated to a role that is the "materialistic equivalent of divinity" (Jordanova, 1989; Tresch, 2012).

Lamarck's environmentalism

The contribution and allure of Lamarck within this trend are difficult to overestimate. Lamarckism gave an enormous causal power to what Lamarck called *circonstances influentes*, which raised the notion of direct external effects to an unprecedented extent. This not only offered naturalists like Darwin an attractive intellectual solution to the problem of evolution, but also strongly resonated in wider society. It became a flag for social groups often leaning toward political radicalism, as in the British context, aiming to challenge the medical and theological establishment with a strong naturalistic theory (Desmond, 1992). However, in the longer perspective addressed in this book, Lamarck's discontinuity with past tropes, at least at the level of his wider philosophy, seems less profound. Lamarck's dependence on an ancient materialistic and physicalistic view of life, with roots in Greek philosophy and chemistry, and his "faith in anything but body" (cited in Burkhardt, 1977: 189), have been largely emphasized (Gillispie, 1959; Corsi, 1988: 119; Gould, 2002). In spite of Lamarck's own emphasis on "le pouvoir de la vie" and other vitalistic themes, his framework was strictly mechanistic, stressing the power of "the motion of fluids in the animal body which would carve channels and cavities in soft tissues, and gradually lead to the evolution of increasing organizational complexity" (Koonin and Wolf, 2009: 42; see also Gould, 2002). The mechanical linkages that connected the interior of the organism to its external environment are reminiscent of the humoralist pores and channels. They were described by Lamarck following a sort of hydraulic model, made of "pipes, tubes, canals, and other equivalent spaces" (Gissis, 2011: 24). If one adds to this materialistic undertone the absolute predictability and lack of randomness in the organism's responses to external changes (Lennox, 2015), we find once again a typical trope of the Hippocratic tradition, in which *the possibility of a disentanglement between the organism and its milieu* is very unlikely. It is true that, in higher organisms, the environment's demands were mediated by subjective needs. However, while it is fair to recognize that in Lamarck there were tensions between mechanism and vitalism, forces and wants, it is also the case that the environment "changes first" (Gould, 2002: 177). The anthropological implications of this position in terms of individual spontaneity are noticeable. For Lamarck, "people have no real creativity or imagination" of their own; "all ideas come from nature, with the consequence that transcendence of the material world is impossible" (Jordanova, 1984: 87). It is worth mentioning here that later in the century, French neo-Lamarckism (in contrast to its American counterpart) continued with, and further radicalized, a bold materialistic model. Organisms not only bore the marks of their milieu, but in a more than metaphorical sense, they digested and metabolized it, imprinting its features (via nutrition) into heredity: "milieu, via la nutrition, informe directement les structures plastiques propres au mond vivant" [the milieu, by means of food, directly shapes the plastic structures of the living world], French neo-Lamarckians claimed (Loison, 2010). Significant neo-Lamarckian influences can also be found in late nineteenth- and early twentieth-century geography, which drew on use-inheritance to make sense of the "interaction between particular physical environments and local cultures" (Campbell and Livingstone, 1983; Peet, 1985; for France: Buttimer, 1971; Conry, 1974; Archer, 1993). It was to this state of affairs and context – a radical embedding and absorption of the organism in its surroundings – that Darwin's selectionism spoke through its repositioning of the relationship between life's forms and life's conditions.

The autonomy of the living: Selectionism as disentanglement

In his *Notes for Philosophy 4 (Psychology: 1878–79)*, William James introduced a crucial distinction between two ways of understanding the environment in evolution: as a "producer" and as a "regulator" (or "preserver") of variations. The first is the notion largely shared by pre-Darwinian authors. The environment directly produces the organism as a sculptor the statue. Here, the organism is "plastic to environment", perfectly corresponding to its surroundings (1988: 137). The second – the environment as regulator or preserver – is the genuine view originating from the *Origin of Species*. I suggest that Darwin's break with the Hippocratic imagination, and its nineteenth-century evolutionary versions, should be read along the lines of James' interpretation. With its apparatus of indirect effects, random variations, a much less harmonious view of nature, and a more complex understanding of adaptation (Worster, 1985; Bannister, 1988; Ospovat, 1995), Darwinian selectionism severed the deep imbrication of organism and milieu posited by traditional environmentalist models. In so doing, it precipitated a crisis in the totalizing view of the environment shared by pre-Darwinian authors. It has to be recognized that Darwin's position is very complex. It is undeniable that we can find plenty of ecological themes in his view of life, evidenced by the famous metaphor of the entangled bank and other biocentric and organicistic analogies (Worster, 1985). It is also true that his break with the Hippocratic imagination is more than partial, given his adhesion to pangenesis (1868) when it came to explaining hereditary mechanisms. Nonetheless, with all the due caveats, Darwinism opened a hole in the environmentalist trend. Darwin transformed ecology into a much less romanticized science (Worster, 1985). The environment (life's conditions, external circumstances) lost much of its creative force, becoming, as critics notice today, something "separable from – and external to organisms [...] a selective force that is passive rather than generative" (Moczek, 2015: 1). Darwin did not overlook the importance of external conditions (such as climate, soil and nourishment); however, he considered them "only in connection with natural selection" (Kelly, 1981: 33). The complex steps through which Darwin came to distance himself from an early belief in the direct effects of the environment to conceive alternative ways of thinking about variation and adaptation, that is, natural selection, have been analysed by historians (Ospovat, 1995). The reasons behind this epistemological break were manifold and include a) biogeographical observations showing great organismic variation in environmentally similar regions and, vice versa, similarity of organisms in highly heterogeneous areas (Darwin, 1845 [1937]; see also, for context, Amundson, 1994; Hodge, 2009); b) the analogy with breeding practices in domesticated production; and c) the crucial influence of Malthus, and political economists in general, in highlighting the priority of relations with other living beings over those "with the environment conceived as a collection of physical forces" (Canguilhem, 2001: 13). If one were to reread the *Origin* today in light of the longevity of environmentalist trends to which I have pointed in the preceding pages, and widespread notions of plastic adaptation of the organism to its life's conditions (with James), what would strike the reader is the absolute confidence with which Darwin dismisses the direct role of external conditions. In the following and several other passages, Darwin overtly confesses to have "not much faith" or "to lay very little weight on the direct action of the conditions of life" (1859[1985]: 105). As he writes:

> Naturalists continually refer to external conditions, such as climate, food, &c. as the only possible cause of variation. In one very limited sense, as we shall hereafter see, this may be true; but it is preposterous to attribute to mere external conditions, the structure, for instance, of the woodpecker, with its feet, tail, beak, and tongue, so admirably adapted to catch insects under the bark of trees.
>
> (1859[1985]: 5)

In other passages in *Origin* Darwin claims that "physical conditions" are insufficient to explain species' distribution; that "direct effects of the conditions of life" are "unimportant" compared with the laws of reproduction, growth and inheritance; and that "quite opposite conditions produce similar changes of structure" and thus only "some slight amount of change may [...] be attributed to the direct action of the conditions of life" (1859[1985]: 31). Finally, Darwin states that it "would be a bold man who would account by such agencies [the external conditions of life, and habit]" to explain completely organic change. Only "little effect", Darwin reiterates, can be attributed to those agencies (1859[1985]: 51). A historical treatment of Darwin's personal oscillation in making room for direct environmental effects in his evolutionary view is beyond the scope of this chapter.[2] Since Darwin never held that natural selection was *the only* evolutionary mechanism, some room for direct effects was always left open. In fact, this space became greater in his later writings, particularly in *The Variation of Animals and Plants* (1868), in combination with Darwin's interest in pangenesis, an obvious place to look for this environmentalist vein (see Winther, 2000).

In spite of Darwin's intellectual fluctuations, the discovery of natural selection as a new "paramount" cause for evolution introduced a radically different way to conceive the power of the environment. No longer was the environment an immediate creator of organismic change; it was now a selector acting indirectly via the reproductive system. This shift had fundamental consequences for the way the relationship between the organism and the environment was conceived. Firstly, variations were now seen as indifferent to environmental changes: they occurred regardless of any adaptive bias (Gould, 2002: 145). The pre-established synchronization between milieu and organism was subverted, and the same notion of adaptation was now to be understood according to a more pragmatic, "less-than-perfect" model (Ospovat, 1995). Secondly, organisms' propensity to change was no longer seen as a direct response to "altered external conditions", but as a spontaneous force largely exceeding the direct pressure of external change (Ospovat, 1995; Amundson, 1996). Thirdly, variations were not only indifferent but also "indefinite" (Olby, 2009). This indefiniteness opened a major crack in the edifice of deterministic explanations. Natural selection anticipated a probabilistic view of the relationship between environment and organism based on tendencies rather than fixed effects (Lennox, 2015). More importantly, both selectionism and probabilistic thinking conceived of organisms as spontaneous "sources of variation, not merely as reactors to outside stimuli" (Amundson, 1996: 33). The distance from Lamarckism (and from previous biopolitical connections of people and places) couldn't be wider. For Lamarck, given a certain environment, "all individuals basically acquire the same structures and adaptations" (Kroenfeldner, 2007: 499; see Mayr, 1972). For Darwin, however, "living organisms of the same species exposed to very different conditions often vary not at all; and the offspring of living organisms of the same species subjected to nearly identical external conditions sometimes vary a great deal" (Johnson, 2015: 65). This move implies an element of accidentality that is unheard of in long-term environmentalist and climatological trends. It disrupted any unilinear causal process and, crucially, against a simplistic understanding of selectionism, introduced a stronger role for the autonomy of the organism, whose potential for change was no longer a direct resultant of the power of circumstances. It is at this level, in my view, that Darwinism acted as a crucial complement to the making of a modernistic body by displacing previous environmentalist models and aligning biology with some key tenets of liberalism. In contrast even to Darwin's own romantic understanding of an entangled nature (1859 [1985]: 489), in the selectionist view, organisms (humans included) were now less entangled in, and imbricated with, their surroundings. The conditions of life acted mostly in an indirect way. It was not long before the repercussions of this break for the environmentalist imagination became apparent.

A selectionist critique of the moral idiom of environmentalism: James and Weismann

The impact of selectionism outside biological disciplines has been mostly considered in relation to the erosion of "evolutionary social science" (Ingold, 1986; Kuklick, 1996; Lewis, 2001; Sanderson, 2007; Bowler, 2009; Bannister, 2014). What is insufficiently investigated, however, are the wider social values that were woven into this debate, and their reverberations for ideas of human agency, social change and even racial differences. What were the moral implications of the rise of selectionism against the venerable doctrine of direct climatological and environmental effects on the human body and mind? The ambiguous moral baggage of climatological and environmentalist themes has been explored in previous chapters within the context of ancient and early modern times. The moral ambiguity of environmentalism and its inclination to hierarchical views of racial relationships continued well into the nineteenth century, however, although this was often obscured by the rise of hereditarian theories of racial differences. In particular, the way in which environmentalist arguments were mostly (not always) associated with the monogenist camp (Stepan, 1982; Zammito, 2006) has obfuscated the ease with which environmentalism remained embroiled in arguments for the acquired inferiority of specific groups and races, in Darwin's time and beyond, because of their geographical or historically acquired disadvantage. In such arguments, growth and stasis, and the development and regression of specific civilizations, were strongly tied to direct environmental pressures. External conditions, American neo-Lamarckian geographers claimed, "strongly impressed themselves on the character of a race" and were reflected in people's "way of living" (Nathaniel S. Shaler, 1892, cited in Campbell and Livingstone, 1983: 272). The founding mother of American geography, Ellen C. Semple, extended such views by claiming that nature

> has entered into his [man's] bone and tissue, into his mind and soul. On the mountains she has given him leg muscles of iron to climb the slope; along the coast she has left these weak and flabby, but given him instead vigorous development of chest and arm to handle his paddle or oar.
>
> (1911, cited in Campbell and Livingstone, 1983: 274)

The emergence of acclimatization theories in colonial medicine since the late eighteenth century was also an important tool to reinforce such a trend (Livingstone, 1987; Anderson, 1996). The meaning of acclimatization was quite diverse in different European countries: in England it was mostly anti-transformationist and conveyed, more conservatively, the meaning of a simple transfer of an organism; in France it had a more structural meaning, referring to physiological and biological changes in organisms (Osborne, 2000). The connection between ideas of acclimatization and Lamarckian and neo-Hippocratic perspectives has also been often emphasized in the relevant literature (Osborne, 2000: 137; see also Anderson, 1996). Importantly, the meaning of acclimatization has also shifted over time, with a hardening since the nineteenth century of the racial distinction between European and native physiology, for instance in the case of India (Harrison, 1999), and increased concern about colonizers' vulnerability in tropical settings (Anderson, 1996). In general, in the context of the colonial endeavour, the narrative of acclimatization tended to oscillate between an optimistic hope for the adaptability of people to new world areas and the reinforcement of a moralistic connection of people and places between *latitude* and *lassitude* (Livingstone, 1991; Bale, 2002).

Without minimising the impact of hereditarian theories, in Darwin's time, it was the intellectual landscape of acclimatization and wider environmentalism that had to be confronted by those wishing to explore the relationship between people and place. As historians have made clear, the Darwinian revolution, meaning the impact of selectionism in the second half of the nineteenth century (Bowler, 1989), was largely a mirage, as the power of older developmentalist and environmentalist tropes remained dominant. Much emphasis has been placed on the unpleasant moral implications of selectionism, its hijacking by a crude militarist rhetoric or for racial hygiene arguments, or its unique favouring of a passive view of the organism; yet the specific moral idiom of environmentalism enjoys less problematic status. This has become especially true since the mid-twentieth century, when a stable association of values between environmentalism and liberal social attitudes crystallized (Toynbee, 1934; Pastore, 1949). However, this professed connection of values is seriously misleading when projected retrospectively, especially before the twentieth century. The notion that the environment impressed its effects directly on people was a key tool of nineteenth-century racialism. It promoted an important conflation of " 'race' and 'nation' [...] natural history and national history" (Campbell and Livingstone, 1983: 271). Where was Darwin's selectionism situated within these debates? In order to unearth the ethical complexity of the selectionism–environmentalism debate from under the weight of historical stratification, I now focus on two texts discussing the development of mental faculties in the aftermath of Darwin's work. The two documents are a) William James' short text *Great Men, Great Thoughts and the Environment* (hereafter GM) and b) August Weismann's essay *Thoughts upon Musical Sense in Animals and Man*, published in

1889 in the political journal Deutsche Rundschau. James and Weismann are two quintessentially selectionist authors. While the selectionism of Weismann,[3] the proponent of the all-sufficiency of natural selection, does not need further explanation here, the case for James as quintessentially selectionist is subtler, though just as strong (Richards, 1987; McGranahan, 2011, 2012). By the age of twenty-three James had already "reached a fairly full acceptance of Darwin's transmutation theory and rejected the most insidious argument of social Darwinism" (Richardson, 2006: 27). This capacity for freeing natural selection from its most simplistic usages makes James a unique conceptual lens through which to see the wider implications of the selectionism–environmentalism debate. Before an analysis of the two texts, a few more words on their context may help. Firstly, it is important to notice that while there are no references to James in Weismann's work, James was overtly appreciative of Weismann's experimental results in the last pages of his *Principles of Psychology* (James, 1890: 686–687). Although Weismann's analysis occupies only a few pages, James adds Weismann's contribution and his "captivating theory of descent" in the successive edition of his *Principles*, after becoming acquainted with Weismann's work (ibid.: 686). This is made all the more interesting given that one of James' teachers at Harvard was the French-American physiologist Charles Brown-Séquard, of whom Weismann was a critic. Charles Brown-Séquard's experiments (Menand, 2001: 382) on the transgenerational effects of epilepsy in guinea pigs were rejected by Weismann, and James agreed with Weismann's scepticism (1890: 687). Besides their rejection of the work of Brown-Séquard, it is in their respective criticism of the work of Herbert Spencer that the two authors find common ground. Spencer's biology and psychology are the common targets of James' and Weismann's critiques: the "foil to set off what seems to me the truth of my own statements", as James writes in *Great Men and Their Environment* (cfr also James, 1878). With his successful combination of psychological associationism and Lamarckian evolution (Peel, 1971; Bowler, 1993; see also Burrow, 1966; for the global diffusion of Spencerism, see Lightman, 2015), Herbert Spencer is probably the most outstanding representative of nineteenth-century theories of the influence of external relations over internal ones within theories of biological growth, psychology and education. He championed the notion that the environment was the key agent of organismal change: in Spencer, environment appears 185 times in *The Principles of Psychology* (Pearce, 2010). Life itself was defined by Spencer, in a thoroughly environmentalist fashion, as "the continuous adjustment of internal relations to external relations" (Spencer, 1855: 80). Even innate factors, in such a view, are not actually innate but "generated" by the deeds of our ancestors (Spencer, 1886). Spencer's environmentalism is apparent in his assessment of moral and cultural development. For Spencer, morality has a physiological basis, or, rather, it is "a development of physiological truth" (Spencer, 1851/1883: 31.6). Human characteristics are malleable to the environment, but not for everyone and not in the same way in any given place: when it comes to intellect and customs, "higher" civilizations are deemed more plastic than others. When it comes to the direct effects of the biophysical environment instead, "inferior" races are more permeable. Spencer and other Lamarckians at the time, such as Topinard, were therefore establishing a hierarchy of civilizations based on plasticity (Staum, 2011; see also Haller, 1971; Bowler, 2009; Gissis, 2003). This scale of educability is not only geographical but also temporal. As Spencer wrote in his "The comparative psychology of man", the capacity of human races and classes to "be impressible by the new circumstances of advancing social life" has changed over time and space:

> Many travelers comment on the unchanging habits of savages. The semi-civilized nations of the East, past and present, were, or are, characterized by a greater rigidity of custom than characterizes the more civilized nations of the West. The histories of the most civilized nations show us that in earlier times the modifiability of ideas and habits was less than it is at present. And, if we contrast classes and individual around us, we see that the most developed in mind are the most plastic.
> (1876: 305)

So while "savages" are at the "mercy of the milieu", the capability for continuous adjustment to new external influences is a characteristic of "higher races". This double-edged view – progress for some but not for everyone – underpinned the characteristic mixture of optimism and pessimism, regeneration and degeneration, in neo-Lamarckian discussions of race and social progress in the second half of the nineteenth century.

It is within this context that I situate James' and Weismann's critique of Spencer's worldview. A long passage in Spencer's *Principles of Psychology*, cited at length by James, is particularly significant because it perfectly combines the three targets of James' and Weismann's parallel attack on Spencer's emphasis on external conditions. The first target is the environmentalist view, supported by Spencer, that it is "experience's moulding finger" (James, 1890: 620) that directly shapes the human mind. The second, related target is the Lamarckian radicalization of this environmentalist view, and particularly the notion that the mind owes its current shape not only to present experiences but to the acquired effects of past generations' experience. The third target concerns the subtle moral repercussions of this version of environmentalism, a crude organicism that confuses cultural acquisitions with the brain's size and attributes human excellence not accidentally to single talented individuals but congenitally to whole populations.[4] According to his use–disuse model, the human brain, Spencer writes, is the

> organized register of infinitely numerous experiences received during the evolution of life, or rather, during the evolution of that series of organisms through which the human organism has been reached. The effects of the most uniform and frequent of these experiences have been successively bequeathed [...] and have slowly amounted to that high intelligence which lies latent in the brain of the infant. ... Thus it happens that the European inherits from twenty to thirty cubic inches more brain than the Papuan. Thus it happens that faculties, as of music, which scarcely exist in some inferior races, become congenital in superior ones.
>
> (1855: 470–471)

It is against this problematic Spencerian legacy regarding mental faculties that I suggest reading the parallel attack advanced by James and Weismann.

James' critique: Great Men, Great Thoughts, and the Environment (1880)

The key argument of James' text, originally a lecture before the Harvard Natural History Society, is a "remarkable parallel [...] between the facts of social evolution on the one hand, and of zoölogical evolution" (GM: 441). The theme is not unique in James' work. A few years later, in his *Principles of Psychology*, James clearly distinguishes between two mechanisms of evolution: a) "the way of 'adaptation,' in which the environment may itself modify its inhabitant by exercising, hardening, and habituating him to certain sequences, and these habits may, it is often maintained, become hereditary"; and b) "the way of 'accidental variation' [...] in which certain young are born with peculiarities that help them and their progeny to survive" and in which causes of variations are "molecular and hidden" (1890: 626–627). GM can be understood as an attempt to apply this latter method to what James calls elsewhere "psychogenesis" or "the factors of mental evolution" (1890: 627). The remarkable parallel announced at the beginning of the text is the following: just as there are two ways of conceiving organic change in zoological evolution, there are two ways to conceive the production of human genius in social evolution. One is the way of adaptation or the Spencerian "law of intelligence". In this view, "great men" are a direct "resultant" of certain "outer relations", exactly, James polemically writes, "as the pressure of water outside a certain boat will cause a stream of a certain form to ooze into a particular leak" (GM: 449). This is a view of the origins of intelligence that makes it thoroughly subject to the "incident forces" of external stimulation. However, there is another way to look at mental evolution, and this is Darwin's selection principle. Darwin's "triumphant originality", James claims, was in showing "the utter insignificance in amount of […] changes produced by direct adaptation, the immensely greater mass of changes being produced by internal molecular accidents, of which we know nothing" (GM: 444). The anti-determinist gains of this gesture are obvious: "The causes of production of great men lie in a sphere wholly inaccessible to the social philosopher. He must simply accept geniuses as data, just as Darwin accepts his spontaneous variations." The potential for genius and its environmental determination are radically disentangled: the first is a "stroke of evolutionary luck", while the second is no longer a creator but a mere selector. "No geographical environment can produce a given type of mind", James writes; "It can only foster and further certain types fortuitously produced, and thwart and frustrate others" (GM: 451).

Against a simplistic reading of James as another nineteenth-century "hero-worshipper" (in the line of a Thomas Carlyle), it is important to insist here that not only is James' analysis entirely naturalistic but it is also far from being sociologically naïve, as Spencerians like the American John Fiske claimed (1881). It is true that James' main worry in the text is Spencer and his sociological school, which posits a necessary relationship between external pressures and genius (and vice versa, it excludes the emergence of genius where these outer relations are missing). Nonetheless, James is far from denying that a "social environment" is fully required to make social evolution work. "Social evolution", James writes,

> is a resultant of the interaction of two wholly distinct factors, – the individual, deriving his peculiar gifts from the play of physiological and infra-social forces, but bearing all the power of initiative and origination in his hands; and, second, the social environment, with its power of adopting or rejecting both him and his gifts. Both factors are essential to change. The community stagnates without the impulse of the individual. The impulse dies away without the sympathy of the community.
>
> (GM: 448).

What James is offering here is a view of social relationships that is more fine-grained than the one held by the Spencerian school, in particular by philosopher and scientific popularizer Grant Allen (GM: 448). James' polemic is against a nondialectical view that, as in the case of Spencer, "makes the outer relations do all the work. The inner ones are plastic and without spontaneity." For James, this lack of spontaneity is not just a psychological problem, however. If the mind is just a mechanical reflection of the outside world, (supposedly) poor human talents will invariably correspond to poor environments. Hence Spencer's racist cartography of the musical faculty: congenital in superior civilizations and impossible in inferior ones, with the brain's size mirroring perfectly this unbalanced development. Indeed, this point emerges even more clearly from Weismann's critique.

Weismann's critique: Thoughts upon the Musical Sense in Animals and Man (1889)[5]

Weismann's text has a more specific focus than James' *Great Men*: not genius in general but musical sense and its historical development. Beyond specific biographical sources (Weismann's predilection for music and the piano in particular; see Conklin, 1915: 4), the essay must be located within a series of exchanges that addressed the evolutionary origins of music in the second half of the nineteenth century, and included Spencer (1857) and Darwin (1859[1985]). Weismann's position is rather unique in this debate. He fully recognizes the role of natural selection in the growth of human intelligence, and of sexual selection in the development of musical sense in animals (and partly in its human origin). However, he disagrees that either natural or sexual selection can explain the "immense growth" in the musical sense in humans "since the earliest times" (1892: 37). This is exactly what makes the essay interesting. If the reproductive value of the musical talent seems nil, how can the consistent naturalist explain its "increased refinement and growth" (1892: 39)? There is obviously one way left, and it is Spencer's, that is, "the inherited effects of practice" (Weismann, 1892: 48). Spencer had famously defended this argument since his *Principles of Biology* to explain the extraordinary musical advancement in the period between Bach and Beethoven. Something so spectacular, Spencer argued, "cannot rationally be ascribed to the coincidence of 'spontaneous variations'" (1886: 250). It is exactly in countering this claim that the richness of Weismann's selectionism comes into view, not as a direct explanation of the growth of musical talent, but as a radical occlusion of Spencer's way. It is this occlusion that makes the search for an alternative mechanism to explain mental evolution necessary. To make this alternative mechanism visible, Weismann makes an important distinction in the essay: between musical expression and musical talent. The latter has always been "inherent in man from the beginning", so the question about its supposed growth is ill posed. The former has, in fact, "undergone progressive increase and development", but this growth has nothing to do with the Spencerian increase in brain size because of the cumulative effects of practice. "Man possesses a tradition", Weismann writes; "he improves and perfects his performances by passing on the gains of each generation to those which follow" (1892: 49). *Tradition* is a very significant word in the German anthropological culture. Herder often refers to the term to convey the idea of a chain of knowledge (art, language) being handed over and refined through generations (Herder, 1778 [2002]). It is exactly in this sense that Weismann – the alleged destroyer of human progress and the value of education, as claimed by the neo-Lamarckians – uses the term to establish a new "method of progress". In his use of "tradition" in this way, Weismann presents an alternative to the inheritance of acquired characteristics, one in which everyone can "seize upon the acquirements of his ancestors at the point where they left them, and [...] pursue them further" (1892: 51). It is because of this heritage, rather than a supposed hereditarian "increase in the capacity of the human brain", that "we can now solve more difficult problems than at the beginning of this century, or in Aristotle's day". Similarly, it is because of this heritage (which also includes technological advancements), not because of a "recent improvement in the dexterity of the human hand", that our pianists can produce better performances than in Bach's or Mozart's day.

Weismann's notion that "music is an invention and rests upon tradition" has several profound implications vis-à-vis Spencer's view. It is important here, however, to highlight the political dimension of the break of selectionism with the long-standing environmentalist tradition. It was not only that selectionism "jettisoned biological analogies" (Bannister, 2014) in the study of society, or put a wedge between cosmic evolution and human ethics (Thomas Huxley). The impact of selectionism is wider. Ideas of racial difference that implied a confusion between race and nation, talents and places, were threatened. The environmental determinism of the Spencerian position seems to imply a rather crude truth: given that mental talent is just the result of a number of environmental stimuli, and given that the nervous system and brain size merely reflect this relation, a musical genius is not possible among savages. The racist potential of this combination of association psychology and inheritance of acquired characteristics in Spencer is palpable. For

Weismann, things are different and much subtler: since musical talent is the result of an undirected mutation, the potential presence of musical geniuses among savages is entirely possible. "From the mere fact that symphonies are not composed by savages", Weismann writes, "we are not entitled to conclude that Mozarts have not existed among them" (1892: 43). What is impossible, Weismann claims, is that this Aboriginal Mozart could do more than produce a "great reform" within the existing "musical environment" of Samoa. To think differently, Weismann claims, is to expect that Archimedes had invented "the modern dynamo as used for the transmission of energy or for electric lighting" (1892: 42). The contrast with Spencer is obvious: the limit of the Aboriginal Mozart is *purely sociological* for Weismann, not organically determined as in Spencer's example of the Papuans. The resonances of Weismann with the anthropological and sociological tradition have been elucidated; in particular, the way in which Weismann helped to purify both disciplines of the "vitiated mixture" of organic and superorganic explanations (Kroeber, 1917; Kroenfeldner, 2009; Meloni, 2016b). This confusing biosocial blend thwarted the emergence of a self-standing notion of culture or social causes disconnected from individual acquisitions. However, there are broader biopolitical implications resulting from Weismann's view. It is true that Weismann's text still belongs within a rather typical Eurocentric canon that thinks in terms of "stages of civilization". It is also true that Weismann, somewhat inconsequently, reintroduces in his conclusion certain arguments about inherent human faculties (Kroeber, 1916: 37; Kroenfeldner, 2009). However, the racist cartography of Spencer's environmentalism, with its logical connection of places and human faculties, is disrupted. It is because human potential escapes the direct determination of places that we are no longer "entitled without further proof to infer that savages never possess high musical talents because their music is but lowly developed" (1892: 43).

After selectionism?

"Only by alienating organism from environment and rigorously separating the ontogenetic sources of variation among organisms from the phylogenetic forces of natural selection could Darwin put evolutionary biology on the right track", Richard Lewontin famously argued (1983: 106). What my reading suggests is that Darwin's genius was in offering a radical critique of the powerful environmentalist tradition without dismissing the role of the environment (as internalists would) but rather, radically repositioning it. Weismann capitalized on this selectionist view to put forward a notion of heredity insulated from direct environmental pressures. It was upon this dual shift that twentieth-century neo-Darwinism established its theoretical basis. This way of thinking has been criticized on different accounts in social theory and philosophy of biology. However, it is undeniable that an alienation of the organism (and mental faculties) from direct environmental pressures also favoured a creative way of thinking about human agency. Selectionism opened up possibilities that were unknown within the framework of the environmentalist tradition. This chapter's historical detour through the moral and sociological implications of the selectionism–environmentalism debate is an important genealogical guide to the next two chapters. As I will argue, in epigenetics and postgenomics the formative power of the environment in instructing the organism in a directed, non-random way is increasingly at the centre of novel evolutionary explorations (Rosenberg et al., 2009; Jablonka and Lamb, 2014), including claims of a return to soft or plastic heredity (Richards, 2006; Lamm and Jablonka, 2008; Bonduriansky, 2012). Bodies are increasingly described as molecularly entangled in their milieu, as "enfold[ing] molecular and social environments into their growth" (Warin et al., 2015: 57; see also Guthman and Mansfield, 2013; Gowland, 2015). The environment that was once utterly separated is now once again flooding over the newly porous organism. Some of the implications of this shift in terms of knowledge production are rapidly coming to light: ideas of culture (or tradition) as primarily extraorganic – as defended by Weismann and later Kroeber in anthropology – are challenged by a novel mixture of biosocial and biocultural approaches that place the body at the centre of the reproduction of culture and social structures (Ingold and Palsson, 2013; Frost, 2016; Meloni et al., 2016). An epigenetics of culture, for instance, although "still in its infancy", is described as being able to show how cultural practices can lead to "molecular epigenetic changes that in turn can contribute to the reconstruction of the system's dynamics" (Jablonka, 2016: 46). Notions of inscription, biological embedding, entanglement and nature-culture, all pointing to a hybrid of bodies and places, meaning and flesh, are increasingly significant in social theory (Meloni et al., 2018). Historians themselves look to epigenetics to replace the modernistic separation of context and content with a thought style now favouring the "imbrication of science with its 'surround'", that is between knowledge and its medium (Alder, 2013: 96) What remains a radical *terra incognita* in this scenario are the moral and political implications of this new entanglement: entanglement between bodies and their milieux but also bodies and bodies, in space and in time, that is, across generations. What does it mean for notions of human agency, social change and racial differences that the immediate and past environment matters more than we previously thought? What shall we expect from claims that past and present social experiences leave a relatively stable imprint on the biology of certain groups and explain racial differences in health (Jasienska, 2009; Kuzawa and Sweet, 2009)? What about the mechanistic correspondence between disadvantaged places and abnormal epigenetic expression for whole groups, not just individuals, claimed today in epidemiological epigenetics (McGuinness et al., 2012)? I will explore some of these emerging claims in the next two chapters. What can be taken from this historical excursus is that a longer genealogical perspective reveals the complexity of the moral discourse associated with the selectionist–environmentalist (or nature first/nurture first) debate, pointing to often counterintuitive and paradoxical implications. A decline in selectionist thinking in evolution and views of heredity is not by itself the condition for more pleasant social attitudes.

Notes

1 Another more directly sociological implication of Weismann's work was strategically appropriated by Emile Durkheim: that heredity is a transcendent force, not the result of accumulated individual efforts (as in a Lamarckian view). If one replaces heredity (or race) with society, here a perfect homology to the Durkheimian view arises (Meloni, 2016b): a modernistic chasm between social fact and individual manifestations that make the former immortal (as in Weismann's germ-plasm) and the second ephemeral (as in Weismann's somatic cells). Durkheim explicitly recognized this filiation in several passages after 1891, claiming (in reference to Weismann) that "our sociological conceptions, without being borrowed from another order of research, are indeed *not without analogies to the most positive sciences*" (1897 [2002]: 320, my italics).

2 One way to look at this is to claim that Darwin was an externalist but of a special kind, given that, as Winther (also) acknowledges, "when dealing with the nature of variation [...] he prioritized the nature of the organism" (2000: 440). In the selectionist tradition, external changes remained the "triggering cause of variation", something that also applies to Weismann (Winther, 2000). This is not unlike what I mean by repositioning the role of the environment, although I think it is fair to place more emphasis on the revolutionary value of Darwin's gesture.

3 I do not underestimate the historical critique (see Winther, 2001) that has offered a more nuanced and complex view of Weismann, quite apart from the popular ideological interpretation. This debate goes well beyond the limits of this chapter. It can be noted in passing, however, that the article by Weismann on music that I am analysing belongs to the "phylogenetic externalism" phase (1885–1891), when

Weismann hypothesized "an (almost) completely variationally-sequestered germ-plasm" (2001: 527), that is, where changes in external conditions were deemed at their lowest.

4 It is paradoxical that it was Herbert Spencer himself who used in his *Principles of Sociology* the term "super-organic" and was for this reason cited by Kroeber as a precursor to the anthropological notion of culture (1952: 3). However, it only takes a careful reading of what Spencer means by the term to agree with authors like Bidney (1953) and later Ingold (1986) that Spencer's super-organic and Kroeber's superorganic (1917) are, in fact, antithetical notions. Spencer, who always uses the term as an adjective (for evolution, growth, products, etc.), means by super-organic literally a superorganism (Ingold, 1986, chapter 6), that is, an extension of the organism beyond the individual level, but not beyond "the organic laws of evolutionary development" (Bidney, 1953: 35). Not by chance, the examples offered by Spencer are typically drawn from animal societies (for instance, social insects, bees, wasps and birds). It is the "coordinated actions of many individuals" that mostly interests Spencer (1877: par. 2). This view has little to do with the superorganic as classically conceived in the Kroeberian tradition (1917), that is, as something that is above the organic world and its laws and is, accordingly, radically absent among animals.

5 Here cited from the English translation in Weismann (1892).

Epigenetics or how matter returned to the genome

4

Genetics and the modernization of the body

If we define the modernization of the body in the second half of the nine-teenth century along the lines described by Cohen (2009) – as a process of corporeal enclosure, a shift from the outer to the inner milieu, an abstraction from local contexts, and a displacement of the Hippocratic imagination – then the construction of the body in genetics was a variation on this broader biopolitical shift. But it was a very specific variation, one whose radicalness is often overlooked. At a certain level, genetics undoubtedly capitalized on the view of life promoted by scientific programmes at the time. This is apparent, for example, from some of its similarity with bacteriology. As sociologists have noticed, both germ theory and genetics "carried similar and familiar assumptions", such as a mono-causal view of aetiology, irrespective of con-text, that saw in a specific physical entity, germ or genetic mutation the direct cause of disease (Conrad, 1999: 231; Cockerham, 2015; Codell Carter, 2017). The resonance of wider social values in genetics and germ theory can also be seen at a broader biopolitical level. Both movements shared a certain view of public policy. In a powerful metaphor (Pernick, 1997; Tomes, 1999), they both moved away from the '*soil*' (the external landscape) as a source of health risk, and increasingly focused on the '*seed*' (the infectious agent or defective heredity residing within the body) as the determinant of disease. This move saw a convergence of the defensive metaphors of eradication of disease and cleansing the individual and social body (Pernick, 1997). Both fields fought common enemies: they shared an aversion to the older gener-ation of sanitationists and social reformers who, with their emphasis on the

environment as a direct source of disease, now looked increasingly incompe-
tent. Hibbert Winslow Hill, a bacteriologist turned public health specialist,
exemplified this shift when he wrote:

> The essential change is this. The old public health was concerned with
> the Environment, the new is concerned with the individual. The old
> sought the sources of infectious disease in the surroundings of man;
> the new finds them in man himself.
>
> (Hill, 1912: 10, cited in Nash, 2006)

The emerging discipline of genetics further strengthened this move toward
the individual and the call to take responsibility for what is inside the body.
However, genetics was not simply mirroring an existing shift in social values;
it also promoted a singular phenomenology of the body, whose unprecedented features remain under-appreciated.

A genetic body

The rise of genetics entailed a radical reorientation in our understanding
of the body – one that undermined the ideas of generation, reproduction
and genealogy that had been hegemonic for centuries among doctors and
naturalists. We saw in previous chapters how, for instance, the ancient view
of *pangenesis* (in which all cells from the body contribute to sexual reproduction) persisted and resurfaced in different guises from Hippocrates to
Charles Darwin (despite opposition by Aristotle, among others). In this
older framework, as discussed, bodies created bodies, one generation after
the other, in an ongoing process of somatic communication. With his idea
that "gemmules [physical bearers of heredity] are supposed to be thrown off
by every cell or unit, not only during the adult state, but during all the stages
of development." (1868, II: 449; Winther, 2000), Darwin did not escape this
framework. Incidentally, Darwin explicitly paid homage to Hippocrates as
the father of his pangenesis theory in his later correspondence (Geison,
1969; Liu, 2008).

  Half a century after Darwin, however, pangenesis appeared laughable.
Danish botanist Wilhelm Johannsen mocked the idea that the "personal
qualities" of a parent's body directly caused "the qualities of its offspring".
This was, he said, "the most naive and oldest conception of heredity"
(Johannsen, 1911). What had taken place in the period between Darwin's

pangenesis and Johannsen's dismissive comment was the making of an alternative view of heredity underpinned by genetics. This also implied the construction of a different body–world configuration in contrast to traditional views of the body as embedded in places and seasons. A good analogy available for sociologists to explain the radical novelty introduced by genetics comes from the sociology of religion. Genetics can be seen as a radical modernization of ideas of heredity and the body in the same measure in which, for instance, Protestantism is said to be a modernization of faith compared with Catholicism (Eisenstadt, 1968). Modernization, or rationalization in the Weberian sense, implies a disenchantment of pre-existing ideas, a disappearance and destruction of magic, and a restriction of the early spontaneity of social life (or for our purposes, the natural plasticity and vitality of organic life).

The connection between Protestantism (and Calvinism in particular) and genetics remains unfortunately overlooked (see for local cases, Taussig, 1997).[1] However, this connection is very visible at the beginning of Mendelian genetics: for instance, in William Bateson's planned (and never completed) popular writings on genetics, which he intended to title "Scientific Calvinism" (Radick, 2016: 165). The notion of scientific Calvinism extends beyond Bateson's anecdotal reference, however. It is also traceable in the overwhelming diffusion of a genetic-based eugenics in all the most important Protestant countries, or in the fact that this diffusion significantly mirrored a Protestant/Catholic divide in religiously mixed nations like Switzerland (Mottier, 2010). There were of course significant exceptions, even in South America (Eraso, 2007), not to mention the participation of a few key (right-wing) Catholic figures in mainstream eugenic discourse in countries like Germany, Italy or the USA (Hasian, 1996; Rosen, 2004; Weiss, 2010). It remains fair to say, however, that Catholic Europe and Latin America generally privileged nurturist forms of eugenics (Stepan, 1991).

My point here is not to establish simplistic or mechanistic sociological connections between religious values and science. Genomics (the heir to genetics) is today a global phenomenon, particularly attractive in emerging Asian powers like China, Singapore and South Korea. Its European and Protestant roots are lost or perhaps diluted in global science. Nonetheless, the way such a radical break with previous views of body and generation came to rapidly conquer Euro-America in the first decades of the twentieth century deserves an understanding that includes wider externalist factors, such as religious and cultural influences. In its historical roots, the relationship between genetics and Protestantism is one of elective affinities.

Genetics and the spirit of Protestantism

At the beginning of the genetic revolution in Northern Europe and America, Protestant values acted as a catalyst for the success of a view of life that represented a radical break with previous body–world configurations. It is possible to individuate at least four points of congruence between Protestantism and the spirit of genetics. Firstly, with its notions of random mutations and a genetic lottery fixed at birth (immutable and independent of human actions or works), genetics reinforced ideas of predestination and the irrationality of salvation (a notion particularly prominent in Calvinism). Rather than the constant management of an open and porous body in which every single work, action and decision mattered to attain health or salvation, genetics inspired a different attitude: the conscientious *scrutiny* and deciphering of an inner script in the search for the *certitudo salutis,* the "recognizability of the state of grace" (Weber, 1930/2001). The term indeed means the certainty of salvation, but also of *health,* as in the original Latin etymology. As we shall see, the careful searching of the inner book of life for a message of salvation or condemnation (what Weber calls the "systematic self-control which at every moments stands before the inexorable alternative, chosen or damned", 1930/2011: 69) came to shape the specific notions of risk and moral intervention that emerged with genetics. This generated a pattern of responsibility quite different from preceding models rooted in corporeal plasticity.

Secondly, genetics underpinned ideas of the uniqueness and privacy of the individual as the owner of a stable and intimate private property: an unchangeable genetic material, "always the same in a given individual in whatever place at whatever time" (Lillie, 1927: 367, cited in Buss, 2014: 11). This, too, is a notion very different from the constant mutability of the humoural body and the elusive nature of its complexion (as a task to attain rather than a starting point at birth). The gene becomes in this way the icon for notions of an essential identity, a sacred space endowed with an exceptional status that brings new life and a scientific validation to ideas of irreducible depth, thus consolidating the "move toward inwardness" of the modern subject (Nelkin and Lindee, 2010; Elliott, 2004; see Taylor, 1989).

Thirdly, both Protestantism and genetics promoted a form of asceticism of the flesh that deprives the "superficial" corporeal body (as opposed to its determining genetic structure) of any significant power vis-à-vis heredity (Gudding, 1996) or God's inscrutable will. In genetics, each individual's set of chromosomes becomes in a sense *the true body,* the body itself, in relation to which the fleshy body of ordinary language stands like an "excrescence" along an imperishable germinal line (Ansell-Pearson, 2003: 36). This is the same relationship of absolute verticality that Calvinism in particular posits between God and the world: a purely tangential relationship, or a chasm, with nothing in between. As Protestant theology said: finitum non est capax infinity. It is the opposite of the large number of mediations that Catholicism posits between God and the believer ("the gradual accumulation of individual good works" Weber, 1930/2011), or the entanglement that humoralism establishes between behaviours and humoral balance. This asceticism of the flesh is obvious in the eugenics movement, where the whole body evaporated as a meaningful target of intervention, to the advantage of the precious sub-units – chromosomes – that lay at its very core and became in a sense the true body. The new regime of perceptibility (Murphy, 2006) inaugurated by genetics moved the focus away from the whole phenotype to germ cells. Social reform was now to be achieved in a non-ephemeral way, through "germinal choice" (Muller, 1963/2008; Carlson, 1981, 2009), rather than by wasting time intervening on the whole body (somatic cells) through wider environmental policy.[2]

Finally, at a more complex level, the synthesis of genetics, hard heredity and selectionism that took shape at the turn of the twentieth century resonates with the Protestant breaking of the "umbilical cord" between individual and community. What the synthesis of selectionism and genetics promoted was a view of life that is not an incremental succession of collective experiences from ancestors to descendants (as in Lamarckism), but "is contained within the bounds of its particular existence". In this view, the individual,

> far from being built on the foundation of ground covered by previous generations [...] is constructed "from scratch" on a template formed from the recombination of elements from past projects, and is in turn expended in the reproductive transmission of these elements in the future.
>
> (Ingold, 1986: 7)

This eradication of layers of collective experiences in particular was a major shift in the common understanding of generation and reproduction that was predominant prior to and during the nineteenth century. For this reason, it was attacked and derided by a vast group of sociologists, educators and intellectuals for its supposedly catastrophic implications for social values and the growth of knowledge. Lester Frank Ward (1841–1913), an influential neo-Lamarckian and the first president of the American Sociological Association, caricatured the new view of Galton and Weismann. If there is no passage of

acquired characteristics from one generation to the next, and every generation starts from scratch, how did "barbaric Germans hordes of the Middle
Ages" transform into the "great modern race of German specialists"? Why
bother wasting time in education if

> all the labour bestowed upon the youth of the race to secure a perfect
> physical and intellectual development dies with the individual to whom
> it is imparted why this labour?
>
> (Ward, 1891: 66)[3]

Ward's bittered address is telling of the shock caused by the new biology.
The above four points – the disconnection between behaviours and heredity,
the existence of an inviolable biological kernel at the core of each individual,
the shift from the body to its determining sub-units, and the breaking of the
communitarian chains in favour of an insulated view of life – undermined
existing body–world configurations.

A body (or its disappearance), after Weismann and Johannsen

To understand the depth of this shift, it is worth looking once again to the
works of two of its major architects: German embryologist August Weismann
and, one generation later, Danish botanist Wilhelm Johannsen. Both Weismann
and Johannsen had major roles in this transition, and it is worth pondering
once again the depth of their contribution to a rethinking of the relationship
between bodies and hereditary structures. They helped to establish a view
based on hard heredity that now appears trivial but was deeply shocking at
the time. Weismann's doctrine of the continuity of the germ-plasm explained
how "the origin of hereditary individual characters takes place in a manner
quite different from any which has been as yet brought forward" (1891: 268).
Rather than assuming intergenerational somatic communication, it did so by
positing a rift between an "immortal germ-plasm" (whose cells were not used
in the construction of the body) and transient bodily cells, the "mortal part"
of the individual. "Reserved unchanged for the formation of the germ-cells
of the following generation", the immortal germ-plasm was the only link
running through generations (Weismann, 1891: 185). Instead of a model in
which one generation directly produces the next, the bodies of both parents
and children were now like pendants emanating from the same uninterrupted
chain of heredity, "successive offshoots thrown up by a long underground root

or sucker" (Ball, 1890: 66). In the law of germinal continuity, the somatic level came to be a passive container for an immortal germ-plasm, which now stood

> "to all the rest of the body in much the same relation as a *parasite* to its host, showing a life *independent* of the body" as Neo-Lamarckians protested.
>
> (Romanes, 1899: 26, my italics)

Compared with pangenesis, the significance of bodily changes was overshadowed by the power of heredity. But the gains of the move were that each generation was given "an identical starting point"; that is, it started from scratch at each point of replication in the unbroken chain of heredity (Weismann, 1891: 168, unless characters were incorporated into the germ-plasm). What was an accumulation of experiences became now a replication of templates (Ingold, 1986).

While Weismann wrote a few years before the rediscovery of Mendel, Wilhelm Johannsen's work perfectly complemented (and influenced) the empirical research coming from the first generations of classical geneticists (Allen, 1979, 1985). Trained in chemistry, Johannsen aimed at a "'radical' ahistoric" view of heredity, "analogous to the chemical view". Mendelian factors, just like chemical atoms, should "have no compromising ante-act: H_2O is always H_2O, and reacts always in the same manner, whatsoever may be the 'history' of its formation or the earlier states of its elements" (Johannsen, 1911: 139). To achieve this scientific narrowing of heredity to its tractable elements (Müller-Wille, 2007), Johannsen coined a distinction whose influence would be massive: that between the *genotype*, the "inner constitution" of a group of organisms, and the *phenotype*, its manifest morphological expression, which is accessible "by direct inspection" (ibid.). The choice of words is not casual. *Geneá* (which Johannsen used to coin the word *Gen*, "gene", in 1909) means in Greek the act of coming into being. Phenotype comes instead from *phainein*, "to appear", a word littered with meanings in Western metaphysics: in both Plato and Aristotle, phenomena are a mutable spectacle opposed to true forms (Preus, 2007: 295). Johannsen's genotype–phenotype disjunction was embraced enthusiastically by the first generation of geneticists, particularly Morgan's group at Columbia (where Johannsen was invited). It favoured the demarcation of a novel epistemic space that made heredity not a mystical whole but something amenable to analysis (Sapp, 1983; Müller-Wille, 2007). Heredity became equated with the transmission of stable units, while wider developmental and morphological questions were side-stepped (Allen, 1985). A phenotype, critics said, could be now "explained once one has mapped a corresponding Mendelian factor" (Goldschmidt, quoted in Harwood, 1993: 50).

Weismann's and Johannsen's strategies don't entirely overlap. They produced two kinds of dichotomies, operating on different levels: one at the mechanistic level (germ-plasm/somatic cells), the other at the statistical one (genotype–phenotype) (Churchill, 1974). However, in terms of their wider message, they both contributed to *a stratigraphic model* in which an underlying biological essence was deemed to control superficial traits. Genes became *a basis* (and later a blueprint) for phenotypic traits. In particular, the body that came into view after Weismann and Johannsen became *a two-tiered organism*: with an immortal substance at its centre and a somehow transient involucre at its phenotypic (i.e. observable) level. Parity between the body and hereditary material (which was common in pre-Weismannian thought) was replaced by a strict hierarchy of causes and (later) biological information. Other metaphors in the history of genetics for the relationship between genotype and phenotype have included structure and surface, and symbol and symbolized (see, for instance, Squier, 2017). This is why, as commentators have noticed, the story of the body in genetics is not so much the birth of a new view "but the drama of its disappearance". In the "delamination within the organism between its genotype and phenotype", the body eventually disappears "as a seat of agency, morality, and identity" (Gudding, 1996: 525). This is a unique phenomenology of the body, on the opposite end of the spectrum to the extreme embodiment of humoralism, where any fleshy details of the body mattered and carried agential power, but no less radical.

Delamination of the body in molecular genetics

In the transition from classical to molecular genetics, the notion of the body or the whole organism as "a physical manifestation of the action of a central directing agency, instantiated by the notion of the 'genetic program'" (Nicholson, 2014: 347) was further consolidated. The discovery that DNA, rather than chromosomal proteins, is the hereditary substance (Avery et al., 1944) and the deciphering of its double helix structure by Watson and Crick in 1953 represented an important trend toward turning the body into a fragile and ultimately superfluous entity, albeit in quite a complex manner. In the context of the emergence of post-World War Two communication sciences, the gene was increasingly understood as a message, and DNA sequences as a "code that carries genetic information", in Watson and Crick's words (1953, cited in Griffiths and Stotz, 2013: 39). Not only were bodies carriers of chromosomes, but chromosomes themselves became the carriers of a final layer of biological DNA information.

From a technical metaphor for biological specificity, the information paradigm became "a rich repository for the scientific imaginaries of the genetic code as an information system and a Book of Life" (Kay, 2000: 2). The history of how biology was reframed as information from the 1950s has been covered by a number of historians and goes beyond the scope of this chapter (Kay, 1993; Keller, 1996, 2000; see also Garcia Sancho, 2015; Stevens, 2016). The late Lily Kay in particular highlighted the complex conceptual and infrastructural transition from early biochemical views of protein to the emerging information framework through which the key problem of heterocatalysis was solved. The notion of genetic code, with its complex system of replication, transcription and translation mechanisms, suggested an elegant answer to the question of how only four chemical bases of DNA "could specify the assembly of 20 amino acids into the myriad proteins present even in as simple an organism as a bacterium" (Kay, 1993: 170). In the information model, the three-dimensional shape of the protein can be entirely reduced to the sequential order of the amino acids "provided it takes place as the newly formed chain comes off the template" (Crick, 1958: 144; cfr. Olby, 1974). The making of proteins – the basic material of which bodies are made – is hence entirely resolved bottom-up by the linear transmission order in DNA information: "the variability in the phenotypes made from proteins had to be passed on as variability embodied in DNA" (Barnes and Dupré, 2008: 27; cfr. Rheinberger and Müller-Wille, 2017).

In its enormous complexity, the rise of molecular biology and its information framework can be seen here from two possible angles. Firstly, the so-called Central Dogma of molecular biology encapsulated the theoretical framework of the molecular age by claiming that protein synthesis is the result of a one-way flow of information from DNA via RNA, and never in reverse (Crick, 1958, 1970). The DNA text message is transcribed into an RNA message and this into proteins and hence, bodies. No change in protein sequence could determine alterations in nucleic acid sequence (Olby, 1970). This straightforward chain of translation – "DNA makes RNA, RNA makes proteins, and proteins make us" (Keller, 1996: 18; see also Watson quoted in Strasser, 2006) – further legitimated the notion of an insuperable causal chasm between the molecular gene and its organismic readout, the body or phenotype.[4]

Under the Central Dogma, bodies are hierarchically reduced to underlying information, and the environment external to DNA plays a passive role. At most it is a backdrop for differential gene expression. As Keller noticed, what the Central Dogma denied was

> the possibility of a substantive influence on genes either from their external or from their intra- or intercellular environment. Instead of circular feedback, it promised a linear structure of causal influence.
>
> (1996: 93).

This framework is conceptually an isomorph of Weismann's doctrine of the sequestration of the germ-plasm, and actually a molecular duplication of it (Griesemer, 2002): somatic events cannot influence the germline. The body is made even more fragile, under the control of a transcendent and disembodied replicator, DNA, which is impervious to environmental inputs. This split was brought to its extreme consequences by the neo-Darwinian notion of the body (or any organism) as a mere vehicle through which DNA implacably reproduces itself: individual organisms are just survival machines for their genes (Williams, 1966; Dawkins, 1976). This is a different "cosmetic of life" that came over time to alter "the percepts of the body, in terms of how [it] is juridically, medicinally, and otherwise, generally perceived and understood" (Gudding, 1996: 526). The ascetic nature of this view in which the body is reduced to a "silhouette" (ibid.) can be seen as quite complementary to some of the "flesh eating" tropes of cybernetics (Kroker and Kroker, 1996; Muri, 2003). There is historical continuity but also a growth in ambition here, from early geneticists' attempt to map every phenotypic trait back to corresponding changes in Mendelian factors, to 1930s biochemists' expectations to write (in the future) human biography "in terms of structural chemistry" (Armstrong, 1931, cited in Gudding, 1996: 545), to the Human Genome Project (HGP) notion that the genome was the true autobiography of the species (Gilbert, 1992; Ridley and Matthews, 1999; cfr. Angrist, 2010).

The second noticeable sociological implication of molecular genetics was that the informatics model of the gene was also an "anthropomorphic" model. By attributing human-like powers to DNA as the *master* molecule that *directs* growth and development, it exploited images taken from our tacit knowledge of "social or hierarchical relations between people, when describing the relations between things" (Barnes and Dupré, 2008: 74). Imbuing biological terms with anthropomorphic or teleological meaning is obviously not new in the history of biology. Powerful metaphors taken from politics or gender differences have shaped our understanding of basic life processes, and, vice versa, the naturalizing effect of drawing on biological metaphors has validated political knowledge (Martin, 1991). However, an anthropomorphic view of genes as leaders ends up obscuring more

> naturalistic account[s] that are the norm in chemistry, where molecules are simply molecules and there is no justification for identifying some as possessed of fundamentally different powers from others or for anthropomorphizing the role of some and not others. The constituents of molecular systems demand understanding as fundamentally the same sorts of objects, and cells are such systems and never mere repositories of DNA.
>
> (Barnes and Dupré, 2008: 62)

This point deserves great attention, especially in the light of recent changes in the understanding of genome functioning, which I will describe in detail later. It is an argument about the tension between two different frameworks for understanding DNA: 1) as a *carrier of information*, which exploits human-like metaphors such as the blueprint or the computer program; and 2) as a *real physical object* in the world, subject to changes in space and time and embodied in real matter, a macromolecule "squeezed into the cell nucleus".

While both approaches may be meaningful in their own way, the pervasiveness of the information metaphors (as good or dangerous as any metaphor) has obscured the fact that the gross properties of macromolecules of DNA need to be constantly taken into consideration, even when DNA is described as merely "transferring information" (ibid.: 83). Without its material structure, DNA would not be stable enough to store information or be sufficiently flexible "to take many forms including packed down forms spooled around protein cores" for storage and transcription of information (ibid.: 80–81). In neglecting its gross material properties and their spatial organization, the informational genome not only contributed to a disappearance of the body (or the whole organism) but also *lost its own material body, or the genome's phenotype* (Jablonka and Lamb, 1995).[5]

How the postgenomic genome got its body back

However, biologists increasingly claim today that this model is a "considerable abstraction" and hence biologically incomplete. Treating DNA "as a text [...] written in three-letter words employing a four-letter alphabet" (Barnes and Dupré, 2008: 83) means neglecting the fact that only "a very small part" of DNA is protein-coding sequence DNA.[6] It is telling testimony to the dominance of this narrow information model that the vast majority of DNA that did not fit into the information metaphor was called "junk DNA". Noncoding regions were considered to be DNA stretches "littered" with a number of useless "untranslated pseudogenes" and other bits of "junk tandem repeat DNA" of no use to the body itself (Dawkins, 2010). This view of extragenic DNA has turned out to be increasingly problematic. There is more to DNA stretches than simple texts and letters, or in other words, there is more to genetics than "genes" (Keller, 2015). Junk DNA has emerged as a key factor in gene control and regulation (Mattick, 2004; Biémont and Vieira, 2006). The new view emerging in postgenomics is that a huge amount of "dark matter" (Carey, 2015) surrounds protein-coding regions. Its biomedical and evolutionary implications are starting to be appreciated, although still debated (Esteller, 2011; Germain et al., 2014).

Of course, it would be naïve to conceive of the relationship between information and matter only in oppositional terms (Hayles, 1999; Kay, 2000). And it would be even more facile to imagine that epigenetics and other postgenomic developments are inherently oppositional to the information paradigm. Many researchers today remain comfortable with control, switches, signals and other information metaphors when describing epigenetic functioning. Several social science commentaries on postgenomics have highlighted this growing enthusiasm for genes and genomes through an informational lens only (Richardson and Stevens, 2015). Moreover, there is definitely a cybernetic legacy in emerging postgenomic discourses (Landecker, 2016). At the same time, however, it is unclear whether this integration into the existing informational paradigm is really enough to make sense of the "cross-talk" between the dark matter of the genome and the whole epigenetic machinery of the cell (Carey, 2015).

I suggest in the following pages to look at epigenetics and postgenomics in terms of an ontological drift toward a new "holistic materialism" of the genome (Gilbert and Sarkar, 2000; Barnes and Dupré, 2008). Epigenetics' importance can be seen precisely as a window into the wider body within which DNA is tightly wrapped – a material body that was neglected at the peak of the information genome. However, it is not only the site of study that is different (or wider) in epigenetics. It is the content that exceeds the previous framework. As the focus of research moves from understanding the functions of elements within naked DNA sequences to a broader consideration of how DNA sequences are expressed within the complex scaffolding of chromatin, the notion of genomic matter as reactive becomes theoretically and experimentally salient. While the *linear sequence* of DNA does not change during a lifetime, in different cells or in response to environmental signals, there are cell-type- and cell-state-specific differences in the packaging of DNA in different tissues and across the lifespan, which may change in response to environmental inputs. Investigating how this wider variation in the regulatory machinery influences gene expression is what makes epigenetic research so significant in the life-sciences today (Jablonka and Lamb, 2014).

Beyond the gene: The roots of epigenetics in the twentieth century

It would be wrong to think of "genetics" and "epigenetics" as oppositional disciplines reducing twentieth-century genetics to a caricatural and monolithic affair. Genetics has been mostly a tentative science too often reconstructed in terms of a progression of scientific successes. However, it is more helpful to see it as a continuous process of branching, which, at each juncture, left several possible lines open and several others forgotten, likely to be rediscovered in more propitious times. For sociologists, this offers a much more intricate landscape in which the interaction between sociology and genetics can unfold as an open matter, beyond stereotypes or dichotomies. Such fine-grained historical analysis also helps us to understand the present postgenomic landscape as the temporal concretion of a number of alternative lines that were forgotten during the twentieth century and may be resurfacing today.

Moving beyond an essentialist view of genetics can help to correct our perception of a staunch opposition between genetics and notions of environmental regulation. Even within the context of Central Dogma, or among genetic hardliners, there were a number of complex theoretical and experimental models that can be seen as supporting current approaches. Jacob and Monod's work on gene regulation by transcription factors in 1960s is a case in point (1961). Much earlier, Muller's pioneering work in the 1930s on position-effect variegation was also particularly significant, because it showed how gene functioning is affected by location on the chromosome. This pointed to the importance of wider chromosome regions to explain genetic functioning, one of the hot topics of contemporary epigenetics (Felsenfeld, 2014). Excited by Muller's discovery of position effects, controversial geneticist Richard Goldschmidt (1937; 1940) speculated on the physical bases and spatial patterns of heredity (Deichmann, 2015; Dietrich, 2003; Allen, 1974). Interestingly, some of his holistic views about the physical structure of chromosomes, and his interest in chromatin rearrangement, may be particularly important in contemporary epigenetics. Another group of dissenters, less speculative than Goldschmidt, included geneticists who were dissatisfied with the mainstream transmission model of genetics. Among them, there was American geneticist Tracy Sonneborn (1905–1981), who studied forms of non-Mendelian inheritance in the ciliate protist *Paramecium* anticipating some of today's work on epigenetics (Felsenfeld, 2014). Sonneborn titled an article in 1949 "Beyond the Gene" to suggest a revision of gene theory. He aimed to emphasize the importance of extra-nuclear factors such as the cytoplasm in regulating genes and controlling hereditary traits. The times, however, were not favourable for such work (Sapp, 1987). Sonneborn and similarly oriented researchers were among the 1950s casualties of the Cold War, and particularly the Lysenko affair (when non-Mendelian heredity was propagandized as a state doctrine by Stalin). From that Cold War scenario, several Western geneticists drew the lesson that the search for alternative theoretical frameworks in heredity was at best "unpalatable", if not utterly "suspect" (de Jong-Lambert and Krementsov, 2011; de Jong-Lambert, 2012; Peterson, 2017: 173).

The Waddingtonian root of epigenetics

Epigenetics can be seen within this wider scenario, as one of the many dissenting lines that challenged the narrow view of transmission genetics and strove to propose a more integrated view of biological processes. Epigenetics was originally designed as a conceptual space to bridge heredity and development and avoid the "black boxing" of the organism. Rather than looking at development as the simplistic unfolding of a genetic program, it focused on the complex and non-linear interactions between genes, bodies and environments. This view included top-down regulation mechanisms in which "genes are not only actors, but they are acted upon" (Gilbert and Sarkar, 2000: 8). The notion of epigenetics was firstly coined by embryologist and polymath C. H. Waddington (1905–1975) in the 1940s as a neologism from *epigenesis*[7] to define, in a broader *non-molecular sense*, the "whole complex of developmental processes" that connects genotype and phenotype (reprinted in Waddington, 2012). For Waddington, epigenetics was "the branch of biology which studies the causal interactions between genes and their products which bring the phenotype into being" (Waddington, 1968). In this original Waddingtonian sense, epigenetics was thought of as an interdisciplinary program to occupy the "no man's land" (Gilbert, 1991) between genotype and phenotype. Because of this innovative and interdisciplinary nature, epigenetics was perceived with scepticism by institutions that heavily funded mainstream molecular genetics, such as the Rockefeller Foundation, and funding was never forthcoming (Gilbert, 1991). Mainstream molecular geneticists saw little to gain from Waddington's work: Francis Crick labelled his landscape a "useful idea in the Thirties", which has now "long outlived its usefulness" (cited in Peterson, 2017: 209). The complexity described by epigenetic models, according to Crick, was a pointless metaphysical detour that covered a ground already successfully covered by DNA mutations and translation errors. Crick believed a new model was pointless (ibid.).

The wider cultural context for Waddington's work is now being rediscovered in light of the growing importance of the term in contemporary life sciences (Peterson, 2017; see also Baedke, 2013; Squier, 2017; Buklijas, 2018). The focus is particularly on the so-called "Theoretical Biology Club", a network of British scientists, philosophers and polymaths (including Joseph Needham, J. D. Bernal and Waddington himself) of the 1930s. The Club aimed to open a third way to cut across the mechanism–vitalism debate: a "new way of seeing" that could escape the facile answers of reductionism and mechanism without embracing vitalism (Peterson, 2017: 7). Its wider philosophical aim was to "understand living systems in their more complex and richer forms" (Waddington cited in Squier, 2017) and to create an innovative synthesis of genetics, evolution and developmental biology (Gilbert, 1991).

There were several philosophical influences behind this search for a third way. Whitehead's processual or interactionist ontology is an explicit example, but so is Needham's fascination with Chinese notions of order, emergence and organicism (Peterson, 2017). An iconic representation of epigenetics is the "epigenetic landscape" proposed by Waddington since the 1940s (Baedke, 2013 and Squier, 2017). Waddington uses a number of images (a river flowing from a mountain, an abstract landscape with a ball rolling downhill, and an empty landscape with pegs representing genes at the bottom) to describe "the processes by which a population of homogeneous cells differentiates into the diverse cell types of the organism" (Gilbert, 1991: 139). Cell differentiation is "canalized" through a number of genetically controlled pathways (Waddington, 1957). Canalization describes how the cell is

> 'buffered' such that it would be difficult to get out of the channel once into it. Once the pathway had been entered, cell fate was rigidly fixed if the pathway were sufficiently canalized.
>
> (Gilbert, 1991: 140–141).

As I will discuss next, this is definitely a view of plasticity, but one that emphasizes the stabilization of forms rather than its potential reversal as in the current view of pluripotent stem cells (Takahashi and Yamanaka, 2006). Unlike the Waddingtonian account of cell differentiation, in the latter, cells can dedifferentiate (reprogram to pluripotency) and travel back the inclined surface from the basin up the hill. For this reason, Waddington's topography deserves attention, because it offers a different take on the concept of plasticity, one that emphasizes *restriction of potentialities* at each branching, rather than self-renewal and reversibility as in today's understanding (MacArthur et al., 2009). Notably, in stem cells, this reprogramming can occur by breaking the epigenetic barrier that otherwise protects cell identity (Watanabe et al., 2013). Waddington's epigenetic landscape describes instead a form of "embryonic determination" or developmentally led "entropy" (in Needham's words, cited in Peterson, 2017: 148; Banerji et al., 2013), in which the gravity of cell fate cannot be lowered (Takahashi, 2012). It is important to consider the specific pattern of biological temporality that emerges from Waddington's landscape vis-à-vis the contemporary usage of plasticity as a constant ability to change. Waddington's landscape, as I will show later regarding the biological embedding of historical trauma, shows instead a view of assimilation of environmental inputs into long-term biological trajectories that emphasizes the lasting impact of contingent events, rather than self-renewal and reversibility as in today's understanding. In the Waddingtonian view, "alternative fates remain present somewhere on the landscape", but they remain inaccessible (Ferrell, 2012: R 462). This does not deny that a hidden genetic potential can be reactivated by environmental exposures (Baedke, 2013), as Waddington believed, but the capacity to change was limited at each bifurcation, and temporality across the landscape was not seen as reversible.

The molecular root of epigenetics

Waddington's embryological work is not the only root of contemporary epigenetics. Alongside this tradition, a parallel line of research took place not outside but within molecular biology, quite distant from the developmental debates that fascinated Waddington. This latter strand, which understands epigenetics more narrowly as an amendment of molecular mechanisms (Griffiths and Stotz, 2013; Peterson, 2017), is probably having a stronger influence on the present than the Waddingtonian line. It originates with Nanney's (1958) paper on "Epigenetic control systems" and refers more specifically to epigenetics as that which occurs on the top of genes, that is, a second non-genetic system, at the cellular level, that regulates gene expression beyond what happens in the "genetic library" (Nanney, 1958: 713; Haig, 2004; Griffiths and Stotz, 2013). Nanney aimed to complement "the current concept of a genetic material (DNA), replicating by a template mechanism" with a more sophisticated "homeostatic system operating, by [...] self-regulating metabolic patterns" (1958: 716). He labelled this homeostatic regulation "epigenetic". Nanney's approach established the debate in terms that still prevail today, that is, looking at epigenetics as a second inheritance system beyond nuclear DNA (Maynard Smith, 1990; Peterson, 2017). In this second understanding, epigenetics concerns "the transmission of phenotype through mitosis or the germline by mechanisms that did not involve changes in the DNA sequence" (Felsenfeld, 2014; cfr. Jablonka and Lamb, 1989). In line with this view, a number of articles were published in the 1970s by Robin Holliday and colleagues (see for instance Holliday and Pugh, 1975) investigating the molecular mechanisms for gene control. Holliday focused in particular on the heritability of the "methylated and non-methylated state of DNA" – a key area today – and its relationship to the pattern of gene activities (Holliday, 2006). Holliday did not speak, however, of "epigenetic", but of "enzymic modifications of specific bases" (Holliday and Pugh, 1975; see Buklijas, 2018).

It is this second molecular meaning, put forward in works from Nanney to Holliday, that is becoming pervasive in the contemporary literature. This is why it is probably more accurate to call contemporary epigenetics "molecular epigenetics" to differentiate it from the broader Waddingtonian sense and the developmentalist-embryological tradition in which the term was first conceived. However, the two meanings are not, in principle, irreconcilable, as they both emphasize the context (molecular or organismic) in which genetic functioning takes place (Hallgrímsson and Hall, 2011).

Contemporary epigenetics: A molecular link between the environment and the genome

With a delay of almost fifty years since its coining, epigenetics has become one of the fastest-growing fields in the life sciences (Haig, 2011) and a "buzzword" for twenty-first-century biology (Jablonka and Raz, 2009). While the term was used only occasionally until the 1990s, since 2000 an exponential growth of publications in the area has occurred (more than 20,000 papers by 2016, depending on search criteria), along with the worldwide launch of epigenetic consortia, journals, professional bodies and research centres (Meloni and Testa, 2014; Skinner, 2015). A standard, often repeated definition of epigenetics is "the study of heritable, reversible forms of gene regulation that are not dependent on the DNA sequence" (Heerboth et al., 2014: 9). However, this definition has various limitations. Firstly, it takes for granted the distinction between epigenetic and genetic changes. Secondly, it continues to use DNA sequences as a reference point to define what epigenetics does. A richer and more accurate view is that epigenetics is the complex machinery that spatially rearranges and regulates chromatin – the moving and malleable matter of chromosomes, as I will claim later.

In its applied dimension, epigenetics is often described as the "molecular link" (Ling and Groop, 2009) between the environment and the genome, or the mechanistic pathways by which environmental factors and experience become biologically embedded, that is, "get under the skin" (Hertzman and Boyce, 2010). In both evolutionary and developmental debates, epigenetics has filled a void in a number of unexplained areas of classical or molecular genetics: how cells remember their identity, and why cells with the same DNA code manifest different phenotypes (Nanney, 1958); phenotypic differences between monozygotic twins; and alternative phenotypes in genetically identical animals such as sterile worker and fertile queen honeybees (*Apis mellifera*) (He et al., 2017).

The most well-known mechanisms in epigenetics include DNA methylation, modification of histone proteins, X chromosome inactivation, parental imprinting and nucleosome positioning, often working interactively with each other (Richards, 2006). These mechanisms organize the packaging and regulation of gene expression (Esteller, 2008; Portela and Esteller, 2010). DNA methylation, the most recognized and studied mechanism of epigenetic mutations, describes the addition of a methyl group to a DNA base, resulting in de-activation of gene transcription. Methylation, which is essential in early development, is often described as a "physical barrier to transcription factors" (Gluckman et al., 2011). Although DNA methylation has been studied since the late 1960s (Holliday, 2006; Buklijas, 2018),[8] the notion that this mechanism is driven by wider environmental changes (food, stress, toxicants) is more recent (Champagne, 2018). A large number of epidemiological studies using epigenetic data focus on DNA methylation, given its more stable nature compared with other epigenetic changes (Li et al., 2014) and the availability of high-throughput technologies that allow its measurement (Bibikova et al., 2006).

Epigenetics occupies a wide terrain, and it is therefore important to sketch a few distinctions among different research communities. A large area of the discipline is concerned with cancer epigenetics, an area that is booming in the biomedical fields (Esteller, 2008; Rodríguez-Paredes and Esteller, 2011; Kiberstis, 2017). Cancer epigenetics moves on from the assumption of an insufficiency of traditional genetic explanations for tumorigenesis and suggests instead looking at the wider disruptions of the epigenetic machinery. It focuses on global alterations in the epigenetic landscape, and particularly low DNA methylation levels, as a possible "hallmark of cancer" (Sharma et al., 2010). Cancer epigenetics has strong implications for diagnosis; for instance, the early detection of abnormal epigenetic profiles as effective cancer biomarkers. Moreover, given the expected reversibility of epigenetic mutations such as DNA methylation and histone modifications, the field carries strong expectations for the design of effective drugs (Rodríguez-Paredes and Esteller, 2011). A second emerging area with important biomedical implications is the study of epigenetic changes in a number of well-defined syndromes in mental health, an area that can be loosely described as "neuroepigenetics". Emerging epigenetic studies address Rett syndrome, a postnatal disorder affecting the motor and cognitive system and associated with abnormal methylation levels in the brain (Pohodich and Zoghbi, 2015). Besides connections to other rare diseases linked to intellectual disability, such as Rubinstein–Taybi syndrome and Coffin–Lowry syndrome (Urdinguio et al., 2009; Park et al., 2014), abnormal epigenetic changes have been linked with a wider range of neurodegenerative disorders: Alzheimer's, Parkinson's and Huntington's diseases and, more recently, autism spectrum disorders (see, respectively, Sanchez-Mut and Gräff, 2015; Feng et al., 2015; Buckley et al., 2010; Loke et al., 2015).

A third sub-field of epigenetic research does not cover specific pathologies but rather, wider effects on epigenetic functioning of environmental contaminants and toxicants, with long-term health implications for chronic disease (Marsit, 2015). This is one of the key areas that highlight the long-term significance of environmental exposures, and often frame their results at the transgenerational level. A transgenerational phenomenon is usually defined as the "ability of an acquired physiologic phenotype or disease to be transmitted to subsequent generations through the germline, such that the subsequent generation is not directly exposed to the environmental factor or toxicant" (Skinner, 2007).[9] Key studies in animals and humans concern the impact on epigenomic dysregulation of mercury (Carvan et al., 2017), arsenic (Reichard and Puga, 2010), pesticides, DDT in particular (Skinner et al., 2013), and dioxin (Manikkam et al., 2012).

A related area – social and behavioural epigenetics – addresses the biological embedding of various effects related not to chemical contaminants but to, widely defined, social relationships, social experience and behaviours. These include the epigenetic changes induced by psychosocial stress, trauma, differences and changes in socioeconomic status, mothering, parent–offspring relationships, social adversity, social instability, poverty, bullying and racism (McGowan et al., 2011; Borghol et al., 2012; McGuinness et al., 2012; Ouellet-Morin et al., 2013; Saavedra-Rodríguez and Feig 2013; Stringhini et al., 2015; Stringhini and Vineis, 2018). The borders of this area are obviously vast and in constant expansion. Frances Champagne (Columbia University), a key researcher in the field, defines social epigenetics as the discipline that

> explores the relationship between the quality of the social environment, epigenetic variation, and behavioral variation and is part of the broader study of how environments come to induce phenotypic variation at the level of the organism (i.e. growth, metabolism, health, behavior) via epigenetic mechanisms.
>
> (Champagne, 2018: 228).

Interestingly, a number of sociologists, anthropologists and social theorists are proposing to establish cross-disciplinary relationships with this literature to focus in a more complex way on social phenomena (Niewöhner, 2011; Niewöhner and Lock, 2018; Roberts and Sanz, 2018). Social epigenetics is being mobilized to look at the possibility of avoiding "nature versus nurture debates and deadlocks and better understanding the entanglement of institutions, social forms and practices, relationships and bodies" (Youdell, 2018: 299). Notions of the biosocial or biocultural are being used to suggest the need for a richer analysis of social phenomena that may take into account the entanglement between affective and relational forces and epigenetic, hormonal, neurobiological and metabolomic processes and pathways (Frost, 2016; Youdell, 2018).

Nutritional epigenetics – how food and diet "can reverse or change epigenetic phenomena such as DNA methylation and histone modifications" – is also central in a further related wing of epigenetic studies (Choi and Friso, 2010; Landecker, 2011). Animal and epidemiological models have highlighted the epigenetic impact of folate, alcohol and protein restriction on embryonic development; of folate and calorie restriction on ageing; of a methyl-deficient diet on cancer; and finally, of a high-fat or methyl-deficient diet on obesity (see a review in Choi and Friso, 2010). A key focus of research is on the link between early nutrition and the onset of adult non-communicable disease as mediated by epigenetic effects, particularly the so-called metabolic syndrome (type 2 diabetes, obesity, cardiovascular disease and insulin resistance) (Canani et al., 2011; Godfrey et al., 2011). The most significant (but not the only) epidemiological study in the area is on the long-term effects of the Nazi blockade of West Holland in the winter of 1944–1945 (Dutch Hunger Winter). During the Nazi occupation the local population suffered a decrease in caloric intake to below 800 calories per day. Epigenetic studies are today looking at the chronic effects of this nutritional shock on babies born to mothers who were exposed to the effects of famine in their early stages of their pregnancy (first trimester). The lingering effects of the Dutch famine – increased metabolic and cardiovascular disease associated with epigenetic changes – have been observed beyond the offspring of those exposed, involving increased neonatal adiposity and poor health in adult life in the second generation after the event (Painter et al., 2008).

In parallel to these studies, an emerging body of literature is examining the impact of biological ageing as measured by epigenetic changes. A recent model of "epigenetic clock" uses DNA methylation as a biomarker of ageing to investigate individual differences between chronological and biological ageing. The epigenetic clock, designed at University of California, Los Angeles by Steve Horvath, aims to offer "accurate age estimates for any tissue across the entire life course". It uses blood, saliva and brain tissues, not just blood as in earlier models. The ambition of Horvath's work is huge in social and health terms, as it seeks to apply these data to address sex and racial differences in all-cause mortality (beyond chronological age), particularly risk factors such as incidence of cardio-metabolic disease (Horvath, 2013; Horvath et al., 2016). This field is also imbued with expectations that, given the reversibility of epigenetic changes, it "might thus be useful for identifying or validating anti-ageing interventions" (Horvath, 2013; Horvath and Raj, 2018).[10]

Finally, in connection with breakthroughs in the availability of aDNA (ancient DNA) technologies, the very last wave of epigenetic interest has been in ancient epigenomics. Ancient epigenomics or paleoepigenetics can be defined as the study of epigenetic patterns in subfossil materials with the goal of complementing genetic information on ancient populations or extinct organisms (Gokhman et al., 2016). This emerging discipline is said to "provide novel molecular phenotypes of the age at death, diet restriction, and other stress conditions, including sociocultural changes" (Hanghøj and Orlando, 2018). Smith and colleagues' study of methylation in ancient DNA of five Native American groups has been the first study to move from isolated samples to whole populations (living up to 4,500 years ago). According to the authors, the study provides evidence that methylation measurements are recoverable in aDNA samples, making it possible to study the lifestyle and health of ancient populations (Smith et al., 2015).

Epigenetics on the rise: summary of the overview

It is evident from the above overview that epigenetic studies are pushing their boundaries to cover an increasingly wide range and large number of areas. This multiplication of foci obviously comes with a price in terms of epistemological consistency. Some of these disciplines are very much in their infancy, and it is difficult to predict their substantial contribution to knowledge in the near and mid-term future. Other areas, such as epigenome-wide association studies, have been criticized for suffering "from multiple problems in design and execution that severely limit their interpretability", particularly a confusion between correlation and causation (Birney et al., 2016). These critiques are important and need to be addressed by emerging epigenetic studies if they want to stand up to scientific scrutiny in the near future. The discipline is far from being unitary, and overall reflects a state of effervescence typical of pre-paradigmatic phases of scientific development. Pre-paradigmatic phases, if one follows a Kuhnian view, are characterized by being open ended, "non-directed and flexible", with a lack of overall consensus and little guidance or standards offered to the community of practitioners (Marcum, 2005: 61; Kuhn, 2012).

However, with these caveats in mind, it is undeniable that the expanding universe of epigenetic studies is adding something significant to our understanding of the biology–society relationship, not only covering new fields compared with genetics, but also proposing a different way of thinking. These differences can be summarized as:

1) the extreme *openness of genetic functioning* via epigenetic mechanisms to the nested levels *of social structures*. In an epigenetic view, social structures are no longer irrelevant to genetic functioning, but a causal source of gene regulation and expression that makes every biological process socially patterned (Landecker and Panofsky, 2013);

2) compared with the standard view of genes, the epigenome is a much more *fine-grained molecular archive* that synchronizes human biology with a very particular micro-history made up of local and recent events, such as our own diet (famine, obesity), habits (smoking, alcohol) and lifestyle or those of our most direct ancestors (Meloni, 2017);

3) *the potential reversibility* of epigenetic marks such as methylation patterns makes them particularly prone to becoming amenable to pharmacological and social intervention, in contrast to practically unchangeable genetic variations (Szyf, 2001).

These are important novelties with far-reaching implications not only for biomedicine (*Nature* Editorial, 2012) but also for long-standing debates between biology and society. Their significance is consolidated not only by the increasing numbers of researchers from several disciplines, centres and countries who are converging on epigenetic studies, but also by their epistemic location within a wider shift called postgenomics.

Genomes in a postgenomic age

Postgenomic ideas are often read in a purely chronological sense: they describe the period following (post) the completion of the HGP in the early 2000s, when the entirety of the three billion bases of human DNA was first sequenced. But is postgenomics just a way to demarcate one period from the other? In an impressive number of scientific publications, the term "post-genomics" or "postgenomics" is used without a clear specification, often just with a rhetorical function to emphasize novelty, a new "era", and to relaunch promissory discourses about the power of yet-to-be biological findings (see, for instance, Plomin and McGuffin, 2003; Plomin et al. 2003). Is postgenomics an empty term? Even in important social science critiques, the construct appears too vaguely defined, as if its meaning were obvious and therefore not in need of a clear specification (Sunder Rajan, 2006). We are told that the postgenomic condition is one of increasing scepticism in relation to the promises of the HGP to explain life processes and offer biomedical applications though knowledge of gene sequencing (Reardon, 2017). But in making the rise and failure of the determinist dream of the genomic project so central, this approach mostly perpetuates the same terms of debate. What comes after genomics seems to be just the same, only more complex, uncertain and blurred. While critical attention is always to be recommended, it is also possible to interpret postgenomics in a different way, as the rise of an alternative model of thinking through the relationship between genomes and their environment. Postgenomics implies a shift from "looking for causes in DNA sequence [towards] how sequences are used (...) by the varied mechanisms which control gene expression". (Griffiths and Stotz, 2013: 70). In the wider context of the emergence of a number of research programs in epigenetics, microbiomics and chromatin modelling, postgenomics appears as the catalyst for a distinct thought-style, one that emphasizes the dependence of genomic functioning on a wider regulatory architecture that extends to the whole cell and the external environment (ibid.). It carries a different focus in evolutionary theory, with stronger attention to the power of the organism, the body or the phenotype not just as a result but as a source of genetic variation (West-Eberhard, 2003; Nicholson, 2014). It explores heredity not only as the narrow transmission of nucleotide sequences but as something related to the whole cellular architecture, including DNA, chromatin structure and so on. It addresses biological information not as "a linear flow of information from the DNA sequence to its product", but as something "created by and distributed throughout the whole developmental system" (Stotz, 2006: 914; Griffiths and Stotz, 2013).

Commentaries insisting that the differences between genomics and postgenomics are largely quantitative or about technological breakthroughs – bigger infrastructural investment, faster and larger scale of sequencing methods and whole genome technologies (Richardson and Stevens, 2015) or the emergence of big data research (Ankeny and Leonelli, 2015) – are in this sense too narrow. There is a transformative meaning of postgenomics that needs to be brought into the limelight.

A new ontology for the genome?

In order to appreciate this transformative meaning of postgenomics, it is important to rethink what genes are and do (Moss, 2003; Griffiths and Stotz, 2006; Keller, 2014). This rethinking has been mostly generated by the perception that "simple assumptions about genetic causality" have been overturned in postgenomic times (Landecker, 2016). In particular, the discovery that there "were too few genes to explain whole-organism traits in simple genetic determinist terms" (Wynne, 2005: 87; Guttinger and Dupré, 2016) has been a major blow to a reductionist understanding of the genome. If the genome is the book of life, and it turns out that humans have fewer genes than simpler organisms like fruit flies, what sort of book is this? And if "major changes in the phenotype" are "apparently compatible with relatively minor changes in the genotype" (Rheinberger and Müller-Wille, 2017: 85) was the basis of the whole HGP project misguided?

While studies of wider genomic association continue, and geneticists remain hopeful that the so-called "missing heritability" (the lack of correlation between genetic variants and common traits or complex diseases) may be solved by more complex studies of gene–gene interactions (Kaiser, 2012), postgenomics research has in fact moved rapidly elsewhere. Awareness of the limitations of the HGP framework has pushed investigation beyond mere DNA sequences to cover newly emerging areas: the *-omics*, a suffix that indicates completeness or wholeness in Greek (Lederberg and McCray, 2001; Yadav, 2007).

Omics research covers all the entities occupying the space between DNA and its wider regulatory context (Baker, 2014; Guttinger and Dupré, 2016; Stallins et al., 2016). This includes research in *proteomics* (large-scale studies of the totality of proteins, their structure and interaction), *transcriptomics* (transcribed RNAs), *metabolomics* (metabolic profile of the cell), *interactomics* (interaction among proteins), *epigenomics* (whole set of epigenetic modifications of the DNA sequence) and more recently, *exposomics*, the epidemiological study, at the molecular level, of "life-course environmental exposures (including life-style factors), from the prenatal period onwards" (Wild, 2005: 1848; 2012).

It is significant that, as a consequence of the shortcomings of the HGP, the environment is being rediscovered in postgenomic research as a factor as "crucial as the DNA sequence" (LaFreniere and MacDonald, 2013). It is also remarkable how these approaches in system biology may favour a return to the probabilistic nature of epigenetic landscape models (in the sense of Waddington) to address the cascades of large-scale phenomena driven by whole-genome technologies (Squier, 2017).

Yet, this "explosion of complexity" (Landecker, 2016) in postgenomic research does not amount to an elusion of the digital logic of the informational age. It is unclear whether this emerging plethora of -omics will just mimic, on a larger scale, this digital logic, or lead to more complex ways of thinking about the entanglement of biological and social matter. Cases like exposomics or epigenomics are quite representative of this dilemma. For, however strong the rhetoric of the environment in epigenetics is, many epigenetic models have only a very narrow way to bring the environment back into the limelight. What they ultimately do is capture the "vastness of what seemed irreducibly analogic (the social, the environmental, the biographical, the idiosyncratically human)" and make it into code-compatible molecular representations (Meloni and Testa, 2014: 435). In this way, the proclaimed environmental turn ends up being just a way to reinforce "that same digitally friendly language of maps, codes or blueprints that enabled the gene-centric paradigm to rise in the first place" (ibid.). This is a problem that a number of anthropologists and sociologists have raised over the last few years. To the extent that whatever is beyond DNA is operationalized in the same *lingua franca* of information theory, bringing the environment and experience back into biological matter is not enough. Molecularizing the environment and social experience is seen as problematic. It is criticized as the emergence of miniaturized and impoverished versions of biography and milieu that make them decontextualized, standardized and portable "between labs and into the wider public discourse" (Niewöhner, 2011: 291; Landecker, 2011; Lock, 2012, 2015; Landecker and Panofsky, 2013). Here, it seems we are caught in a conundrum. Sociologists and anthropologists have been criticizing biology for not being open enough to the social. Now that this biological matter is seen as necessarily social by biologists themselves (or at least a good number of them), social scientists feel that the social is turned into a digital travesty of itself, miniaturized in impoverished experimental settings and ultimately molecularized. In Landecker's words:

> "The social" is being entified and concretized by its experimental capture within a signaling framework [...] The ontology of the signal flattens difference between different kinds of worldly things, such that the more tangible (the chemical odorant, the nutrient, cocaine) provides form for the less tangible (parenting behavior, stress), and all can equally reshape the template.
>
> (2016: 95)

My understanding is that we will not be able to sort out this dilemma unless we redefine the meaning of molecularization. An alternative ontology of the genome would serve exactly this goal – to have a different take on how the social may be instantiated into the biological (Frost, 2016); not in a linear text, though, but in a three-dimensional and malleable body.

After naked DNA: Chromatin as impressionable matter for postgenomic times

Is a code, a library or some other digital metaphor the only possible framework to describe molecularization in emerging postgenomic research? Probably not. After all, as I have highlighted above, even when it conveys information, DNA is not merely a unit of information but a molecule, and as such, it displays gross material properties that need to be considered to understand its functioning (Barnes and Dupré, 2008).

So what really is molecularization? Just a way to make the analogic vastness of the environment into a digital linear text? Or an experimental way to record material changes in the external milieu as changes to another (molecular) body? One possible way to look at molecularization differently, beyond the digital logic of information language, may come from chromatin research. Although this so far remains a minority area of research, in recent years there has been growing interest in the complex interactions of

DNA with proteins within eukaryotic chromosomes (Dekker et al., 2013; Lappé and Landecker, 2015). Chromatin – the macromolecule into which DNA fibers are folded – is a complex of nucleic acid and proteins in the cell nucleus of all eukaryotic cells: DNA + RNAs + proteins and other associated molecules (Jablonka and Lamb, 2014; Deichmann, 2015). It can be defined as "the physiological template of all eukaryotic genetic information" (Jenuwein and Allis, 2001: 1074). While recognizing that research on higher-order chromatin structure is still in the making, some recent works open a fascinating perspective on the *molecular impressionability* of biological matter in the post-genomic age. As Barnes and Dupré write,

> The dominant view of genomes is that they are objects made of DNA. But the actual material objects we encounter in the cell nucleus are made of chromatin, not DNA. In chromatin, DNA exists in association with various other substances including small RNA molecules and proteins, and in particularly close association with the histone proteins that provide something like a spool around which the DNA strands are coiled, and which thus facilitate the packing of DNA into the restricted space available in the cell nucleus.
>
> (2008: 105)

Chromatin research is not a postgenomic novelty. Far from it. It dates from the last decades of the nineteenth century, when, as a consequence of technological developments in the use of microscopes in cytology, chromatin (from the Greek *khroma*, colour) was discovered by German biologist Walther Flemming, who described it as a "substance in the cell nucleus which is readily stained" (Olins and Olins, 2003; Deichmann, 2015). Flemming didn't put much hope into this new term: he believed that the concept was just transitory, destined to disappear "once its chemical nature is known" (Olins and Olins, 2003). However, the word did not disappear. Instead, it produced a significant line of research, sometimes at the margin of mainstream genetics, but also entangled with its key development. For instance, the notion that higher-order packaging structures of chromosomes have important regulatory functions dates back to Muller's research on position-effect variegation studies in fruit flies, yeast and mice in the 1930s. This was an important contribution to the idea that genes were not really independent; rather, their activities depended on wider topographical arrangements and movement in the proximity of active or inactive regions of chromatin. This was taken by some, including controversial geneticist Richard Goldschmidt, to mean that "all so-called gene mutations will turn out to be chromatin rearrangements"

(Deichmann, 2015). After World War Two, chromatin research focused on the role of histones in regulating nuclear functions and the effect of acetylation and methylation on histone actions (Morange, 2013; Deichmann, 2015). This research had limited impact at the time. However, since the mid-1970s, novel electron-microscopic visualization technologies and the discovery of the nucleosome, "the fundamental subunit of chromatin" where base pairs of DNA are wrapped around histone proteins, have provided a significant boost to chromatin research (Olin and Olin, 2003). The nature of this interest has further changed in the last decade. With the growing focus on epigenetic mechanisms, methylation, acetylation and histone modifications, the area previously covered by chromatin research has found a true rebirth, making epigenetics a placeholder for chromatin research (Deichmann, 2015).

If a number of historians and philosophers of science have described the postgenomic genome as a "responsive germline" (Jablonka, 2013) or a "vast reactive system", always changing in response to environmental changes (Keller, 2014), it is probably the emerging research on chromatin that offers the most effective material counterpart to such a theoretical framework.

This is because DNA is topologically and functionally constrained by chromatin architecture. It is the form assumed by the body of chromatin (tightly packed or transcriptionally open) that generates biological meaning, that is, changes in genome function and expression (Tark-Dame et al., 2011). The material density of chromatin acts as "a barrier to [DNA] machinery that either transcribes, replicates, or repairs DNA" (ibid.). Where chromatin is less dense and more accessible (euchromatin), genes are activated; in more dense regions (heterochromatin, usually in the nuclear membrane), genes are inactive (Cortini et al., 2016). Interestingly, however, though there are discrete domains of condensed and de-condensed chromatin, chromatin condensation is not an on/off phenomenon, but something that allows a range of different states to be implemented: an overall remodelling of the molecule as a consequence of subtle cellular and environmental influences. Chromatin configuration resembles an analog rather than a digital device: more like an old fax copying system (Meyer, personal communication) or a column of mercury. It is this analogical sensitivity of chromatin states that allows chromatin to act not only

> as a protective sheath to guard against these [regulatory] processes occurring in an untimely manner, nor simply a packaging tool, but [...] also a dynamically adjusted entity that reflects the regulatory cues necessary to program appropriate cellular pathways.
>
> (Margueron and Reinberg, 2010: 285)

This is where epigenetic changes (DNA methylation, histone modifications) can be seen not just as adding a further layer of complexity in DNA sequences, or the fifth letter of the genetic code. These metaphors are inadequate as they leave flat DNA sequences at the centre of the description, making epigenetics an addition to an unvarying structure. A much better image is that of epigenetics as the modulation and reconfiguration of the chromatin structure.[11] Epigenetic changes are therefore not so much "tags" or "bookmarks" added to linear DNA sequences as changes to the whole three-dimensional chromatin structure. Epigenetic regulation is "the active perpetuation of local chromatin states" (Richards, 2006: 395), a "chromatin-marking system" that is active both at the level of cellular physiology and in the wider heredity system (Jablonka and Lamb, 2014: 130).

The plastic scaffolding of DNA

Chromatin is not an "inert structure" but "an instructive DNA scaffold that can respond to external cues to regulate the many uses of DNA" (Bannister and Kouzarides, 2011: 381). Alteration and topological reorganization of the body of chromatin change the transcriptional capacity of DNA (Gómez-Díaz and Corces, 2014; Jablonka and Lamb, 2014) while at the same time depending on and registering the physical impact of environmental and developmental cues. DNA strings are wrapped up and regulated by flexible fibers, chromatin, whose study "allows quantitative measurement of the physical registration of environmental experience originating outside the body as shifts in conformation deep inside cells" (Lappé and Landecker, 2015: 153).[12]

This full *rediscovery of the material and morphological density of the genome* and attention to the material scaffolding of DNA are crucial to the discontinuity between genomics and postgenomics. In genomics, while the same genotype could express several phenotypes through a range of environments, each of those environments remained an external background for an otherwise static, and ontologically prior, genome. In postgenomics, by contrast, the "excitable" nature of chromatin (among other changes) brings into question the ontological priority, and boundedness, of the genome. Social matter, and the wider biophysical environment, impinge on biological matter and impress its regulatory architecture. This implies a shift from the linear and disembodied logic of DNA information to a different model of biological memory. DNA is re-embodied in chromatin as "the dynamic physical body of the genome" in Lappé and Landecker's (2015) felicitous expression. As they continue:

> What we wish to highlight here is the contrast drawn between DNA that is mutated versus chromatin that is reshaped after environmental input. The mutation bears no functional relationship to the environmental exposure, whereas the change in shape is called forth in some functionally specific way: it is a logic of imprint, not one of error. These are two different models of memory. Where the linear sequence information can remember only itself [...] the imprint carries experience forward via three-dimensional impressions linked to gene transcriptional responses to experience.
>
> (Lappé and Landecker 2015: 157)

At the very core of postgenomics, chromatin as a material-semiotic object is enabling a return to ancient metaphors of plasticity such as imprinting, marking, (re)modelling and erasing, rather than just a flat digital language of copying, editing and translating. Chromatin is an impressionable matter. It is because of this shift to a reactive genome (to which chromatin offers its body) that plasticity and the entanglement of biosocial matter are not just ephemeral or fashionable labels but a structural effect of a transformation in concepts and experimental practices in some emerging areas of postgenomic research.

In light of the postgenomic complication of the boundaries between the genome and its wider regulatory network, the dualism between a stable DNA sequence and a plastic epigenome has been challenged (Griffiths and Stotz, 2013; Lappé and Landecker, 2015). Not just the epigenome but *the genome itself has become a dynamic and impressionable organ*. The change is visible in new renderings of genomic functioning. In classical molecular genetics, gene functioning was described visually by a long series of rows representing nucleotide sequences, a string of information that dictated the inner program of each organism (Keller, 2000). The three-dimensional structure of the protein encoded by gene action was necessary for regulatory functions, but the key determinant remained linear DNA sequences. If, in principle, genomic sequencing could be captured by a flat series of letters, postgenomics necessitates a multidimensional representation showing "the changing landscape of loops" that regulates gene expression (Gómez-Días and Corces, 2013; Pennisi, 2017). This necessarily includes a temporal representation, for instance of the "fluctuation of chromatin density": this is what is currently happening, for instance, with studies in three-dimensional spatio-temporal organization and architecture of genome folding driven by interest in epigenetic landscape and chromatin research (Gómez-Díaz and Corces, 2014; Cortini et al., 2016).

Conclusion: Baroque genomes, Baroque bodies? For a postgenomic aesthetics

We started this chapter with an analogy between Protestantism and the spirit of genetics based on the idea of a transcendence of the germline to the body. This morphology was rendered by images of a chasm between genotype and phenotype, and later views of the genome as stripped of any unnecessary material scaffolding beside DNA bases. This austere formalism made difficult an entanglement of social and biological matter. It could allow either an inter-action between two clearly separated entities (gene and environments) or a flattening of the analogic richness of the environment into digital readouts (informational molecularization).

In the light of my previous considerations on epigenetics and chro-matin, in postgenomics a different aesthetics emerges. At every scale, postgenomic writings exhibit a richer morphology, which privileges looping, entanglement and curvilinear forms over rectilinear tracks (as in quintessentially Calvinist Central Dogma). *Folding*, and derivative forms like *enfoldment* and *scaffolding* (but also adjectives such as *entrenched* and *entangled*), are terms often employed to describe the complex architecture of gene functioning: chromatin is the folding matter of DNA. Genomes are highly looped into this regulatory architecture. It is this folding and looping that explains genomic properties (Tark-Dame et al., 2011). Genomes are no longer naked matter.

This complex morphology also applies at a different scale, as we shall see in the final chapter: that of organismic relations to their spatial and temporal contexts, as well as to other organisms (Griesemer, 2014; Chiu and Gilbert, 2015). The postgenomic organism, we are told in eco-evo-devo accounts, is always situated "in a complex supraindividual web of relationships [...] that determine its ontogenetic and even transgenerational destiny" (Baedke, 2017). Developmental processes are not "self-unfolding" but rather, "involve the interaction of a developer with scaffolding", both a noun and a verb that includes the assemblage of the organism and all the "external" material entities (including other organisms) that enable its growth; for instance, hosting some of its functions (Caporael et al., 2013; Griesemer, 2018: 38). Emerging interest in maternal–foetal microchimerism is also situated at this level (Martin, 2007, 2010 and 2011; Yoshizawa, 2016).

This is a different morphology. Rather than a modernistic separation of inner and outer, visual representations of postgenomic models of life are better rendered with a Baroque morphology in which the outside is never an absolute limit but instead "a moving matter", a fold understood recursively as an ongoing succession of "folds always folded within other folds" (Deleuze, 1993: 6). Reiteration of movement, and the notion of entanglement, also connects Baroque aesthetics and postgenomics. In Baroque morphologies, entanglement refers to a

> point of view that involves two mobile positions. It neither entails something that is simply relativism nor allows universalism or absolutism to assert itself ... Entanglement proceeds in the knowledge that *we are always within the histories we make*, enfolded in their spatio-temporal frame and engaged in their production.
>
> (Meskimmon, 2002: 698; italics added)

This profound situatedness is essential to understand postgenomic writings and is the source of new notions of plasticity inherent in them. This is the topic that I will discuss in the last chapter through an analysis of the complex sociological implications of emerging views in epigenetics and related postgenomic programmes.

Notes

1 It is, moreover, obscured by the simplistic idea that, at least formally, genetics "began" in 1859 thanks to the discoveries of Mendel, an Augustinian friar. I say "began" in inverted commas because the complex relationship between Mendel and the reconstruction (rather than rediscovery) of genetics in 1900 are well known to historians (Bowler, 1989). Jokingly, one could add, for that matter, that Protestantism began in the same way, that is, with the work of an Augustinian monk (i.e. Luther).

2 H. J. Muller made this point clear in his famous letter to Stalin in 1935, in which he attempted to win the attention of the dictator to the cause of genetics and eugenics. Investing in bodily changes, he claimed, is just ephemeral success for a real and durable social transformation:

> The usual environmental influences that affect the body or mind of the individual, such as *education, better nourishment* etc., although they are extremely important in their effects on the individual himself [mostly a lip service paid to the dictator, NM], *do not result in improvements or in any definite kinds of changes*, of the genes within and so the generations following such

"treatment" start in with the same capacities as their forefathers. Genes can, to be sure, be changed by certain drastic means such as x-rays, but these changes are brought about in a random fashion, the product more usually being harmful. And as random changes also occur to some extent without any interferences on our part, there is little use in our attempting to produce them so long as enough products of natural change are already in existence.

(Glad, 2003, my emphasis; see Meloni, 2016a)

For stable socialist progress, the only viable alternative was through a "conscious socialized control" of germinal choices. This would imply only a "minimum disturbance of personal lives":

Many a mother of tomorrow, freed of the fetters of religious superstitions, will be proud to mingle her germ plasm with that of a Lenin or a Darwin, and to contribute to society a child partaking of his biological attributes,

Muller argued (ibid.).

3   This was, however, not the only reaction to the reconfiguration of the ties between generations after the emergence of hard heredity and genetics. Some saw the possibility of a more liberating side in this shift. In brief, if it is not the "individual" but the "generic type" that is reproduced in the new heredity, then the "individual is tied less strongly to his past" (Durkheim, 1893/1997: 256). This was Durkheim's insightful reading of Weismann's work. Heredity's importance "is less great, and science, as we shall see, reveals nothing that contradicts this view", Durkheim claimed, paralleling Weismann's perspective with overt references to his work (ibid.; cfr. Meloni, 2016b). Other authors, too, saw an attractive emancipatory side to the idea that the lifetime experiences of each generation are cancelled in the next, a modernist message about autonomy of the individual and the breaking of the chains of the past. Alfred Russel Wallace argued that it was a "relief" that lifetime experiences are not transmitted from one generation to the other, since this implied that "all this evil and degradation [of our present social arrangement] will leave no permanent effects whenever a more rational and more elevating system of social organization is brought about" (see Meloni, 2016).

4   As Olby has highlighted, the Dogma is actually not one but *two theses*, both of which, however, imply the disappearance of the organism. The first is the reduction of the stereochemical properties of the protein to its basic DNA sequence. The second is, more speculatively, that "once information has passed into protein it cannot get out again"; that is, the transfer from "protein to nuclei acid is impossible" (1974: 432). It is important to highlight how, historically, the dogma has always been open to challenges and contestation (Keller, 1992; Strasser, 2006). However these contestations have greatly expanded over the years, becoming "major chasms" since the turn of the century (Keller, 2000: 55 and ff; Koonin, 2012). Technically speaking, what we know today about the Dogma is that, while there is no reverse translation from protein sequence to DNA (in this sense the dogma does hold),

transfer of information from phenotype to genotype, and also from phenotype to phenotype (e.g. protein to protein), has been individuated through a number of molecular processes. These include direct DNA translation to protein, transfer of information from protein sequences to the genome, genetic assimilation of prion-dependent phenotypic heredity, reverse transcription, non-protein-coding RNA (ncRNA) transcription, and transplicing – all of which have disproved molecular biology's "linear logic" (respectively, in Pigliucci and Muller, 2010; Koonin, 2012; Brosius, 2003; Mattick, 2003).

5 Regarding some of the wider historical and disciplinary reasons for the disinterest in the "material and morphological bases of heredity" well before the molecular gene, see Deichmann (2015).

6 This is all the more so in higher mammals (as opposed to worms and yeast, for example). In humans, it is just above 1% of the genome (Germain et al., 2014; Carey, 2015), a surprising fact that has pushed a few authors to establish connections between non-coding DNA and organism complexity (Keller, 2015).

7 There are two terminological confusions around epigenetics. The first originates from the fact that the term "epigenetics" is new, but not the adjective "epigenetic". This latter term has been used since early modernity as the adjectival form of *epigenesis* (not epigenetics), a construct coined by William Harvey in the seventeenth century to describe, in an Aristotelian fashion, "the conception of development as a gradual process of increasing complexity from initially homogeneous material in the egg" (Deichmann, 2016). Epigenesis as *de novo* formation was famously devised in opposition to preformationism (the notion of the full presence of a miniaturized organism in the initial egg or semen) (Pinto-Correia, 1997).

Another widespread but wrong idea is that epigenetics means on the top of genes, epi + genetics, which is merely folk etymology (as the term was coined by Waddington from epigenesis, not genetics).

8 This is true as well for histone modifications, which were studied from the 1960s, particularly through the work of Vincent Allfrey at Rockefeller University (Allfrey et al., 1964). In the past two decades, the notion of a "histone code" has emerged to capture the idea "that multiple histone modifications act in combination to regulate chromatin structure and gene transcription" (Forger, 2016; see Strahl and Allis, 2000).

9 There is, however, some confusion over, or at least a flexible use of, terms like "intergenerational", "multigenerational" and "transgenerational" in the epigenetic literature. While transgenerational effects relate to "the germline transmission of epigenetic information between generations in the absence of direct environmental exposures" (Skinner et al. 2013), intergenerational effects would instead be

those that do not pass through the germline (egg or sperm). In the case of intergenerational effects, progeny can be exposed as gametes through nongenetic factors present in egg or sperm, through nutritional or hormonal influences during gestation, or through caretaking after birth.

(ibid.)

A parallel definition focusing on the number of generations is offered by Heard and Martiennsen (2014): transgenerational effects in mammals can be defined as referring to phenotypic changes observed in the *third* female (F3) or *second* male (F2) generation of unexposed individuals. While transgenerational effects are well established in plants as persistent changes propagated through the germline (Rapp and Wendel, 2005), their provenance in higher mammals is hotly debated. It is here that caution about the generalizability of these findings is perhaps greatest (Heard and Martiennsen, 2014; Kazachenka et al., 2018), but it is also the area in which some of the most exciting research is being carried out (for instance: Dias and Ressler, 2014).

10 Identification of drugs that inhibit epigenetic changes (DNA methylation inhibiting drugs, histone modification drugs) is still in the making. Some have been approved for cancer treatment by the Food and Drug Administration (FDA). See for theoretical overview Tollefsbol (2017) ch. 37, and for a review of classes of epigenetic drugs, Heerboth et al. (2014).

11 Although what comes to the body of chromatin from the environment is a cybernetic signal, as Landecker notes (2016), this does not rule out the possibility that its transduction into the three-dimensional body of chromatin with its continuous rather than discrete changes may fundamentally alter the digital nature of informational genomics.

12 For emerging research on the significance of chromatin dysregulation and neurodevelopmental disorders, see Gabriele et al. (2018).

A sociology of the body after the genome **5**

For most of the twentieth century, genes have been considered the controlling force and basis of life processes, and the transfer of DNA through generations the definitive explanation for biological heredity. Such views helped shape the politics of human heredity: at the peak of the eugenic era (1910–1940), controlling heredity meant intervening in the distribution of "good" and "bad" genes. In the post-World War Two landscape, a medicalized and more horizontal form of eugenics took place in advanced liberal democracies (Rose, 2007), focusing on genetic counselling and screening, selective abortion, and prophylactic surgery for cancer mutation carriers. Irrespective of changes in the wider political landscape and the ensuing ontological transformations (from Mendelian to molecular), for the last twelve decades the gene has remained a pivotal actor and a powerful "cultural icon" (Nelkin and Lindee, 1995; Keller, 2000). This period of ascendency culminated in the launch of the Human Genome Project in the 1990s, with all its promise and hype.

However, since the turn of the twenty-first century, the centrality of genes has turned out to be much more problematic. The existing concepts of gene and gene control have become blurred, distributed in the wider regulatory architecture that controls gene expression beyond DNA sequences (Griffiths and Stotz, 2013; Moore, 2015). The notion of a "reactive genome" (Griffiths and Stotz, 2013; Keller, 2014), and the increasing focus on the developmental space between genotype and phenotype, is well exemplified in a number of "postgenomic" programmes, particularly social and environmental epigenetics, microbiomics and Developmental Origins of Health and Disease (DOHaD). Even though epigenetic and other postgenomic research programmes have some roots in twentieth-century languages such as cybernetics (Landecker, 2016), what is new in the present configuration is the scale of analysis and level of integration between these programmes.[1] What were just a few heretic lines of enquiry during the century of the gene are now gathered together, often under alternative evolutionary frameworks that offer to these emerging disciplines a credible level of theoretical integration (Jablonka and Lamb, 2014). Added to this is a new generation of scientists, less engulfed in major twentieth-century ideological obstacles such as the Cold War opposition of hard and soft heredity and the subsequent practical impossibility of exploring non-Mendelian heredity in the West. In light of these factors, emerging postgenomic themes represent a quasi-paradigm shift, or at least a "profound disturbance" (Lock, 2015) of the genetic view of life.

The sociological implications of this shift for novel body–world configurations and biology–society debates is significant. This new discourse holds potentially paradigmatic implications for the understanding of human health, development and policy. Social epigenetics and DOHaD are contributing, often in triangulation with findings from microbiomics, to a shift from notions of biological fixedness to ideas of corporeal plasticity and the "impressionability" of biological material – notions that seemed forgotten during most of the twentieth century. At the level of societal circulation in particular, these notions are rewriting the human body as permeable to its genomic core. In so doing, however, they emphasize that the body is vulnerable to new risks and open to new forms of intervention. With the rise of these programmes, the ways in which we understand *the management of bodies* and *reproduction of social norms* are at stake. For instance, if epigeneticists claim that when I am eating, "I am eating for two" (Rando and Simmons, 2015), meaning that a future parent's diet has an impact on the offspring's wellbeing, how does this affect notions of responsibility and risk, normality and pathology (Rose, 2007; Rothstein et al., 2009)? If not only brains but also genomes can be damaged through junk food or optimized through exercise, can we not prevent damage and create ideal bodies through policing people's lifestyles (Wastell and White, 2017)? And whose lifestyles should be policed? Not all bodies are considered equally permeable, and plasticity appears highly gendered. How will the focus on *in utero* epigenetic programming intensify attention to and obligations on pregnant women (Richardson et al., 2014)? Will this reinforce, and possibly exacerbate, pre-existing discourses of maternal blame and other gendered prejudices (Lupton, 2012; Richardson, 2015)? At the population level, questions about social management are also being asked, with deep political implications. If, in epigenetics, social factors are massively engaged in producing aspects of our own individual biology, are there clear-cut boundaries between collective and individual responsibility? What of groups exposed to famine or violence? Are they damaged *and therefore in need of reparation*? Should they benefit from principles of justice "in the remediation of exposures causing epigenetic changes" (Rothstein et al., 2017: 8)? Or are they damaged and *therefore the bearers of an "acquired inferiority"*, unresponsive to any intervention? And what does it mean that race is a "social construction", as generally held by sociologists, if social constructions are now described as biologically embedded in genomic changes?

In search of a postgenomic lexicon

These and similar questions exemplify how emerging postgenomic topics are undermining established intellectual coordinates in the biology–society debate. Many of these coordinates became truth during the twentieth century but may no longer hold in the near future: for instance, the existence of a clearly drawn distinction between biological and social causes (increasingly problematized in biosocial or biocultural frameworks); the notion that biological heredity is merely the transmission of DNA and stops at birth (challenged by a number of postnatal factors affecting heredity); or a strict association of values between biological plasticity and progressive policy in debates about development, education and IQ (given how plasticity is used to make arguments about the incorporation and biosocial transmission of social damage).

A new landscape may be emerging in the biology–society debate, and often in disconcerting ways. On the one hand, the new biology of plasticity seems to fulfil some of the desiderata of sociologists concerning a biology that is less gene-centric, more plastic and sensitive to contextual factors. On the other hand, it is because of this potential erasure of modernistic boundaries between biology and society (or culture) that this shift may entail more pernicious consequences in terms of class-, gender- and race-based forms of moralization science and the stigmatization of vulnerable groups than genomics had in the recent past. The ethical, epistemological and biopolitical quandaries of the emerging postgenomic landscape can be summed up as follows.

The *ethical* problem of the postgenomic condition can be articulated in the question: how does one live with a porous body, a body in which social things are reconstituted at the molecular level as having a durable impression on cellular processes (Landecker, 2011)? This is, at least in principle, different from the framing of the problem posited by the modernistic body, for which at stake there was how to prevent pathogens from entering into the immured sovereign body (Roberts, 2017). This is instead similar to the ancient humoralist perception of a fragile body and displaced biosocial identity, one that always assumes that the inside is already an effect of the outside, and hence aims at a subtle governance of these blurred boundaries through intense day-to-day vigilance and (unavoidable) inner/outer transactions.

The *epistemological* perspective is also different in postgenomic writings. Given that the epigenome is described as a "biosocial archive" of past experiences (Relton et al., 2015), is it still possible to neatly parse gene and environment, self and world? Or do bodies and their surroundings need to be rewritten in terms of an indissoluble unity, a more than metabolic exchange that blurs differences? Which language is required to describe this biocultural dimension in which "distinct temporal movements of the biochemical, the metabolomics, the social and the relational, [...] come to be instantiated in the body" (Frost, 2016)? The metaphor in several postgenomic writings is often one of *absorption* in places (geographical, social, experiential) that "call[s] into question how and to what extent the self and the world mix" (Solomon, 2016: 8). Another possible metaphor is that of a "violent entanglement" of bodies and places, in which "outsides and insides are constantly co-constituted across different lifeworlds" (Roberts, 2017: 594). Importantly, to come back to the previous ethical point, these claims are often made not to celebrate the liberatory side of entanglement, but to show how problematic it is for people to survive "so entangled in shit" and "garbage" (the example is toxic exposure in a poor barrio in Mexico City) through a complex everyday management of "what gets inside and what does not" (ibid.: 594).

Biopolitical questions also look different. Governing the postgenomic body displays a specific temporality and spatial articulation. At the individual level, firstly, if our biology is checkered with spots of unique sensitivity to environmental influences (*in utero*, early life, pre-puberty, adolescence, pregnancy, old age and even "pre-pregnancy"), when would it be most productive for the state or the economy to intervene to make the most of these opportunities (Wastell and White, 2017)? And when have things gone too far to protect human capital? These questions easily translate to the collective level: how can we manage populations so permeable to the power of places and experiences? And which populations? Who is permeable to what? If epigenetic studies bring together individuals with a shared social experience now turned into a biological effect (for instance, common exposure to adversity), aren't researchers making up new populations based on epigenetic differences, in a meso-space somewhere in between race and individuals?

Finally, there is the specific profile of the *bioeconomy* of postgenomics. It aims not just to commodify DNA sequences but, more ambitiously, to enclose the whole spatial influence that regulates DNA functioning, the -omics (the epigenome, the proteome, the microbiome and, ultimately, the whole body). In postgenomics the process of enclosure is outward-looking. It "extends away from DNA rather than isolating itself in genes and their DNA sequence" (Stallins et al., 2016: 3). To make "the spaces and histories of life productive", postgenomic bioeconomies proceed upstream rather than tracing, as in previous models, "the downstream economic implications of biotechnology and the big data geographies of DNA" (ibid.). This novel emphasis on what externally regulates DNA can be seen as a new spatial fix for global capitalism, a cartographic endeavour to circumvent crises by mapping "vastly larger biological territory exterior to DNA sequence for countries, institutions, and universities to claim and to integrate into their economies" (ibid.: 5).

A thorough analysis of these emerging lines in postgenomics and their increasingly visible polarities (individual / collective; malleable / fixed; male / female) is obviously beyond the scope of a single chapter or book or an individual researcher's work. It is, rather, a collective endeavour across the natural / social science divide, a creation of networks, institutes and centres that must be promoted to address, in a multi-scaled and multi-sited way, these emerging frameworks of ideas, standards and formal procedures (to use Epstein's formulation, 2007) which constitute the emerging biopolitics in the West and the Global South.

In this chapter I have a more limited task: to sketch some possible research pathways to study the contemporary coproduction of social life and postgenomic plasticity. My analysis will follow three axes: a) shifts in notions of responsibility from genetics to epigenetics (particularly around reproduction) and implications for a new moralized attention to parental lifestyles; b) emerging notions of biolegitimacy connected to demand for social justice and reparation, especially in postcolonial areas; and c) the ethics of postgenomic plasticity as an alternative to modernistic and postmodernist appropriation of biological plasticity, one that promotes notions of biological finitude and radical situatedness.

The convergence of these three axes in outlining an emerging postgenomic landscape illustrates the important need to update the sociology of genetics (and more largely of health) to include these novel areas of contention. It is also telling of the analytical task of going beyond the approaches to genomics (and today epigenetics) of bioethical or "ethical, legal, and social implications" (ELSI) to incorporate the wider coordinates of power, and power struggles, into the bigger picture. This requires the demarcation of a very specific epistemic niche – a medium level of analysis (Fuller, 2018) – between the fetishism of the micro in many science and technology studies and the macro simplifications of biopolitical theorists who lack engagement with the history and sociology of science.

Axis I: Responsibility and reproduction from genetics to epigenetics

A genetic responsibility

Responsibility in a genetic era has been a complex phenomenon. To navigate the complex demands, risks and anxieties generated by genetic knowledge, particularly around reproductive technologies and pregnancy outcomes, true forms of genetic citizenship, reflexivity, and ethical pioneership have emerged (Kerr and Cunningham-Burley, 2000; Rapp, 2000; Löwy, 2017). Since the incorporation of human genetics into wider medical programmes (Lindee, 2005), sociologists and historians have illuminated the intricate relationships between the geneticization of pathologies (the framing of health problems in genetic terms) and widespread forms of risk, prudence and obligation. These have invested not just the single individual but also "family histories and potential family futures" (Novas and Rose, 2000: 487; Löwy, 2014). Technologies of disciplinary and post-disciplinary power have been formed, either to shape the behaviour of the genetically at-risk person (Rose, 2007) or to enable them to live with a genetic condition (Paul and Brosco, 2013). Rayna Rapp's important work on the social and cultural impact of amniocentesis at the Prenatal Diagnosis Laboratory (PDL) of New York City is an exemplar of this wave of studies on the complex moral stance generated by the assessment of preconception genetic risk (2000). Rapp's analysis persuasively shows how emerging genetic knowledge both "constrained and empowered" pregnant women, turning them into "moral pioneers" to traverse the norms of a new technological order. Part of this navigation into unknown techno-scientific order included facing maternal blaming. Genetic rationality definitely did generate forms of moralization and blaming, mostly through the idea of pregnant women as carriers of genetic defects. This shaped ideas of responsibility and inter-connectedness to past, present and future generations (Petersen, 1998; Hallowell, 1999; Petersen and Bunton, 2002; Hallowell et al., 2006; Mozersky, 2012).

But what sort of responsibility? Within what limits and of what magnitude? Responsibility, firstly, *to know* the content of one's hereditary script (using the body as a window into this script), and secondly, to act on this knowledge. This call to action has taken on different forms, but has been mostly limited to the medical (rather than behavioural) sphere: using available reproductive technologies to prevent the transmission of the disease-causing genes, terminating pregnancy in response to the risk of congenital malformations, undergoing prophylactic mastectomy to reduce the risk of cancer in at-risk families. In a few cases, such as phenylketonuria (PKU) (Paul and Brosco, 2013), this also includes limiting the usage of certain substances, or introducing some others, to prevent the unfolding of disease.

I do not mean to underestimate the global impact of clinical genetics and the reproductive technologies associated with this knowledge. Prenatal genetic diagnosis and amniocentesis have involved tens of millions of women around the world (Löwy, 2017). On a wider non-medical scale, insurance companies have made significant use of genetic knowledge, and so have employers. Ancestry testing has contributed to the rewriting of family and historical genealogies and impacted significantly on notions of race (Nelson, 2016). The twentieth century has produced forms of personhood that take into consideration genetic knowledge "and use it to make decisions concerning reproduction" and life plans (Novas and Rose, 2000: 504, 507). Numerous forms of resistance to genetic rationality have emerged too, and various identities and biosocialities have been built as a consequence of the increasing appeal of genetic knowledge.

And yet, what is often missing from these analyses is a wider perspective on how the rise of the genetic view also produced intense forms of de-responsibilization and secularization of heredity and morbidity. It did so by disconnecting pathology from the moralizing effect of direct human action; by severing the maternal body from the physiology of the foetus and protecting it from past speculations about the maternal power to mark the unborn; by supplying the modernistic body with a reservoir of genetic talent unaffected by adverse social circumstances, and hence ready "to blossom into actuality as soon as improved conditions provide an opportunity" (Huxley, 1949: 187).

Genetics displaced views of impressionable biology through a complex historical process of de-personalization of heredity. Even in the growing medical control of the female body in the twentieth century, this phenomenon deserves a more objective understanding, especially now that molecular versions of the "maternally marked" foetus may be unfolding again, along with related ideas of a direct behavioural influence on genomic functioning.

We need to remember a few facts. With the due exceptions and caveats, the overall message that doctors and geneticists conveyed to the wider public in the twentieth century was, invariably, that 1) genetic diseases are rare and 2) when they occur, they are for the large part the result of random errors in DNA replication (Keller, 1991), which are independent of direct selective pressures. Obviously, rare does not mean unimportant (Löwy, 2017: 102), and the denial of environmental effects did lead, in some cases, to catastrophic consequences for foetal development (as the thalidomide crisis showed in the late 1950s and early 1960s). On the other hand, a genetic style of reasoning made clear that there is not much one can read into, or unveil from, a mistake in our DNA copy-system. While there are genetic diseases directly amenable to environmental intervention through diet, such as PKU, in the long run, genetic rationality helped minimize the impact of parental misbehaviours (especially those of mothers) on developmental abnormalities and pathology in general. In genetics, it is the "randomness of nature", not a woman's action that threatens the foetus. Intervention "is not behavioral but biomedical" (Mansfield, 2017: 359); that is, opting for a number of available medical choices (abortion, etc.), rather than embarking on a long list of everyday prescriptions. As it refers to a nature that is largely unaffected by events occurring in a lifetime or in a few generations, genetics decentres and marginalizes earlier ideas of maternal (and more broadly familial) responsibility. This is what I mean by *secularization* and *de-personalization* of heredity: a general freeing of the hands of parental responsibility, and a strong containment (which does not mean elimination) of their capacity to inflict harm.

The moral landscape of the genetically at-risk pregnant woman was constructed under the guiding perception that chromosomes are unaffected by controllable human behaviours. As Rapp wrote in her monograph, while

> holding a woman accountable for a pregnancy's outcome is undoubtedly helpful in linking some health problems like smoking or alcohol consumption to low birth weight or some congenital problems [...] it doesn't aid in understanding chromosomes, whose patterns and pathologies are *unaffected by maternal behavior*.
>
> (Rapp, 2000: 42, my italics)[2]

As we saw in chapter 4, the knowledge derived from twentieth-century genetics implied mostly *a chasm* (mechanistic but also moral) between what a body could do and its genomic effects, with little connection between the two. This chasm which insulated genes from life's circumstances turned to have unexpected sociological consequences. Firstly – and this can be taken as a standard rule of the history of eugenics – it was mostly doctors, social reformers and puericulturists who didn't see this chasm and rather, believed in direct environmental effects on heredity, who suggested the most extensive forms of surveillance of maternal behaviours, often with the best possible intentions. On the contrary, "bad" hard-hereditarian eugenicists kept repeating that children could be very smart or very strong regardless of any maternal or paternal lifestyle (alcohol, schooling, etc.), given the largely statistical nature of heredity and the denial of the inheritance of acquired traits (Meloni, 2016a, ch. 4). Secondly, this insulation of heredity paralleled another important historical phenomenon: it severed parental responsibility from the morbidity of heredity. Genetics happily coexisted with a view of the foetus as a "perfect parasite", something that could develop and grow regardless of maternal diet and lifestyle (Paul, 2010). Although the "parasite paradigm" of foetal growth, prevalent in obstetrics during the last century (Luke and Johnson, 1991), does not have a direct origin in medical genetics, it actually perfectly corresponds to the view of heredity underpinned by genetics. It well complements ideas of reproduction as the hosting of an "alien" body by a mostly passive carrier with no capacity to shape its growth unless tangentially. On the one hand, this may have enabled the emergence of notions of foetal personhood and autonomy in the second half of the last century. On the other hand, it has favoured a boundary-process between mother and foetus that confined a mother's responsibility for the generation of disabilities and malformations to only a few selected cases. Extensive medical beliefs about the impermeability of the placenta further consolidated this trend (Dally, 1998). At the end of the last century, typical Darwinian accounts of pregnancy highlighted the perfectly shielded nature of the embryo from toxins and bacteria, minimizing the importance of women's avoidance of teratogens as critical in preventing birth defects (Profet, 1995; Oaks, 2001: 37). Although there is limited research in this area, it would not be far-fetched to explore connections between these forms of immunization and de-responsibilization of pregnancy and the entry of vast numbers of women into the workforce on a global scale, particularly after World War Two.

Thus, while in former medical views the consequences of maternal (and sometimes paternal) actions were all-encompassing, affecting any single behaviour (from emotions to food) and constantly reminding mothers how imperfect their management of the womb could be, genetic diseases were seen as fundamentally disconnected from any detailed set of rules about managing everyday life or changing lifestyle and behaviours. To avoid ionizing radiations, thalidomide or other dangerous drugs may, of course, be considered as a set of maternal responsibilities undertaken to avoid damage to the unborn morphology before or during pregnancy. However, it cannot be compared in terms of extension and pervasiveness to early modern notions that a pregnant woman should avoid passion, anger or melancholic thoughts because they may affect foetal physiology. Nor can this be compared to emerging ideas, which we will explore in a moment, that maternal pre-pregnancy nutrition or paternal smoking shapes the metabolic trajectory of the unborn child. As I will argue in the next section, making the womb (molecularly) imperfect seems again a possibility in postgenomic times (Warin et al., 2012; Richardson et al., 2014; Mansfield, 2017).[3] This occurs in a widespread scientific shift toward the notion of direct parental effects on the physiology of future generations.

This is why the sociology of genetics may be in need of an important rethinking in postgenomic times. When sociologists write that "early eugenicists developed all sorts of events to encourage individuals and families *to reflect on themselves* (....) with a view to enhancing healthy procreation" (Rose, 2007: 139, my emphasis), they might be overlooking a key novelty: that there can be more than one view of the genome and heredity, and for some of them, to reflect on oneself *is no longer enough*. If our genome is understood as impressionable to present and past social events, then everyday action and constant behavioural vigilance are needed, way beyond the conscientious scrutiny and biomedical control triggered by twentieth-century genetics. This may be seen not necessarily as a break with a twentieth-century culture that made bodies and selves reflexively recreated through lifestyle and consumer choices (Turner, 1983; Featherstone et al., 1991; Giddens, 1991). However, in contrast to the modernism of consumeristic culture, in postgenomics there are not so much individual atoms, fluid identities and an abundance of life-projects that one can start from scratch and endlessly negotiate, unconnected to past histories and circumstances. Instead, there are more biologically enfolded individuals whose degree of freedom and control is shaped by the cumulative weight (inertia) of past experiences and present environmental forces into which they are fully absorbed. This points to a "new spatial and temporal politics of risk and responsibility" with important implications for social and medical surveillance of bodies and individual decisions (Lappé, 2016).

An epigenetic responsibility

In the current postgenomic scenario, notions of responsibility and risk are being rewritten and possibly expanded. In his *The Politics of Life Itself*, Rose tracked the birth of the genetically at-risk individual at the crossroads of (at least) three distinct lines of development: 1) *the societal level*: "the growing belief" and its circulation in society in the genetic basis of many undesirable conditions; 2) the *scientific community*: the "researchers' claim" that they can now identify the genetic sequences or markers associated with the rise of many conditions at the molecular level; and 3) *medical beliefs and practice*: the "doctors' claim" that they can turn this knowledge into practice by being increasingly able "to identify specific individuals" at genetic risk before the onset of the disease (2007: 106 and ff).

If we take Rose's analysis as a criterion to assess the emergence of the epigenetically at-risk person, it seems possible to say that of these three claims, the first two are also accurate in relation to epigenetic risk, although we may need to wait and see how medical beliefs and practice will build on this knowledge (at present, DOHaD is the most obvious, but not the only, channel through which epigenetic knowledge may percolate into practice).

After offering a quick summary of the societal belief in epigenetic responsibility, my focus in the remaining part of this section will be on the escalating number of *scientific claims* (the second level of Rose's analysis) about epigenetic effects across generations. What is impressive about these claims is the avalanche-like rate by which they have proliferated in just the last decade (I will purposely not use any study published before 2010), and their widespread diffusion among different research communities, institutions and disciplines (molecular or developmental biologists, biochemists, psychologists, etc.). This occurs in a context where allocation of funding toward laboratory research in epigenetics has also grown substantially in the major international public agencies, such as the National Institutes of Health (NIH), the European Research Council (ERC) and the Australian Research Council (ARC).[4]

While controversies and uncertainties are significant in the epigenetic community (Tolwinski, 2013; Pickersgill, 2016), it is doubtful that these are more than what has always happened in "normal science" like genetics, Mendelian and molecular, not to mention applied fields like behavioural genetics (see Panofsky, 2014). Uncertainty in epigenetics may reveal a magmatic phase of epistemic transition across paradigms but cannot be turned into an alibi against the depth and worldwide circulation across different scientific communities (especially for a younger generation) of expanded notions of heredity that no more than fifteen years ago were seen as speculative and held only by a theoretical avant-garde with little empirical support (see Jablonka and Lamb, 1989, 1995). Even factoring in cycles of hype and the regime of promises that typically fill the life-sciences landscape (Fortun, 2008), and their connection with market bubbles in the area,[5] it is plain to see that the genie of *more-than-DNA heredity* is out of the bottle, and it will not be easy to put it back.

The societal circulation

In just a few years, epigenetics has turned into a global success in communication (Haig, 2011), with its "stories for the masses" (Davey Smith, 2012) featuring Audrey Hepburn[6] and genetically identical mice changing colour or size due to different diets. A study conducted by Rachel Yehuda and her colleagues on the altered methylation levels in descendants of Holocaust survivors (Yehuda et al., 2014) was taken up in just a few weeks by *The Guardian* (UK), *Il Corriere della Sera* (Italy), *Le Monde* (France), *A Folha* (Brazil), *Maariv* (Israel) and *Gazeta* (Russia). But each news outlet had its own distinctive set of concerns. In Israel it was received as cutting-edge evidence of the existence of second-generation trauma ("Holocaust Trauma is passed on through genes" (Isrovich, 2015). In Russia, a growing interest surrounds the long term effects of the siege of Leningrad, albeit so far evidence is only genetics (Khlustova, 2015). The trajectory of such claims can be complex and troubling. Dias and Ressler's (2014) influential study carried out at Emory University on inheritance of fear in mice was used in the Russian political debate to claim "that the political passivity of Russian citizens [...] can be explained by fears inherited from ancestors who endured the Stalinist repressions" (Graham, 2014; see also, Graham, 2016; Kolchinsky et al., 2017). The same study in India was understood as scientific support for the existence/concept of karma (https://pparihar.com/2014/06/09/memories-can-be-passed-down-through-generations-in-our-genes/[7]). But also in strict Euro-American contexts, there is certainly no shortage of simplified translations of epigenetic studies, often sensationalized by scientists themselves (or their institutions). Among the claims that have appeared are that "obese grandfathers pass on their susceptibility to junk food" (Klein, 2016), and that "pre-pregnancy diet permanently influences a baby's DNA" (Briggs, 2014). The notion that biological heredity may include whole lifestyle information is common: "Sperm can carry Dad's stress as well as genes", reported *The Wall Street Journal* (Sapolsky, 2014). Several decades after the notion of racial or hereditary poison was employed, and then forgotten, in eugenic debates (see, for instance, Saleeby, 1914), *The Economist* published an article titled "Poisoned Inheritance" commenting on an epigenetic study on folate deficiency in mice, certainly unaware of the past connotations of the term (2013).

However, the communication of epigenetics-based claims is characterized by more than just sensationalism. Epigenetics-related approaches are starting to figure within policy debates, often in the form of pre-existing frameworks, such as "early intervention", but also in challenging the wisdom of previous public health interventions (Wastell and White, 2017). The French Senate and French Parliamentary Office for the Assessment of Scientific and Technological Choices (26 May 2015) and the UK House have discussed epigenetics-related findings and their impact for public health (debate in Lords Chamber, 10 May 2016).[8] In global health initiatives, international campaigns such as the "First 1000 days" movement, the UN's Scaling Up Nutrition Programme and the World Bank are using epigenetic and DOHaD findings. So are private companies such as Danone and Nestlé (Pentecost, 2018; www.nestle.com.au/media/newsandfeatures/nestle-boosts-research-into-cutting-edge-maternal-nutrition-and-epigenetics). The focus on the first 1000 days reflects the notion of a specific window of plasticity (i.e. most intense epigenetic programming) from conception until the second year of age, when intervention would be the most beneficial for future health and the protection of human capital. The harnessing of these themes at different levels contributes to the emergence of a new framework, a "biology of social adversity" that addresses how chronic poverty or racism "get under the skin" via brain and epigenetic mechanisms and often stay for the rest of life (Boyce et al., 2012). The application of these studies in the Global South is also visibly growing, particularly via DOHaD studies of the enduring effects of famine, war, trauma and nutritional change, as discussed in Chapter 1. A whole new area of global political economy and public affairs takes inspiration from DOHaD studies to make assumptions about the long term "scarring effect" (Almond and Currie, 2011: 165) of *in utero* programming. This new area is concerned with "cost-effective" economic interventions in key windows of human plasticity – particularly "pregnant women, or perhaps even women of child-bearing age" (ibid., 167).

Notions like "epigenetic load" (Bohacek and Mansuy, 2013) or "dysbiotic effects" (Prescott and Logan, 2016) are featuring in recent debates in epigenetics and microbiomics to convey ideas of accumulated stressors and "difficult living" over a lifetime and beyond. Arguments on "cumulative risk assessment" have also featured the notion of epigenetic load (Environmental Protection Agency, September 2015[9]). Private investors and insurance companies are also moving in on this new terrain. According to a recent study by Dupras and colleagues, since November 2016 a US insurance company based in Minneapolis (GWG Holdings, Inc.) has, through its subsidiary Life Epigenetics, "secured an exclusive license over the exploitation of a new epigenetic technology allegedly allowing for the prediction of a person's life expectancy through DNA methylation profiling" (Dupras et al., 2018). This is based on the innovative work on the so-called "epigenetic clock" of University of California, Los Angeles biostatistician Steven Horvath, discussed in Chapter 4. According to Dupras and colleagues, GWG Holdings has begun to collect saliva samples from policy owners in order to determine via epigenetics the "true 'biological age'" of clients. The goal is to differentiate between those "epigenetically younger than their 'chronological age'", who should be rewarded with an insurance premium, and those whose epigenetic clock instead signals a higher biological age compared with their chronological age, a discrepancy that "implies" a higher risk in terms of future health perspectives and life expectancy (Dupras et al, 2018). Epigenetic data are considered to unveil something significant about the lifestyle behaviour and risk attitude of individuals, not just random mutations. These conclusions may be hyped or distorted as a consequence of commercial interests, but are not entirely disconnected from the underlying (moralistic) association of behaviours and genomic effects that the thought-style emerging in epigenetics is introducing.

The claims from researchers

In the early 2000s, two major studies stood out in demarcating the emergence of an epigenetics of social behaviours, that is, the study of a nongenomic transmission of an altered phenotype across generations. The two studies are Waterland and Jirtle's agouti mouse study (2003) on the next generation effects of diet in pregnancy for obesity and diabetes, and Meaney and colleagues' study (Weaver et al., 2004) on the epigenetic transmission of stress and anxiety in rats via maternal behaviours. Waterland and Jirtle's experiment showed how exposing a pregnant mouse to a low-methyl diet resulted in epigenetic changes correlated with offspring that were yellow and fat rather than slim and brown like their parents (Waterland and Jirtle, 2003). Meaney and colleagues' study highlighted the different epigenetic effects on glucocorticoid receptors (with implications for sensitivity to stress) in pups of different styles of nursing (high vs. low licking and grooming) in rats. The study also highlighted the reversibility of these effects via cross-fostering (Weaver et al., 2004; see an updated review in Lutz and Turecki, 2014).

These two pioneering studies, which have accrued around 2000 and 5000 citations respectively, have now been used as the basis for a huge number of cases and situations. Interestingly, while those studies focused only on the behavioural or nutritional role of mothers, a more recent wave of research is increasingly targeting the male germline. Overall, these new studies offer a window into what may be called a new impressionability and re-personalization of heredity. Impressionability and personalization are the two sociological sides of the same epigenetic coin. The first aspect, impression-ability, highlights the porosity of the epigenome to the effects of present and past environments (Soubry, 2015). The second, personalization, emphasizes the subjective side, the actual deeds and often "sins" (Hughes, 2014) of (grand)fathers and (grand)mothers on the establishment of next generation phenotype(s); hence, researchers' claims to have established a direct relation-ship between choices and disease (Grayson et al., 2014).

This emerging area of epigenetics is very diverse. The mechanistic focus of these studies may vary between DNA methylation patterns, microRNAs, histone modifications and chromatin remodelling. The scien-tific background of the research group is also diverse, spanning molecular genetics, developmental biology, behavioural sciences, neuroscience and psychology. A common thread, however, is the complex temporal pattern of biological causation that turns individual life into a folded figure carrying different historical times into each other (Mansfield, 2017). This figure is imagined as a fragile, presently impressionable genome, the sen-sitivity of which is modulated across different critical periods of biological vulnerability. Parental physiology, both maternal and paternal, has a role to play in it.

Mothers and fathers in epigenetics

The novel impressionability and re-personalization of heredity runs across both the male and the female line. As is well known, there are many prom-inent studies on maternal effects, particularly in the area of DOHaD or "foetal programming", where pregnancy is considered a key moment of epigenetic programming and a channel for present and future disease risk (Hanson and Skinner, 2011). In the DOHaD official journal alone (https://dohadsoc.org/journal-of-dohad/), maternal effects are mentioned in approximately one third of all publications, while "paternal effects" are pre-sent in a very small fraction and are commonly mentioned alongside *in utero* effects rather than in isolation. Studies in the DOHaD literature include, for instance, those dealing with the impact of maternal diet on induced obesity and general susceptibility to metabolic disease in offspring (Blackmore and Ozanne 2013; Lillycrop and Burdge, 2015; partly independently of postnatal diet, Liang et al., 2009); prenatal maternal stress and behavioural and neurodevelopmental disorders, including aspects of theory of mind (Simcock et al. 2017); and depression and anxiety in gestating mothers and foetal growth restriction (Lewis et al., 2016).

Other recent studies beyond the DOHaD literature have looked at how pre-natal and early postnatal food habits in mothers may shape food preferences in offspring well into adolescence. Emphasis is commonly on the potential risks generated by "mothers who eat a 'junk food' diet during pregnancy and lac-tation" (Beauchamp and Mennella, 2009; Mennella, 2014). Prenatal cigarette smoking has not escaped epigenetic investigation, with researchers claiming that modifications in DNA methylation associated with prenatal maternal smoking "may persist in exposed offspring for many years – at least until ado-lescence" and are the cause of the onset of adult chronic diseases (Lee et al., 2015; see also Joubert et al., 2012). Similarly, *in utero* alcohol exposure and the aetiology of Fetal alcohol spectrum disorder (FASD) are being increasingly rewritten in epigenetic terms (Ungerer et al., 2013). DNA methylation levels, measured from buccal swabs in children, are considered by some as a bio-marker for risk of FASD (Laufer et al., 2015[10]).

But it would be reductive to say that mothers are the only focus. This may remain true for most of the DOHaD area but is increasingly less so in the wider epigenetic community. It is probably in relation to paternal effects that the most fascinating studies are coming to light from a huge number of diverse and often unconnected research groups. According to Oliver Rando (University of Massachusetts), one of the emerging leaders in the field and recipient of the first major National Institutes Health grant on paternal nutrition and offspring metabolism (2014–2019),[11] what we know today is that "sperm carry not only genetic information to the next generation, but also carry some imprint of a male's prior experiences in the form of epigenetic information carriers" (Rando, 2016; see Rando, 2012).

In the words of another researcher in the field, the sperm epigenome is "a messenger of ancestral exposures" (Soubry, 2015). Research on the transfer of information through the male germline is often based on animal models (rodents in particular, and in a few cases Drosophila). As in the maternal area, the research focuses on diet, stress, and exposure to alcohol or drugs. Some of these studies have highlighted, for instance, the effects of different paternal exposure to food – from obesity to fasting, from overnutrition to a low pro-tein diet – on the next generation DNA methylation, with implications for metabolic alterations and longevity (Kaati et al., 2002; Pembrey et al., 2006;

Carone et al., 2010; Ng et al., 2010; Rando and Simmons, 2015; see a comment in Moore and Stanier, 2013; see also Pembrey et al., 2014); the impact of pre-adolescent smoking on the sperm quality of first and second generation off-spring (Soubry et al., 2013); and the effects of paternal stress on offspring behavioural and metabolic responses (Gapp et al., 2014a and 2014b) and hypothalamic–pituitary–adrenal stress axis regulation (Rodgers et al., 2013).

Pathology and resilience

Even at a mechanistic level, these models often imply a "vicious cycle" in which the establishment of a certain "suboptimal" phenotype in the first generation (social defeat, metabolic abnormalities, stress, etc.) is invariably repeated into the next (cfr. Rando, 2016). It seems that if "like begets the like", it is mostly in a negative sense. However, while this may be true for the majority of studies, not all of them reflect this dark deterministic logic. Sometimes genuine differences are believed to appear in the next generation through a cascade of events. Two studies in particular are worth highlighting here, both of which hinge, from different angles, on the notion of "epigen-etic compensation" (Vyssotski 2011, cited in Jablonka and Lamb, 2014: 432). Epigenetic compensation may be understood as a form of evolution of resist-ance or "epigenetic learning", in which, rather than an intergenerational reproduction of the phenotype, there is a shift from one phenotype to its opposite ("phenotypic inversion"). For instance, in their study of self-administration of cocaine in rats, Vassoler and colleagues (2013) found that there was a better capacity to deal with drug effects ("delayed acquisition and reduced maintenance") in the male progeny of rats that had ingested cocaine. A "reduced drug-seeking behaviour" was developed in the new generation (Jablonka and Lamb, 2014: 497). In another study, Katharina Gapp (Wellcome Sanger Institute) and colleagues (2014b) analyzed whether "traumatic stress in postnatal life can have behavioural benefits in the offspring of mice". They exposed newborn mice to a model called "unpredictable maternal separ-ation and stress" (MSUS), noticing an improved capacity to cope with stress ("improved flexibility and better adaptation to new rules") in the second generation. Unpredictable MSUS may favour "goal-directed behaviours and reversal learning in the offspring, suggesting an effect on behavioural flexi-bility" (2014: 1). In some circumstances, early trauma can have "inoculating" effects that may confer some advantage not only later in life but also in the new generation when adult (ibid.).

Heredity expanded?

Whatever the societal and ethical implications one might draw from these studies, epigenetic inheritance appears no longer blind or random, but often the result of direct social exposures. Unlike genetic mutations epigenetic marks are more likely to be taken as a scientific-cum-social piece of information that can be moralized or anthropomorphized: one can read social behaviours through them. Often (not always), bad environments generate negative health outcomes; in some cases they can be reversed or compensated for through "environmental enrichment" (Gapp et al., 2016). How long it will take for these claims to become available to medical practice and, more extensively, to percolate in a systematic way into the areas of public policy and health is hard to say. It is difficult to anticipate when a form of knowledge will reach sufficient appeal, stability and persuasiveness for policy-makers, legislators, public health officers and citizens (Jasanoff, 2009). Political, medical and legislative processes are often outpaced by the advancements of scientific knowledge (Rugg-Gunn et al., 2009; Dupras et al., 2018). Historical experience – early eugenics for instance – tells us that sudden changes in socioeconomic circumstances may render pressing the adoption of a form of biopolitical knowledge that just a few years earlier seemed far-fetched.

If DOHaD appears the easiest pathway to channel epigenetic knowledge into available medical models, in sociology and social policy, epigenetic studies could prove attractive in debates around the persistence of inequality across generations, and even offer evidence for, or reinforce, old ideas like the "culture of poverty" (Welshman, 2013; see Perkins, 2016). Unlike sociological analysis, however, what is at stake in emerging epigenetic models of inequalities is not the psychological, economic or sociological attachment to places (Sharkey, 2014), but very material biological or phenotypic memories (Kuzawa and Quinn, 2009; Thayer and Kuzawa, 2011), literally passed on through a certain number of generations.

There are, finally, a number of tensions in emerging models of risk and responsibility implied in social and environmental epigenetics. Three, in particular, stand out. The first is between *paternal* and *maternal* responsibility, as we saw above. The second, in terms of social causation, is between the *individual* and the *collective* levels. Sociologists and anthropologists have often criticized how, especially in DOHaD models, social responsibility is "telescoped" to individual bodies, particularly the maternal womb (Warin et al., 2011). However, an increasing number of studies also look at collective causes, especially in environmental epigenetic studies of repeated exposure to toxicants (Manikkam et al., 2012; Skinner et al., 2013). As researchers in the field increasingly recognize, these works raise questions about not only individual but also collective responsibility "to minimize known health risks, develop human capabilities, and apply principles of distributive justice for current and future generations" (Cunliffe, 2016: 67). Finally, another tension in these findings is apparent between change and stability, what is *malleable* and what is *stabilized* (or hardened) and therefore unresponsive to social intervention (Jasienska, 2009). Within the latter, a further conflict emerges between a rhetoric of hope and one of fate, especially deployed at the collective level, as I will now explore.

Axis II: Culture and politics: Molecular suffering and biosociality in epigenetics

In this section, I observe two of the tensions we have sketched above – i) a subtle slippage in epigenetics from the individual to the group level in producing forms of responsibilization and stigmatization, but also ideas of victimhood and resilience, and ii) an oscillation between a "political economy of hope" (Novas and Rose, 2000) and a more sombre appreciation of the viscous power of traumatic events in "marking" the biosocial identity of certain groups. I am also interested in the objectification of epigenetic findings into a form of historical testimony about the impact of past colonial violence and quests for reparation: the turning of the epigenome into an object of compassion and the creation of notions of "molecular suffering" (that is, a suffering made "truer" by biological validation). This form of objectification of epigenetic findings is occurring within the context of a wider shift toward an ethics of victimhood and trauma as "one of the dominant modes of representing our relationship with the past" (Fassin and Rechtman, 2009: 15). In order to see the significance of epigenetic findings at the collective level, we must diffract epigenetic knowledge through the prism of its manifestations beyond Euro-American mainstream science, and particularly in the discourse of under-represented ethnic minorities in settler-colonial contexts and beyond. After all, one of the guiding hypotheses of this book has been that of a specific affiliation between contemporary forms of corporeal plasticity and subaltern or non-Western epistemologies of the body and health, before and alongside the rise of modern biomedicine.

A postcolonial epigenetics?

Following this insight, one of the most interesting cultural aspects of epigen-etics is the way in which it is perceived as aligned with Indigenous epistem-ologies and approaches to health, unlike genetic knowledge. As Australian anthropologist Emma Kowal has noted:

> For the last two decades, Indigenous peoples have consistently resisted genetics on local, national and international scales [...] Adding the prefix "epi", however, makes a big difference. In the last few years, epigen-etics has struck a chord within Indigenous scholarship and Indigenous media. Compared with the fear of genetics, the embrace of epigenetics is remarkable. Indigenous scholars, writers and leaders from Australia, New Zealand, the United States and Canada have expressed enthusiasm for epigenetics as a biological mechanism that explains [...] both the effects of early life on disease risk and "inter-generational Indigenous disadvantage".

Kowal continues:

> Most prominently, epigenetics is seen to align with Indigenous world views. As Justin Mohamed, Chairman of the Australian National Aboriginal Community Controlled Health Organisation, said [...] "in many ways the science backs up what's long been known." In a similar vein, Red Cliff Tribe of Wisconsin Ojibwe member Mary Annette Pember writes, "Folks in Indian country wonder what took science so long to catch up with traditional Native knowledge."
>
> (Kowal, 2016)

In Aotearoa /New Zealand, for instance, several authors have challenged a separation between "'scientific' epigenetics from 'non-scientific' indigenous knowledge" (Warbrick et al., 2016: 400; Ker, 2017; cfr. Gillett and Tamatea, 2012). They suggest that a number of Indigenous concepts, particularly "whakapapa", the Māori term for heredity, can be used "alongside empir-ical science to generate unique knowledge at the interface of indigenous and Western ontologies" (Ker, 2017: 11). According to these authors,

> it is not difficult to see the theoretical link between epigenetic determinants of health and a Māori view [...] which locates the health

of individuals within the context of whakapapa; a term concerned with the links between environment, genealogy and posterity.

(Warbrick et al., 2016: 400)

As a relationship with ancestors and places (cfr. Roberts, 2013), whakapapa has obvious resonances with epigenetic notions of the embodiment of environmental influences, genealogical transmission of these effects (Ker, 2017: 13 and ff.) and their continuous impact on the present (Roberts, 2013: 97). The porous relationship between personhood and the physical and relational whole expressed in whakapapa makes it somehow closer to notions of soft heredity than to hard genetic transmission. At the same time, however, it displays a value-laden meaning and narrative that exceeds the narrower scientific context of biological heredity (Ker, 2017: 64–65; albeit see Roberts, 2013: 97). Similar affinities between epigenetics and local understandings of the porous relationship between environment and personhood have been analysed in China (Lamoreaux, 2016) and Aboriginal cosmologies in Australia (Warin et al., 2018; see Arabena et al., 2016).

The biology of historical trauma?

However, it is probably through the construct of "Indigenous historical trauma" or, more broadly, "postcolonial distress" (Kirmayer et al., 2014) that Indigenous and epigenetic knowledges are finding important connections.

Constructs of historical trauma have proliferated in the last two decades, both in academia and among health activists, in the context of an increasing pervasiveness and cultural legitimation attached to ideas of traumatic victimhood (Fassin and Rechtman, 2009). In postcolonial debates particularly, historical trauma is used to "describe the impact of colonization, cultural suppression, and historical oppression of many Indigenous peoples" (Kirmayer et al., 2014: 300; cfr. Prussing, 2014). Historical trauma encapsulates a number of different processes, aetiological factors, kinds of trauma responses, and pathways of transgenerational transfer (Walters et al., 2011). It has emerged at the confluence of four different trajectories: 1) the recognition of a specific "colonial injury to Indigenous peoples by European settlers"; 2) a radical alteration in "identities, ideals, and interactions" of entire Indigenous communities as a consequence of this event; 3) "cumulative effects from these injuries" that "snowball" throughout a complex historical landscape made of dispossession, forced relocation and everyday racism; and finally 4) "cross-generational impacts of these injuries" in terms of a perpetuating legacy of risk and vulnerability across multiple generations (Hartmann and Gone, 2014 cited in Kirmayer et al., 2014: 301).

There is a significant analogy between the morphological description of historical trauma, with its cumulative and stabilizing effect in downward pathways, and views of temporality coming from epigenetics, as seen for instance in transgenerational versions of the Waddingtonian landscape. Historical trauma becomes a sort of *morbid version of developmental robustness* (morbid because the concept is usually taken to describe a buffering *against* environmental disruption) in which the sculpting power of past events is maintained and perpetuated beyond the individual lifespan, with little chance to move the ball back along its epigenetic pathway.

Possibly because of this isomorphism, or in general the allure of biological explanations, a good number of Indigenous researchers (particularly mental health and epidemiology scholars) seem positively attracted to the explanatory capacity of epigenetics. In the context of debates around trauma and reparation, they position their Indigeneity alongside emerging views of postgenomic plasticity (Warin et al., 2018). They often see in epigenetics a better way to integrate environmental or psychological analysis with biological explanations and give an additional, more reliable, truth and validation to the historical suffering of their people, a molecular document of historical violence (cfr. Fassin and Rechtman, 2009).

In an influential article, Amy Bombay and colleagues (2014) have explored the enduring effects of the Indian Residential Schools (IRS) system, the century-long forced removal of Indigenous children from their families to be assimilated into Canadian schools where they were systematically exposed to various forms of abuse. Bombay, an assistant professor of Psychiatry at Dalhousie University and a member of the Anishinaabe people, offers a compelling analysis of the long-term chronic effects of IRS attendance on the present wellbeing of Indigenous populations in Canada. The article is an attempt to look beyond individual-level reactions to the collective effects of trauma experiences on "family dynamics and on whole communities". While the article recognizes the potential difficulties of involving Indigenous groups in such studies, epigenetic changes in gene expression are postulated in the conclusions as an additional factor to be investigated in the study of historical trauma (Bombay, 2014: 332; cfr. also Brockie et al., 2013). In a more recent CBC interview ("Lasting effects of trauma reaches across generations through DNA"), Bombay claims that knowledge of epigenetic intergenerational effects of trauma may become a healing force eliciting "forgiveness within families and communities" (CBC News 2015).

Another influential researcher in this field is Karina Walters, an epidemiologist at the Indigenous Wellness Research Institute (University of Washington) and a member of the Choctaw Nation. Walters and colleagues, in their "Embodiment of Historical Trauma among American Indians and Alaska Natives" (2011), have mobilized epigenetics as a possible explanation for the embodiment of historical trauma among First Nations groups, reflected in their disproportionately higher rates of poor health, both mental and physical. A slippage between individual and collective analysis is very palpable in their work, particularly the way in which individual traumatic events constitute a wider fabric of "sustained cultural disruption and destruction directed at AIAN [American Indians and Alaska Natives] tribal communities" (Walters et al., 2011: 181). Epigenetics, understood as a non-genomic multigenerational transmission of responses to stress, is postulated as a more promising and comprehensive explanatory framework than traditional social determinants of health approaches to explain the chronicization of historical trauma among Native American communities. If bodies "keep the scores" of historical trauma, epigenetics is selected as a more objective testimony of, or a dangerously naïve shortcut to, collective sufferings along the lines of similar processes in humanitarian psychiatry (Fassin and Rechtman, 2009). This objective rendering of historical violence in the form of laboratory-certified molecular scars is probably considered helpful in a "politics of relief" where scientific evidence will make it no longer possible to blame victims for their symptoms (Fassin and Rechtman, 2009). Perhaps it will even "foster improved intergroup relations by increasing understanding of the complicated issues contributing to the health of Aboriginal peoples" (Bombay et al., 2014: 333).

The epigenetic legacy of the Holocaust?

Another area of intergenerational trauma research appropriating epigenetic findings is Holocaust studies, in which much of the original paradigm of historical trauma was actually proposed (LaCapra, 1996, 2001). Natan P.F. Kellermann, former chief psychologist of the Israel's largest mental health support centre for Holocaust survivors based in Jerusalem is the author of the influential article, "Epigenetic transmission of Holocaust trauma: Can nightmares be inherited?" (2013). It focuses on epigenetics as a possible explanation for the transmission of a specific neurobiological susceptibility to stressors (rendered in the article in terms of a specific vulnerability, but also resilience) in the children of Holocaust survivors. Using overt references to Lamarckian ideas, and building on still-contested works on neuroendocrine and epigenetic modifications in infants born to mothers who were pregnant during the Manhattan attacks of 9/11 (Yehuda et al., 2005), war veterans (Yehuda et al., 2010) and adult offspring of Holocaust survivors (Yehuda and Bierer, 2008; Yehuda et al., 2014), Kellermann claims that "epigenetics adds a new and more comprehensive psychobiological dimension to the explanation of transgenerational transmission of trauma" (2013: 33). The indirect effects and severity of trauma across generations, insufficiently explained by psychodynamic or communication models, may instead find validation in the transmission of biological memories typical of epigenetic mechanisms. This positing of corporeal truth as revealing the impact of major historical events across time is rendered rather crudely in the article when the author claims that "instead of numbers tattooed on their forearms [...] they [the children of Holocaust survivors] may have been marked epigenetically with a chemical coating upon their chromosomes, which would represent a kind of biological memory of what the parents experienced" (Kellermann, 2013: 33). The oscillation between doom and hope is well captured in the conclusions of the article, in which the author claims that "the bad news with epigenetics is that we have to carry the load of our parents", while the good news is that "we apparently can do something about it", through a variety of established psychotherapeutic interventions or new psycho-pharmacological drugs, or "a combination of both":

> epigenetics opens up a potentially more optimistic view of health and disease in offspring of trauma survivors. Since epigenetics conveys that human beings are not only predestined, but also highly malleable creatures, they are able to reverse the deleterious effects of trauma and find some closure to the endless multi-generational saga.
>
> (ibid., 38)

Epigenetics, Reparation and Justice

The usage of epigenetics as a form of biolegitimacy in which biologically validated knowledge about suffering is turned into a platform for political recognition (Warin et al., 2018; see Fassin, 2009) may be seen as a complex and problematic strategy from vulnerable groups. Yet, epigenetics does not represent the first instance of this kind of usage of molecular findings. Genetics has also been turned into "a medium through which the 'unsettled past' can be reconciled" (Nelson, 2012). Various forms of slavery reparation activism have emerged that have employed "genetic genealogy evidence in order to elicit recognition of their injuries and experiences [...] by virtue of their shared status as descendants of a slave caste, a collective" (Nelson, 2016: 138).

However, this reparative mode based on notions of "hereditary injury" (Nelson, 2016) may gain strength in the future through epigenetics in light of the stronger alignment between the molecular and social experience in epigenomic data. Epigenetics offers not just a "collision" of history and DNA (Wailoo et al., 2012) but a whole superimposition of the molecular and the experiential that may become a fertile ground for debates on the legacy of historical injustice.

The notion of a shared epigenetic fate is already informing the first claims of epigenetic reparations that are emerging, among no few ambiguities. Alongside a claim from descendants of Caribbean slaves, for instance, white American southerners have also lodged an epigenetic claim (also circulating on violently racist websites) of victimization by the United States federal government during Reconstruction (Meloni, 2017). This confirms what Fassin and Rechtman (2009) have convincingly shown: that an objectivistic usage and naturalization of the category of trauma may end up concealing power differences rather than facilitating political recognition of oppressed groups. More research, however, is emerging in this area, and we should be open to following the incorporation of epigenetic claims by under-represented communities in a dynamic and unpredictable way, rather than using facile formulas such as biological reductionism.

In their ongoing fieldwork in the United States Pacific Northwest, Martha Kenney and Ruth Müller (Müller and Kenney, 2018) have studied the usage of insights from the epigenetics of early life adversity in "initiatives in the fields of trauma-informed care and restorative justice" in schools, juvenile correction facilities and communities that aim, among other things, to interrupt the school-to-prison pipeline. Here, non-profits and other actors in youth services draw on biological research about brain development to reconceptualize common "problem behaviours" of young people as effects of adverse childhood experiences. Yet, instead of pathologizing the individual or focusing on the need for prevention, Müller and Kenney highlight the positive emphasis on "recovery and resiliency" in this biological language and the creative usage of epigenetic knowledge to enable institutions to respond more attentively to demands for justice. Interestingly, these emerging narratives can also become "important resources for reorienting epigenetic research in the lab" (Müller and Kenney, 2018).

Anthropologists are also moving in on this new terrain, not only in terms of lab ethnography (Niewöhner, 2011; Lloyd and Raikhel, 2018) and conceptual framework (Lock, 2015; Niewöhner and Lock, 2018), but also as an empirical and methodological challenge to incorporate epigenetic findings in anthropological research, addressing racial disparities in health and the long-term impact of structural violence (Non and Thayer, 2015; Thayer and Non, 2015). The political significance of this emerging area of epigenetics remains very much open. This is especially true for its looping effects (Hacking, 1996) and potential for reinscription of racial categories. Unlike in the twentieth century, when implications centred on the discovery of discrete genetic differences, the significance of epigenetics is the embodied result of historical events (especially traumatic) on the shared biological fate of certain human groups. Biology is molecularly impressionable at an unprecedented level of historical detail (see Shackel 2017 for the epigenetic legacy of deindustrialization in the US).

Axis III: Ethics: Another plasticity is emerging?

In the last few years, sociologists have produced brilliant analyses of the complex social iterations of ideas of body and brain plasticity, using plasticity to make "visible the ways that cultural norms and social inequalities are mapped onto bodies, how gender is significant in the production of bodies, and how bodies become the object and subject of consumption" (Berkowitz, 2017: 24). Plastic surgery in particular has been analyzed as *giving forms* to a docile body by "an enterprising self", albeit one that is caught in the coercively normalizing effect of marketplace culture. Berkowitz's recent analysis of Botox consumption in the US, for instance, addresses plasticity as the strengthening of an "active and rational consumer seizing control" over an ageing body. This occurs in the wider context of a society where plastic surgery is increasingly understood "as a given", a second nature (ibid.: 116; see Kimmel, 2011), and bodies are rewritten as malleable projects to develop constantly through hard work and anxious surveillance (Brumberg, 1998; Jones, 2008; Dworkin and Wachs, 2009; Berkowitz, 2017: 36).

Moving from plastic surgery to neuroplasticity, we have significant analysis of the incorporation of plastic biology into the neoliberal imperative that we each become the best possible versions of ourselves, reinforcing the privatization of health, the "individualization of risk, and the internalization of responsibility" (Lappé, 2016: 4; Pitts-Taylor, 2016). Taking control of the brain becomes the last step in the neoliberal incitation to govern and optimize oneself, opening up the brain and the body "to personal techniques of enhancement and risk avoidance" (Pitts-Taylor, 2010: 635). At a macro level, this emphasis on plasticity as the capacity to train at will one's body or brain is also seen as "compatible with neoliberal divestments in macro-economic, public health, and community-based programs that address poverty itself" (Pitts-Taylor, 2016: 38). What is common across these different iterations of plasticity and their impact on cultural norms is the notion (or fantasy, as some critics would point out) of choice, autonomy and control over a docile biological matter, something shaped by an agent-master of its own desires. To paraphrase Nikolas Rose, here we find form of plasticity in which a culture of maximization of potentialities goes hand in hand with the penetration and intensification of power relationships (1996: 170).

Yet new forms of plasticity might also liberate us from the power of liberal or neoliberal agency, as they promise "constant renewal" that challenges stability (Rees, 2016) and enables the multiplying and decentring of subjectivity (Watson, 1998). Postmodern readings of plasticity propose a dissolution of the intentional subject-master and a displacement of biosocial identity to the advantage of the generativity and power of life processes themselves. Some readings suggest plasticity in the service of endless potentialities, making it synonymous with a continuous generation of forms even in the adult brain. Plasticity is here taken as having wider ethical implications for ideas of humanity itself. It is the material trace for the emergence of a new neurological human "at home in a novel ethical space, equipped with a whole different [...] ethical equipment for neuronal sense making" (Rees, 2016). We could even associate plasticity with notions of a "vibrant matter" (Bennett, 2009) and similar vitalist or "new materialist" tropes in social theory (Coole and Frost, 2010). Finally, we have claims of plasticity as consistent with forms of resistance: properly secured into a new political consciousness, biological non-determinism can foster social and political non-determinism by disentangling plasticity from its dark doppelganger, capitalistic flexibility (Malabou, 2008). One might reasonably hold any of these positions. However, is the corporeal plasticity that is emerging from social epigenetics and related programmes explainable along the above lines? Is epigenetic plasticity just about modernistic control, neoliberal travesty, or a postmodernist destabilization of the subject or political resistance? As we have noted at the beginning, plasticity "is neither an undisputable fact with a singular meaning nor a mere social construction. Rather, it refers to multiple materialities that are entangled with specific research questions, and practices of scientific measurement" (Pitts-Taylor, 2010). If this is the case, we should be ready to make room for a further pluralization of meanings in plasticity, in accordance with the materiality, politics and temporality entangled with research questions and practices of measurement in epigenetics and related postgenomic programmes. To analyse this last emerging axis, I will follow the remaking of the notion of reproduction in epigenetics and microbiomics as a vantage point from which to look at a mutated relationship between agency and biological matter. My argument is that this emerging plasticity is not about a modernist control of the body or a postmodernist generation of endless forms. It discloses an alter-modernistic experience of finitude, dwelling and belonging: by this, I mean a relational and communitarian dimension of biology that is partly alien to post-Enlightenment modalities. The new biology emphasizes a reincorporation of the body *within histories and milieu* (as it does the postgenomic genome within its wider material context) a view of multiplicity and transgression of inner/outer boundaries that resembles Baroque entanglements rather than a modernistic chasm (Deleuze, 1993).

Life in postgenomic times: From individuals to holobionts

It is through this reincorporation of the body *within histories and milieu* that I suggest reading the specific figure of plasticity that postgenomics paints for us. My starting point is a piece of research that received the 2017 ISHSSPB (International Society for the History, Philosophy, and Social Studies of Biology) Werner Callebaut Prize and focuses on the way in which microbiomics and epigenetics have been recently mobilized to rethink the "human birth narrative". To challenge the myth that childbirth is about "the origins of a new individual", Lynn Chiu and her colleague, developmental biologist Scott Gilbert, describe birthing as the origin of a new community in which what is reproduced is the web of relationships among mother, child and microbe symbionts (see also Gilbert, 2014). Chiu and Gilbert – this latter a leading figure in post-individualist developments in theoretical biology (Gilbert et al., 2012) – challenge the inherent solipsism of the birth narrative, understood as a modernistic "immunization" of one individual from the other. Human birth does not amount to "the heroic travails of the mother or the amazing journey of foetus", or to the supposed emancipation of the foetus from the mother's symbiotic system, but is, rather, "the passage from one set of symbiotic relationships to another" (Chiu and Gilbert, 2015: 192). This is not a simplistic argument about the "programming" of the foetus via maternal biology. As in the Baroque entanglement, what is brought to light here is the mobile, dynamic coproduction of mother and infant, a holobiontic assemblage.[12] The relationship between mother, child and the symbiotic communities of microbes has to be understood as one of "mutual reliance (reciprocal developmental *scaffolding*) and mutual construction (niche construction)" (2015: 194, emphasis added). The foetus, for instance, does not just passively receive the maternal symbiotic system via the mother's hormones, food, antibodies and later, breastfeeding. The foetus actively contributes to maternal development, for instance by modulating, modifying and stabilizing the mother's immune system or changing her blood circulation and metabolic functioning (Nuriel-Ohayon et al., 2016). This is a system of reciprocal "enveloping-developing", in a Deleuzian parlance (Deleuze, 1993: 9), in which each being is making the scaffold for the other (Chiu and Gilbert, 2015). *Scaffold* and *scaffolding* are used nearly fifty times in Chiu and Gilbert (2015) to convey a strong sense of shared material contexts by which development takes place. Birth is defined as "an example of bacterial and symbiont scaffolding in which each is making the scaffold for the other" (ibid.: 204).

What is at stake is the plastic coproduction of a number of beings-in-common, "the unfolding of [a] community structure over time": humans "are holobionts – multicellular eukaryotes with multiple species of persistent symbionts, not merely habitats colonized by microbiota" (Chiu and Gilbert, 2015: 192); hence the notion of *motherfetus* introduced by University of California-based anthropologist Chikako Takeshita (2018) "to release", as she claims, "feminist theory from dualist binds so that reproductive science and politics can be explored in new ways" (2017: 5).[13]

Blurring individual boundaries in epigenetics

This blurring of individual histories within wider contexts is far from being the idiosyncratic outcome of this research. There would be many possible examples of this embedding of personal biographies either in spatial relationships (especially in microbiomics) or in temporal ones (in epigenetics). In epigenetics in particular this situatedness may become even stronger, as ancestral events often seem to linger with delayed effects on the present temporality of other biological beings. Whether, as we saw above, the focus is on the reproduction of obesity (Warin et al., 2011, 2012; Rando and Simmons, 2015), the plasticity of taste preferences moulded via molecular cues across generations (Jablonka and Lamb, 2014; Mennella, 2014), or the intergenerational transmission of famine, racism, slavery or trauma (Kuzawa and Sweet, 2009; Wells, 2010), what emerges is a nested continuum of biological states and forms replicated rather stably from one generation to another (with the exceptions discussed above, pp. 146–7).

Epigenetic temporality "folds in on itself", bringing together in present biological time a multiplicity of generations. Particularly, foetal life is extended "linearly both backward into the period prior to conception and forward into the months and years following birth" (Mansfield, 2017). The image of the Russian dolls, or similar sequential representations of multiple generations folded one into the other (such as in the logo for the 2015 DOHaD conference in Johannesburg), is in fact a recurring one in the DOHaD and epigenetic imagination. Rather than the dematerialization of a field for the free play of desires and unlimited possibilities, plasticity here means a recognition that the past is never wholly elapsed – that a body is embedded in a very material lineage (Warin et al, 2012, 2015) that acts as regulator of the function and morphology of present and future generations (Landecker, 2011). This is not a plasticity of continuous creation of forms (Rees, 2016) or a naively modernistic self-directed plasticity, but one of intergenerational *inertia* (Kuzawa, 2005) in which the physiology of each generation is shaped not so much by present environments as by a sampling of present and past cues "over decades and generations" (Kuzawa, 2005: 12–13). This is a literal, biological version of the famous Marxian passage "the tradition of all dead generations weighs like a nightmare on the brains of the living" (Marx, 1978). It is the weight of historical matter that counts in postgenomic plasticity. It is, for instance, the accumulated inequity of previous centuries of colonialism and exploitations that weighs on the uneven distribution of "somatic capital" and metabolic capacity in different ethnic groups within and between populations. The accumulation and distribution of "somatic capital" is a "slow and steady process, distributed across rather than within generations" (Wells, 2010: 9). Present birth weight in contemporary populations, for instance, a key indicator of future health, "is not only determined just by the current maternal condition, but also by the influence of intergenerational life conditions, i.e., influences integrated across several generations" (Jasienska, 2009: 16). In social-theoretical terms, it is a plasticity of *viscous porosity* rather than smooth fluidity and endless possibility to change (Tuana, 2007). In this way, the postgenomic body becomes not a modernistic abstract point in time, or an instantaneous entity that can start anew at each generation. It is instead the sedimentation, even the concretion, of a long history into which the individual is immersed, if not submerged. This is why this emerging anthropological figure fits better with alter-modernistic frameworks such as the Baroque, or Heidegger's analytics of *Dasein*. As an alternative to the modernistic chasm of subject and object, in which an independent subject disposes of its past as a reified object, Heidegger's concept of *thrownness* (*Geworfenheit*) illustrates well the recognition of a "referential dependence on other beings" (Richardson, 1974) that is characteristic of postgenomic plasticity. Thrownness means that I am always placed in a situation that I have not chosen, found in a terrain that "has already constituted for itself" (Malpas, 2012) and of which I have to recognize its otherness and priority. While for Heidegger, it is *Stimmung* (mood) that reveals this belonging to an already-given situation, its postgenomic iteration is embodied, not psychologistic. It is not a mood like boredom or anxiety, or a linguistic web of meanings that precedes me and discloses my possibilities – rather, it is a very material entanglement with other biologies and other histories: maternal microbiome via the placenta or breastmilk, paternal sperm physiology, the range of exposures that ceaselessly sculpts my identity. This model can be called plastic because my skin is not an insuperable wall but rather, one of the points of entrance for innumerable microbiomic exchanges; my genome is susceptible to developmental and environmental cues; and there is no reset button at each generation, given the inertial effects of past biological histories on present temporality.

Conclusion: A farewell to determinism and anti-determinism?

Emerging models of plasticity in epigenetics are best represented by ancient and early modern morphologies (like the Baroque) of profound situatedness, multiplicity and disruption of dichotomies between the inner and the outer, activity and passivity, determination and openness, malleability and stability (or robustness; Bateson and Gluckman, 2011). In this way, postgenomic plasticity complicates debates on determinism and non-determinism, making somehow unproductive contemporary attempts to either condemn or rescue postgenomics from one of these two extremes. Determinism and anti-determinism, programming and freedom, all imply the modernistic figure of an autonomous body and insular individual that one has to either deny as illusory or defend in its integrity. But this integrity is deceptive, according to postgenomic models in which entanglement (with others and the external world) comes ontologically first. As in older ecological models, bodies are webbed in biological and social stories, neither determined by biology (as if they *couldn't* be) nor abstract from it (as if they *could* be). It is, however, a very ambiguous plasticity. It is capable of undermining atomistic and insulated models of the body in favour of more relational views of personhood and autonomy beyond notions of property and control (see Prainsack, 2017 and for wider debates Nedelsky, 1990). But it is also true that, by re-embedding the individual within a wider lineage of ancestral experiences and reconfiguring it as a multi-species holobiontic assemblage, it may open the way to a problematic space where the subject of emancipation is simply too difficult to define. Moreover, the power of biological heredity may have expanded to the point that it is stronger than in any genetic view. And finally, the experience of plasticity can be so deeply enfolded and layered in racialized and gendered mechanisms, as I have shown in the first two chapters, that it is difficult for it to serve inherently emancipatory goals.

Whatever conclusions the reader might draw from the arguments I have presented, it is fair to acknowledge that the terms of the debate have dramatically shifted from past arguments about genes and/or environments, the innate and the acquired, biological or social explanations. There is no need for epochal claims to realize that what we came to believe as the natural landscape of the biology–society debate was in fact a recent and precarious invention, one of the many possible faces drawn "in sand at the edge of the sea", to cite Foucault's lesson (2002: 422).

Notes

1 On the integration between microbiomics, epigenetics and DOHaD, see, for instance, Majnik and Lane (2015); Flandroy et al. (2018).

2 Although, as Rapp further recognized at the time, "there may well be contributions to chromosome damage which can be socially influenced, but of which we are currently unaware" (ibid.).

3 Some of these trends may draw on already existing arguments about the criminalization of the womb, which, however, largely arose outside of genetic research (Oaks, 2001; Calhoun and Warren, 2007; Golden, 2009).

4 Since 2007 the ERC has funded 110 projects in basic epigenetic research or involving epigenetic areas in the life sciences. Since 2010, the ARC has funded 58 projects in or involving epigenetics (only three before that). To my knowledge, NIH has started funding major research in nutritional epigenetics since 2014: see, for instance, http://grantome.com/grant/NIH/R01-HD080224-05.

5 Epigenetic market products to enable DNA-wide methylation analyses (including DNA-modifying enzymes; next generation sequencers; reagents; kits) were nonexistent in the early 2000s, while they have been valued at $413.24 million in 2014 and are expected to reach $ 1,605 million by 2022 (source: marketsandmarkets.com; Google search on 3 February 2017).

6 Reference to Audrey Hepburn comes from Nessa Carey's popular *The Epigenetics Revolution* (2012). According to Carey, Audrey Hepburn survived as a teenager the

Dutch Hunger Winter (see Chapter 4); the long-term effects of this event, Carey claims, "stayed with her for the rest of her life", visible in her thin figure. This is one of the stories used to popularize epigenetic findings; see, for instance, www.dailymail.co.uk/health/article-2031505/Audrey-Hepburn-Is-key-stopping-obesity-epidemic.html.

7 Accessed February 2016.

8 Thanks to Andrew Bartlett (Sheffield and York) for access to these documents.

9 https://cfpub.epa.gov/ncea/risk/recordisplay.cfm?deid=308271, accessed April 2018. The concept of "epigenetic load" is defined as "accumulated epigenetic marks as influenced by multiple stressors" (EPA Workshop on Epigenetics and Cumulative Risk Assessment on September 2–3, 2015).

10 It is worth noting that this research was conducted on a sample of six children.

11 http://grantome.com/grant/NIH/R01-HD080224-05.

12 The notions of the holobiont and the hologenome are a novel and richer way to look at what was known as symbiosis. A holobiont is considered to be a unique biological consortium of multiple persistent symbionts, generally a host and a number of symbionts. The hologenome indicates "the sum of the genetic information of the host and its symbiotic microorganisms" (Rosenberg and Zilber-Rosenberg, 2014: 13).

13 Albeit the political implications of this move for women's rights (especially abortion rights) remain rather complex, beyond the scope of this chapter.

References

Abu Asab, M, Hakima A and Micozzi MS (2013) *Avicenna's Medicine: A New Translation of the 11th-Century Canon with Practical Applications for Integrative Health Care.* Rochester: Inner Traditions/Bear & Company.

Ackerknecht EH (1982) *A Short History of Medicine.* Baltimore and London: JHU Press.

Adair L and Prentice A (2004) A critical evaluation of the fetal origins hypothesis and its implications for developing countries. *The Journal of Nutrition* 134(1): 191–193.

Adamson P (2018) Al-Kindi. In N Zalta (ed.) *The Stanford Encyclopedia of Philosophy.* Stanford: Stanford University. Available at: https://plato.stanford.edu/archives/sum2018/entries/al-kindi/.

Agamben G (1998) *Homo Sacer: Sovereign Power and Bare Life.* Stanford: Stanford University Press.

Agerholm F (2013) The Sex Res Non Naturales and the Regimen of Health – On the Contemporary Relevance of the History of Ideas of Dietetics. Available at: https://pure.au.dk/ws/files/53611039/The_Sex_Res_Non_Naturales_and_the_Regimen_of_Health_On_the_Contemporary_Relevance_of_the_History_of_Ideas_of_Dietetics.pdf (Accessed May 2018).

Albala K (2002) *Eating Right in the Renaissance.* Berkeley: University of California Press.

Albertus Magnus (1515) *Liber de natura locorum.* Strasbourg: Matthias Schurerius.

Alder K (2013) The history of science as oxymoron: From scientific exceptionalism to episcience. *Isis* 104(1): 88–101.

Allen GE (1974) Opposition to the Mendelian-chromosome theory: The physiological and developmental genetics of Richard Goldschmidt. *Journal of the History of Biology* 7: 49–92.

Allen GE (1979) Naturalists and experimentalists: The genotype and the phenotype. *Studies in History of Biology* 3: 179–209.

Allen GE (1985) Heredity under an embryological paradigm: The case of genetics and embryology. *Biological Bulletin* 168: 107–121.

Allfrey VG, Faulkner R and Mirsky AE (1964) Acetylation and methylation of histones and their possible role in the regulation of RNA synthesis. *Proceedings of the National Academy of Sciences of the United States of America* 51(5): 786.

Almond D and Currie J (2011) Killing me softly: The fetal origins hypothesis. *Journal of Economic Perspectives* 25(3): 153–172.

Almond D, Currie J and Hermann M (2012) From infant to mother: Early disease environment and future maternal health. *Labour Economics* 19(4): 475–483.

Amundson R (1994) John T. Gulick and the active organism: Adaptation, isolation, and the politics of evolution. In P Rehbock and R MacLeod (eds.) *Darwin in the Pacific* (pp. 110–139). Honolulu: University of Hawaii Press.

Amundson R (1996) Historical development of the concept of adaptation. In MR Rose and GV Lauder (eds.) *Adaptation* (pp. 11–53). New York: Academic Press.

Anderson W (1996) Disease, race and empire. *Bulletin of the History of Medicine* 70(1): 62–67.

Anderson W (2002) Introduction: Postcolonial technoscience. *Social Studies of Science* 32(5–6): 643–658.

Anderson W (2006) *Colonial Pathologies: American Tropical Medicine, Race, and Hygiene in the Philippines.* Durham: Duke University Press.

Anderson W (2009) From subjugated knowledge to conjugated subjects: Science and globalisation, or postcolonial studies of science? *Postcolonial Studies* 12(4): 389–400.

Anderson W (2014) Racial conceptions in the Global South. *Isis* 105(4): 782–792.

Anderson W (2016) Simply a hypothesis? Race and ethnicity in the global South. *Humanities Australia* 7: 55–62.

Angrist M (2010) *Here Is a Human Being: At the Dawn of Personal Genomics.* New York: Harper.

Ankeny RA and Leonelli S (2015) Valuing data in postgenomic biology: How data donation and curation practices challenge the scientific publication system. In SS Richardson and H Stevens (eds.) *Postgenomics: Perspectives on Biology after the Genome* (pp. 126–149). Chapel Hill: Duke University Press.

Ansell-Pearson K (2003) *Germinal Life: The Difference and Repetition of Deleuze.* London: Routledge.

Aquinas T (1951) *Commentary on Aristotle's De Anima.* K Foster and S Humphries (trans.). New Haven: Yale University Press.

Aquinas T (2002) *The Essential Aquinas: Writings on Philosophy, Religion, and Society.* JYB Hood (trans.). Westport: Greenwood Publishing Group.

Arabena K , Ritte R, Panozzo S et al. (2016) First 1000 days Australia: An Aboriginal and Torres Strait Islander led early life intervention. *Aboriginal and Islander Health Worker Journal* 40: 21.

Archer K (1993) Regions as social organisms: The Lamarckian characteristics of Vidal de la Blache's regional geography. *Annals of the Association of American Geographers* 83(3): 498–514.

Arendt H (1958) *The Human Condition.* Chicago: University of Chicago Press.

Arens H (1984) *Aristotle's Theory of Language and Its Tradition: Texts from 500 to 1750.* Amsterdam: John Benjamins Publishing Company.

Arikha N (2007) *Passions and Tempers: A History of the Humours.* New York: Harper.

Aristotle (1984) *The Complete Works of Aristotle, Volumes I and II.* J Barnes (ed.). Princeton: Princeton University Press.

Aristotle (1995) *Aristotle: Selections, Translated with Introduction, Notes, and Glossary.* T Irwin and G Fine (eds.). Indianapolis: Hackett.

Aristotle (2014) *On Memory and Reminiscence.* JI Beare (trans.). Available at: http:// classics.mit.edu/Aristotle/memory.html

Armstrong HE (1931) The Monds and chemical industry: A study in heredity. *Nature* 128: 238.

Arni C (2015) Traversing birth: Continuity and contingency in research on development in nineteenth-century life and human sciences. *History and Philosophy of the Life Sciences* 37(1): 50–67.

Arni C (2016) The prenatal: Contingencies of procreation and transmission in the nineteenth century. In S Müller-Wille and C Brandt (eds.) *Heredity Explored: Between Public Domain and Experimental Science, 1850–1930.* Cambridge: MIT Press.

Arnold D (1996) *The Problem of Nature: Environment, Culture, and European Expansion.* Oxford: Blackwell Publishers.

Aspers P (2007) Nietzsche's sociology. *Sociological Forum* 22(4): 474–499.

Attewell G (2007) *Refiguring Unani Tibb: Plural Healing in Late Colonial India.* Hyderabad: Orient Longman.

Avery O, MacLeod C and McCarty M (1944) Studies on the chemical nature of the substance inducing transformation of pneumococcal types: Induction of transformation desoxyribonucleic acid fraction isolated from pneumococcus type III. *Journal of Experimental Medicine* 79: 137–157.

Avicenna (1999) The Canon of medicine (al-Qānūn fi'l-ṭibb), vol. 1. In L Bakhtiar (ed.), OC Gruner and MH Shah (trans.) *Great Books of the Islamic World.* Chicago: Kazi Publication, Inc.

Azzolini M (2013) *The Duke and the Stars: Astrology and Politics in Renaissance Milan.* Cambridge: Harvard University Press.

Baedke J (2013) The epigenetic landscape in the course of time: Conrad Hal Waddington's methodological impact on the life sciences. *Studies in History and Philosophy of Science Part C: Studies in History and Philosophy of Biological and Biomedical Sciences* 44(4): 756–773.

Baedke J (2017) Locating the Organism in the Environment. Paper presented at the Annual ISHPSSB conference, Sao Paulo, Brazil, 16–21 July.

Bagg S (2018) Beyond the search for the subject: An anti-essentialist ontology for liberal democracy. *European Journal of Political Theory.* doi: 10.1177/1474885118763881.

Baker GJ (2014) Christianity and eugenics: The place of religion in the British Eugenics Education Society and the American Eugenics Society, c. 1907–1940. *Social History of Medicine* 27(2): 281–302.

Bakhtin M (1984) *Rabelais and His World.* Bloomington: Indiana University Press.

Baldwin JM (1902) *Development and Evolution*. New York: Macmillan.

Bale J (2002) Lassitude and latitude: Observations on sport and environmental determinism. *International Review for the Sociology of Sport* 37(2): 147–158.

Ball WP (1890) *Are the Effects of Use and Disuse Inherited?* London: Macmillan and Co.

Banerji CR, Miranda-Saavedra D, Severini S et al. (2013) Cellular network entropy as the energy potential in Waddington's differentiation landscape. *Scientific Reports* 3: 3039.

Bannister AJ and Kouzarides T (2011) Regulation of chromatin by histone modifications. *Cell Research* 21(3): 381.

Bannister R (1988) *Social Darwinism: Science and Myth in Anglo-American Thought* (2nd ed.). Philadelphia: Temple University Press.

Bannister R (2014) *Sociology and Scientism: The American Quest for Objectivity, 1880–1940*. Chapel Hill: The University of North Carolina Press.

Bapteste E and Dupré J (2013) Towards a processual microbial ontology. *Biology and Philosophy* 28(2): 379–404.

Baranski M and Peirson BRE (2015) Introduction. (Special Issue: Contexts and concepts of adaptability and plasticity in twentieth century plant science). *Studies in the History and Philosophy of the Biological and Biomedical Sciences* 50: 26–28.

Barker DJ (1995) Fetal origins of coronary heart disease. *British Medical Journal* 311(6998): 171.

Barnes B and Dupré J (2008) *Genomes and What to Make of Them*. Chicago: University of Chicago Press.

Barnes J (1982) *The Presocratic Philosophers*. London: Routledge & Kegan Paul.

Bartlett R (2001) Medieval and modern concepts of race and ethnicity. *Journal of Medieval and Early Modern Studies* 31(1): 42.

Barton T (1994) *Ancient Astrology*. London: Routledge.

Bateson P and Gluckman P (2011) *Plasticity, Robustness, Development and Evolution*. Cambridge: Cambridge University Press.

Beauchamp GK and Mennella JA (2009) Early flavour learning and its impact on later feeding behaviour. *Journal of Pediatric Gastroenterology and Nutrition* 48(Suppl 1): S25–30.

Bennett J (2009) *Vibrant Matter: A Political Ecology of Things*. Durham: Duke University Press.

Berger M, Leicht A, Slatcher A et al. (2017). Cortisol awakening response and acute stress reactivity in First Nations people. *Scientific Reports* 7: 1–10.

Berkowitz D (2017) *Botox Nation: Changing the Face of America*. New York: New York University Press.

Berlin I (2002) *Four Essays on Liberty*. London: Oxford University Press.

Berlucchi G and Buchtel HA (2008) Neuronal plasticity: Historical roots and evolution of meaning. *Experimental Brain Research* 192(3): 307–319.

Bernard C (1949) *An Introduction to the Study of Experimental Medicine*. HC Green (trans.). London: Henry Schuman.

Bethencourt F (2013) *Racisms: From the Crusades to the Twentieth Century*. Princeton: Princeton University Press.

Bianchi E (2014) *The Feminine Symptom: Aleatory Matter in the Aristotelian Cosmos*. New York: Fordham University Press.

Bibikova M, Lin Z, Zhou L et al. (2006). High-throughput DNA methylation profiling using universal bead arrays. *Genome Research* 16(3): 383–393.

Bidney D (1953) *Theoretical Anthropology*. New York: Columbia University Press.

Biémont C and Vieira C (2006) Genetics: Junk DNA as an evolutionary force. *Nature* 443(7111): 521–524.

Birney E, Davey Smith G and Greally J (2016) Epigenome-wide association studies and the interpretation of disease-omics. *PLoS Genetics* 12(6): e1006105.

Blackmore HL and Ozanne SE (2013) Maternal diet-induced obesity and offspring cardiovascular health. *Journal of Developmental Origins of Health and Disease* 4(5): 338–347.

Blank A (2010) Material souls and imagination in late Aristotelian embryology. *Annals of Science* 67(2): 187–204.

Boas F (1912) Changes in the bodily form of descendants of immigrants. *American Anthropologist* 14(3): 530–562.

Bodin J (1576 [1962]). KD MacRae (ed.). *The Six Books of a Commonwealth*. Cambridge: Harvard University Press.

Bohacek J and Mansuy IM (2013) Epigenetic inheritance of disease and disease risk. *Neuropsychopharmacology* 38(1): 220.

Bombay A, Matheson K and Anisman H (2014) The intergenerational effects of Indian residential schools: Implications for the concept of historical trauma. *Transcultural Psychiatry* 51(3): 320–338.

Bonduriansky R (2012) Rethinking heredity, again. *Trends in Ecology & Evolution* 27(6): 330–336.

Borghol N , Suderman M, McArdle W et al. (2012) Associations with early-life socio-economic position in adult DNA methylation. *International Journal of Epidemiology* 41(1): 62–74.

Bos J (2009) The rise and decline of character: Humoral psychology in ancient and early modern medical theory. *History of the Human Sciences* 22(3): 29–50.

Bourdieu P and Passeron JP (1979) *The Inheritors: French Students and Their Relation to Culture*. Chicago: University of Chicago Press.

Bourdieu P (1986) The forms of capital. In J Richardson (ed.) *Handbook of Theory and Research for the Sociology of Education* (pp. 241–258). New York: Greenwood.

Bowler P (1989) *The Mendelian Revolution: The Emergence of Hereditarian Concepts in Modern Science and Society*. Baltimore: Johns Hopkins University Press.

Bowler P (2009) *Evolution, the History of an Idea* (3rd ed.). Berkeley: University of California Press.

Boyce WT, Solokowski MB and Robinson GE (2012) Toward a new biology of social adversity. *Proceedings of the National Academy of Sciences* 109: 43–48.

Braunstein JF (1997) Le concept de milieu, de Lamarck à Comte et aux positivismes. In G. Laurent (ed.) *Jean-Baptiste Lamarck, 1744–1829* (pp. 557–571). Paris: CTHS.

Briggs H (2014) Pre-pregnancy diet "permanently influences a baby's DNA". BBC News: Health. 30 April.

Brockie TN, Heinzelmann M and Gill J (2013) A framework to examine the role of epigenetics in health disparities among Native Americans. *Nursing Research and Practice* 1: 395–410.

Broomhall S (1998) Rabelais, the pursuit of knowledge, and early modern gynaecology. *Limina: A Journal of Historical and Cultural Studies* 4: 24–34.

Brosius J (2003) The contribution of RNAs and retroposition to evolutionary novelties. *Genetica* 118(2–3): 99–116.

Browne J (2002) *Charles Darwin: A Biography, vol. 2. The Power of Place.* Princeton: Princeton University Press.

Brumberg JJ (1998) *The Body Project: An Intimate History of American Girls.* New York: Knopf Doubleday Publishing Group.

Buckley NJ, Johnson R, Zuccato C et al. (2010). The role of REST in transcriptional and epigenetic dysregulation in Huntington's disease. *Neurobiology of Disease* 39(1): 28–39.

Buklijas T (2018) Histories and meanings of epigenetics. In M Meloni, J Cromby, D Fitzgerald et al. (eds.) *The Palgrave Handbook of Biology and Society.* London: Palgrave Macmillan.

Burk RL (2010) *Salus Erat in Sanguine: Limpieza De Sangre and Other Discourses of Blood in Early Modern Spain.* Philadelphia: Publicly Accessible Penn Dissertations.

Burkhardt RW (1977) *The Spirit of System: Lamarck and Evolutionary Biology.* Cambridge: Harvard University Press.

Burns SB, Almeida D and Turecki G (2018) The epigenetics of early life adversity: Current limitations and possible solutions. *Progress in Molecular Biology and Translational Science* 157: 343–425.

Burrow J (1966) *Evolution and Society: A Study in Victorian Social Theory.* Cambridge: Cambridge University Press.

Burton R (1621 [2000]) *The Anatomy of Melancholy.* TC Faulkner, NK Kiessling and RL Blair (eds.). 6 vols. Oxford: Clarendon Press.

Buss LW (2014) *The Evolution of Individuality.* Princeton: Princeton University Press.

Buttimer A (1971) *Society and Milieu in the French Geographic Tradition.* Chicago: Rand McNally and Company.

Bynum WF (1993) *Companion Encyclopedia of the History of Medicine.* Abingdon: Taylor and Francis.

Calhoun F and Warren K (2007) Fetal alcohol syndrome: Historical perspectives. *Neuroscience & Biobehavioral Reviews* 31(2): 168–171.

Campbell JA and Livingstone DN (1983) Neo-Lamarckism and the development of geography in the United States and Great Britain. *Transactions of the Institute of British Geographers* 8(3): 267–294.

Camporesi P (1995) *The Juice of Life: The Symbolic and Magic Significance of Blood.* New York: Continuum.

Canani RB, Di Costanzo M, Leone L et al. (2011) Epigenetic mechanisms elicited by nutrition in early life. *Nutrition Research Reviews* 24(2): 198–205.

Canguilhem G (1955) *La formation du concept de reflexe aux XVIIe et XVIIIe siecles.* Paris: Presses Universitaires de France.

Canguilhem G (1966/2012) *On the Normal and the Pathological.* Dordrecht: Springer.

Canguilhem G (2001) The living and its milieu. *Grey Room* 3 (Spring): 6–31.

Cañizares-Esguerra J (2006) *Nature, Empire, and Nation: Explorations of the History of Science in the Iberian World.* Stanford: Stanford University Press.

Caporael LR, Griesemer JR and Wimsatt W (Eds.). (2013). *Developing Scaffolds in Evolution, Culture, and Cognition.* Cambridge: MIT Press.

Carey, N (2012). *The epigenetics revolution: How modern biology is rewriting our understanding of genetics, disease, and inheritance.* New York: Columbia University Press.

Carey N (2015) *Junk DNA: A Journey through the Dark Matter of the Genome.* New York: Columbia University Press.

Carlson E (1981) *Genes, Radiation, and Society: The Life and Work of H. J. Muller.* Ithaca: Cornell University Press.

Carlson E (2009) *Hermann Joseph Muller 1890–1967: A Biographical Memoir.* Washington: National Academy of Science.

Carone B, Fauquier L, Habib N et al. (2010) Paternally induced transgenerational environmental reprogramming of metabolic gene expression in mammals. *Cell* 143: 1084–1096.

Carvan MJ III, Kalluvila TA, Klingler RH et al. (2017). Mercury-induced epigenetic transgenerational inheritance of abnormal neurobehavior is correlated with sperm epimutations in zebrafish. *PloS ONE* 12(5): e0176155.

CBC News (2015) Lasting effects of trauma reaches across generations through DNA. CBC News, 28 September.

Cecil CA, Smith RG, Walton E et al. (2016) Epigenetic signatures of childhood abuse and neglect: Implications for psychiatric vulnerability. *Journal of Psychiatric Research* 83: 184–194.

Chakrabarti P (2004) *Western Science in Modern India: Metropolitan Methods, Colonial Practices (Permanent Black Monographs: Opus 1 series).* Hyderabad: Orient Blackswan.

Champagne F (2018) Social and behavioral epigenetics: Evolving perspectives on nature–nurture interplay, plasticity, and inheritance. In M Meloni, J Cromby, D Fitzgerald et al. (eds.) *The Palgrave Handbook of Biology and Society.* London: Palgrave Macmillan.

Charney E (2012) Behavior genetics and postgenomics. *Behavioral and Brain Sciences* 35(5): 331–358.

Chimisso C (2003) The tribunal of philosophy and its norms: History and philosophy in Georges Canguilhem's historical epistemology. *Studies in History and Philosophy of Biological and Biomedical Sciences* 34: 297–327.

Chiu L and Gilbert S (2015) The birth of the holobiont: Multi-species birthing through mutual scaffolding and niche construction. *Biosemiotics* 8:191–210.

Choi S and Friso S (2010) Epigenetics: A new bridge between nutrition and health. *Advances in Nutrition* 1(1): 8–16.

Christopoulos J (2010) By "your own careful attention and the care of doctors and astrologers": Marsilio Ficino's medical astrology and its Thomist context. *Bruniana & Campanelliana* 16(2): 389–404.

Churchill F (1974) William Johannsen and the genotype concept. *Journal of the History of Biology* 7: 5–30.

Clark A (1998) Embodiment and the philosophy of mind. In A O'Hear (ed.) *Current Issues in Philosophy of Mind: Royal Institute of Philosophy Supplement 43* (pp. 35–52). New York: Cambridge University Press,.

Clarke AE (2003) *Biomedicalization*. Hoboken: John Wiley & Sons, Ltd.

Clarke AE, Shim JK, Mamo L et al. (2003) Biomedicalization: Technoscientific transformations of health, illness, and U.S. biomedicine. *American Sociological Review* 68: 161–194.

Cockerham W (2015) *Medical Sociology*. New York: Routledge.

Codell Carter K (2012) *The Decline of Therapeutic Bloodletting and the Collapse of Traditional Medicine*. London: Routledge.

Codell Carter K (2017) *The Rise of Causal Concepts of Disease: Case Histories*. New York: Routledge.

Cohen E (2009) *A Body Worth Defending: Immunity, Biopolitics and the Apotheosis of the Modern Body*. Durham and London: Duke University Press.

Coleman W (1974) Health and hygiene in the Encyclopédie: A medical doctrine for the bourgeoisie. *Journal of the History of Medicine and Allied Sciences* 29(4): 399–421.

Comaroff J and Comaroff J (2012) Theory from the South. *Anthropological Forum* 22: 113–131.

Conklin E (1915) August Weismann. *Science* 1069(41): 917–923.

Connell R (2007) *Southern Theory: The Global Dynamics of Knowledge in Social Science*. Cambridge: Allen and Unwin.

Conrad P (1999) A mirage of genes. *Sociology of Health & Illness* 21(2): 228–241.

Conry Y (1974) *L'introduction du Darwinisme en France au XIXe siecle*. Paris: Vrin.

Coole D and Frost S (eds) (2010) *New Materialisms: Ontology, Agency, and Politics* (pp. 92–115). Durham: Duke University Press.

Cooper M (2017) Intervention at the Biopolitics of Epigenetics Conference, University of Sydney, 27 June. http://sydney.edu.au/arts/ssps/news_events/events/index.shtml?id=9489

Corbin A (1986) *The Foul and the Fragrant: Odor and the French Social Imagination*. Cambridge, Mass: Harvard University Press.

Corbin A, Courtine J-J and Vigarello G (Eds.) (2005a) *Histoire du corps. Vol I De la Renaissance aux Lumières*. Paris: Le Seuil.

Corbin A, Courtine J-J and Vigarello G (Eds.) (2005b) *Histoire du corps. Vol II De la Révolution à la Grande Guerre.* Paris: Le Seuil.

Corbin A, Courtine J-J and Vigarello G (Eds.) (2006) *Histoire du corps. Vol III. Les mutations du regard. Le XXe siècle.* Paris: Le Seuil.

Cornaro L (1833) *Sure and Certain Methods of Attaining a Long and Healthful Life. With a Portrait.* London: GA Williams (trans.).

Corsi P (1988) *The Age of Lamarck: Evolutionary Theories in France, 1790–1830.* Berkeley: University of California Press.

Cortini R, Barbi M, Caré BR et al. (2016) The physics of epigenetics. *Reviews of Modern Physics* 88(2): 025002.

Crick F (1958) On protein synthesis. *Symposia of the Society for Experimental Biology* 12: 138–163.

Crick F (1970) Central dogma of molecular biology. *Nature* 227(5258): 561–563.

Crook D (1994) *Darwinism, War and History.* Cambridge: Cambridge University Press.

Crossley N (2013) Habit and habitus. *Body and Society* 19(2&3): 136–161.

Cueto M and Palmer S (2014) *Medicine and Public Health in Latin America: A History.* Cambridge: Cambridge University Press.

Cunliffe VT (2016) The epigenetic impacts of social stress: How does social adversity become biologically embedded? *Epigenomics* 8(12): 1653–1669.

Currie J and Vogl T (2013) Early-life health and adult circumstance in developing countries. *Annual Review of Economics* 5(1): 1–36.

Dales R and Grosseteste R (1966) The text of Robert Grosseteste's Questio de fluxu et refluxu maris with an English Translation. *Isis* 57(4): 455–474.

Dally, A (1998) Thalidomide: Was the Tragedy Preventable? Lancet 351 (18 Apr): 1197–99.

Darwin C (1845 [1937]) *Voyage of the Beagle.* New York: Collier and Son.

Darwin C (1859 [1985]) *The Origin of Species by Means of Natural Selection.* JW Burrow (ed. with introduction). New York: Penguin Books.

Darwin C (1868) *Variation in Animals and Plants under Domestication* London: J. Murray.

Dasgupta A (2017) Can the major public works policy buffer negative shocks in early childhood? Evidence from Andhra Pradesh, India. *Economic Development and Cultural Change* 65(4): 767–804.

Davey Smith G (2012) Epigenetics for the masses: More than Audrey Hepburn and yellow mice? *International Journal of Epidemiology* 41(1): 303–308.

Dawkins R (1976) *The Selfish Gene.* Oxford: Oxford University Press.

Dawkins, R (2010) The information challenge. In *A Devil's Chaplain: Selected Writings.* New York: First Mariner Books.

De Esteyneffer J (1719) *Florilegio medicinal de todas la enfermedades.* Querétaro: Francisco Frias.

Deichmann U (2015) Chromatin: Its history, current research, and the seminal researchers and their philosophy. *Perspectives in Biology and Medicine* 58(2): 143–164.

Deichmann U (2016) Epigenetics: The origins and evolution of a fashionable topic. *Developmental Biology* 416(1): 249–254.

de Jong-Lambert W and Krementsov N (2011) On labels and issues: The Lysenko Controversy and the Cold War. *Journal of the History of Biology* 45(3): 373–388.

de Jong-Lambert W (2012) *The Cold War Politics of Genetic Research. An Introduction to the Lysenko Affair*. Dordrecht: Springer.

De Renzi S (2007) Resemblance paternity and imagination in early modern courts. In S Müller-Wille, H-J Rheinberger and JZ Buchwald (eds.) *Heredity Produced: At the Crossroads of Biology, Politics, and Culture, 1500–1870*. Cambridge, Mass: MIT Press.

Dean M (2003) *Critical and Effective Histories, Foucault's Methods and Historical Sociology*. London/New York: Routledge.

Dean-Jones L (1994) *Women's Bodies in Classical Greek Science*. London: Clarendon Press.

Dekker J, Marti-Renom MA, Mirny LA et al (2013). Exploring the three-dimensional organization of genomes: Interpreting chromatin interaction data. *Nature Reviews Genetics* 14(6): 390–403.

Deleuze G (1993) *The Fold: Leibniz and the Baroque*. London: Bloomsbury.

Deleuze G (1994) *Difference and Repetition*. P Patton (trans.). New York: Columbia.

Dennett D (1995) *Darwin's Dangerous Idea: Evolution and the Meanings of Life*. New York: Simon & Schuster.

Derrida J (1981) Plato's pharmacy. In *Dissemination*. B Johnson (trans.). Chicago: University of Chicago Press.

Deslauriers M (2009) Sexual difference in Aristotle's politics and his biology. *Classical World* 102(3): 215–231.

Desmond A. (1992). *The Politics of Evolution: Morphology, Medicine, and Reform in Radical London*. Chicago: University of Chicago Press.

Desmond A and Moore JR (1991) *Darwin*. London: Penguin.

Detel W (2005) *Foucault and Classical Antiquity*. Cambridge: Cambridge University Press.

Dias B and Ressler K (2014) Parental olfactory experience influences behavior and neural structure in subsequent generations. *Nature Neuroscience* 17(1): 89–96.

Diedrich L (2005) Introduction: Genealogies of disability: Historical emergences and everyday enactments. *Cultural Studies* 19(2): 649–666.

Dietrich M (2003) Richard Goldschmidt: Hopeful monsters and other "heresies". *Nature Reviews Genetics* 4(1): 68.

Doidge N (2008) *The Brain That Changes Itself: Stories of Personal Triumph from the Frontiers of Brain Science*. London: Penguin.

Doniger W and Spinner G (1998) Misconceptions: Female imaginations and male fantasies in parental imprinting. *Daedalus* 127(1): 97–129.

Douglas B and Ballard C (Eds.) (2008) *Foreign Bodies: Oceania and the Science of Race 1750–1940*. Canberra: ANU Press.

Douglas D (2015) *Neuroplasticity. The Secrets behind Brain Plasticity*. Seattle: Independent Publishing Platform.

Dubow S (1995) *Scientific Racism in Modern South Africa*. Cambridge: Cambridge University Press.

Duden B (1991) *The Woman beneath the Skin: A Doctor's Patients in Eighteenth-Century Germany*. Cambridge, Mass: Harvard University Press.

Duffau H (2006) Brain plasticity: From pathophysiological mechanisms to therapeutic applications. *Journal of Clinical Neuroscience* 13(9): 885–897.

Dumont L (1986) *Essays on Individualism: Modern Ideology in Anthropological Perspective*. J Erhardy, P Hockings and L Dumont (trans.). Chicago: University of Chicago Press.

Dupras C and Ravitsky V (2016) The ambiguous nature of epigenetic responsibility. *Journal of Medical Ethics* 42(8): 534–541.

Dupras C, Song L, Saulnier KM et al. (2018) Epigenetic discrimination: Emerging applications of epigenetics pointing to the limitations of policies against genetic discrimination. *Frontiers in Genetics* 9: 202.

Durkheim E (1893/1997) *The Division of Labor in Society*. WD Halls (ed., trans.). New York: Free Press.

Durkheim E (1897/2002). *Suicide: A Study in Sociology*. JA Spaulding (ed.) and G Simpson (trans.). London: Routledge.

Dworkin SL and Wachs FL (2009) *Body Panic: Gender, Health, and the Selling of Fitness*. New York: New York University Press.

Earle R (2012) *The Body of the Conquistador: Food, Race and the Colonial Experience in Spanish America, 1492–1700*. Cambridge: Cambridge University Press.

Editorial (1915) Maternal impressions: Belief in their existence is due to unscientific method of thought. *Journal of Heredity* 3: 512–518.

Eisenstadt SN (1968) *The Protestant Ethic and Modernization*. New York: Basic Books.

Elias N (2000) *The Civilizing Process: Sociogenetic and Psychogenetic Investigations*. Oxford: Wiley Blackwell.

Elliott C (2004) *Better Than Well: American Medicine Meets the American Dream*. New York: W. W. Norton & Company.

Emch-Deriaz A (1992) The non-naturals made easy. In R Porter (ed.) *The Popularization of Medicine. 1650–1850* (p. 134f). London: Routledge.

Epstein J (1995) The pregnant imagination, fetal rights, and women's bodies: A historical inquiry. *Yale Journal of Law & the Humanities* 7(1): 139–162.

Epstein S (2007) *Inclusion: The Politics of Difference in Medical Research*. Chicago: Chicago University Press.

Erasmus Darwin (1818) *Zoonomia; Or The Laws of Organic Life, Volume 2*. William Brown: Philadelphia.

Eraso Y (2007) Biotypology, endocrinology, and sterilization: The practice of eugenics in the treatment of Argentinian women during the 1930s. *Bulletin of the History of Medicine* 81(4): 793.

Eriksen KG, Radford EJ, Silver MJ et al. (2017) Influence of intergenerational in utero parental energy and nutrient restriction on offspring growth in rural Gambia. *The FASEB Journal* 31(11): 4928–4934.

Ernst W (2014) *Plural Medicine, Tradition and Modernity, 1800–2000*. London: Routledge.

Esteller M (2008) Epigenetics in cancer. *New England Journal of Medicine* 358(11): 1148–1159.

Esteller M (2011) Non-coding RNAs in human disease. *Nature Reviews Genetics* 12(12): 861.

Evans B and Reid J (2013) Dangerously exposed: The life and death of the resilient subject. *Resilience* 1(2): 83–98.

Fassin D (2009) Another Politics of Life Is Possible. *Theory, Culture, & Society* 26(5): 44–60.

Fassin D and Rechtman R (2009) *The Empire of Trauma: An Inquiry into the Condition of Victimhood*. R Gomme (trans.). Princeton: Princeton University Press.

Featherstone M, Hepworth M and Turner B (Eds.) (1991) *The Body: Social Processes and Cultural Theory*. London: Sage.

Febvre L (1924) *A Geographical Introduction to History*. London: Routledge, Trench and Tubner.

Feerick JE (2010) *Strangers in Blood: Relocating Race in the Renaissance*. Toronto: University of Toronto Press.

Feher M, Naddaff R and Tazi N (1989a) *Fragments for a History of the Human Body*. Part One. New York: Zone.

Feher M, Naddaff R and Tazi N (1989b) *Fragments for a History of the Human Body*. Part Two. New York: Zone.

Feher M, Naddaff R and Tazi N (1989c) *Fragments for a History of the Human Body*. Part Three. New York: Zone.

Felsenfeld G (2014) A brief history of epigenetics. *Cold Spring Harbor Perspectives in Biology* 6(1): a018200.

Fend M (2015) Marie-Guillemine Benoist's "Portrait d'un négresse"and the visibility of skin colour. In C Rosenthal and D Vanderbeke (eds.). *Probing the Skin: Cultural Representations of Our Contact Zone* (pp. 192–210). Cambridge Scholars Publishing.

Feng Y, Jankovic J and Wu YC (2015). Epigenetic mechanisms in Parkinson's disease. *Journal of the Neurological Sciences* 349(1): 3–9.

Ferrell JE Jr (2012) Bistability, bifurcations, and Waddington's epigenetic landscape. *Current Biology* 22(11): R458–R466.

Finkelstein J (1991) *The Fashioned Self*. Cambridge: Polity Press.

Fischer-Homberger E (1979) On the medical history of the doctrine of imagination. *Psychological Medicine* 9(4): 619–628.

Fiske J (1881) Sociology and hero-worship. *Atlantic Monthly* 47(January): 75–84.

Fissell M (2004) *Vernacular Bodies: The Politics of Reproduction in Early Modern England*. Oxford: Oxford University Press.

Flandroy L, Poutahidis T, Berg G et al. (2018) The impact of human activities and lifestyles on the interlinked microbiota and health of humans and of ecosystems. *Science of the Total Environment* 627: 1018–1038.

Floyd-Wilson M (2003) *English Ethnicity and Race in Early Modern Drama*. New York: Cambridge University Press.

Forger NG (2016) Epigenetic mechanisms in sexual differentiation of the brain and behaviour. *Philosophical Transactions of the Royal Society B* 371(1688): 20150114.

Forsman A (2015) Rethinking phenotypic plasticity and its consequences for individuals, populations and species. *Heredity* 115(4): 276–284.

Forti S (2006) The biopolitics of souls: Racism, Nazism, and Plato. *Political Theory* 34(1): 9–32.

Fortun M (2008) *Promising Genomics: Iceland and deCODE Genetics in a World of Speculation.* Oakland: University of California Press.

Foster ES (1927) *The Works of Aristotle. Vol. VII The Problemata.* Oxford: Clarendon Press.

Foster G (1994) *Hippocrates' Latin American Legacy: Humoral Medicine in the New World.* Amsterdam: Gordon & Breach Science Publishers Ltd.

Foucault M (1973) *The Birth of the Clinic.* New York: Pantheon Books.

Foucault M (1978) *History of Sexuality, Vol. 1. An Introduction.* New York: Random House.

Foucault M (1984) Nietzsche, genealogy and history. In Paul Rabinow (ed.) *The Foucault Reader* (pp.76–100). New York: Pantheon.

Foucault M (1990) *The History of Sexuality Volume 3: The Care of the Self.* London: Penguin Books.

Foucault M (1998) Nietzsche, genealogy, history. In J Faubion (ed.) *Aesthetics, Method, and Epistemology: Essential Works of Foucault 1954–1984, vol. 2* (pp. 369–392). London: Penguin.

Foucault M (2003) *"Society Must Be Defended": Lectures at the Collège de France, 1975–1976.* New York: Picador.

Freeland CA (2010) *Feminist Interpretations of Aristotle.* University Park: Pennsylvania State University.

Freudenthal G (2002) The medieval astrologization of Aristotle's biology: Averroes on the role of the celestial bodies in the generation of animate beings. *Arabic Sciences and Philosophy* 12: 111–137.

Freudenthal G (2009) *The Astrologization of the Aristotelian Cosmos: Celestial Influences on the Sublunar World in Aristotle, Alexander of Aphrodisias, and Averroes.* Brill: Leiden.

Frost S (2016). *Biocultural Creatures: Toward a New Theory of the Human.* Durham: Duke University Press.

Fuller S (2018) Maurizio Meloni's *Political Biology*: The hour of political biology: Lamarck in a eugenic key? *History of the Human Sciences* 31(1): 97–103.

Gabriele M, Tobon AL, D'agostino G et al. (2018) The chromatin basis of neurodevelopmental disorders: Rethinking dysfunction along the molecular and temporal axes. *Progress in Neuro-Psychopharmacology and Biological Psychiatry* 84(Pt B): 306–327.

Gapp K, Jawaid A, Sarkies P et al. (2014a) Implication of sperm RNAs in transgenerational inheritance of the effects of early trauma in mice. *Nature Neuroscience* 17(5): 667.

Gapp K, Soldado-Magraner S, Alvarez-Sánchez M et al. (2014b) Early life stress in fathers improves behavioural flexibility in their offspring. *Nature Communications* 5: 5466.

Gapp K, Bohacek J, Grossmann J et al. (2016) Potential of environmental enrichment to prevent transgenerational effects of paternal trauma. *Neuropsychopharmacology* 41(11): 2749.

García-Sancho M (2012) *Biology, Computing, and the History of Molecular Sequencing: From Proteins to DNA, 1945–2000*. Dordrecht: Springer.

Gavrylenko V (2012) The "body without skin" in Homeric poems. In H Horstmanshoff, H King and C Zittel (eds.) *Blood, Sweat and Tears: The Changing Concepts of Physiology from Antiquity into Early Modern Europe* (pp. 479–502). Leiden: Brill.

Geison GL (1969) Darwin and heredity: The evolution of his hypothesis of pangenesis. *Journal of the History of Medical and Allied Sciences* 24(4): 375–411.

Germain P, Ratti, E and Boem F (2014) Junk or functional DNA? ENCODE and the function controversy. *Biology & Philosophy* 29(6): 807–831.

Giddens A (1991) *Modernity and Self-Identity. Self and Society in the Late Modern Age*. Cambridge: Polity Press.

Gilbert S (1991) Epigenetic landscaping: Waddington's use of cell fate bifurcation diagrams. *Biology and Philosophy* 6(2): 135–154.

Gilbert S and Sarkar S (2000) Embracing complexity: Organicism for the 21st century. *Developmental Dynamics* 219(1): 1–9.

Gilbert S, Sapp J and Tauber I (2012) A symbiotic view of life: We have never been individuals. *Quarterly Review of Biology* 87: 325–341.

Gilbert S (2014) A holobiont birth narrative: The epigenetic transmission of the human microbiome. *Frontiers in Genetics* 5: 282.

Gilbert W (1992) A vision of the grail. In DJ Kevles and L Hood (eds.) *The Code of Codes: Scientific and Social Issues in the Human Genome Project* (pp. 83–97). Cambridge, Mass: Harvard University Press.

Gillett G and Tamatea AJ (2012) The warrior gene: Epigenetic considerations. *New Genetics and Society* 31(1): 41–53.

Gillispie C (1959) Lamarck and Darwin in the history of science. In B Glass, O Temkin and W. Straus, Jr. (Eds.), *Forerunners of Darwin: 1745–1859* (pp. 265–291). Baltimore: Johns Hopkins University Press.

Gilman S (2008) *Fat: A Cultural History of Obesity*. Maiden, MA: Polity.

Gissis S (2003) Late nineteenth century Lamarckism and French sociology. *Perspectives in Science* 10: 69–122.

Gissis S (2011) Lamarckian problematics in historical perspective. In S Gissis and E Jablonka (eds.) *Transformations of Lamarckism: From Subtle Fluids to Molecular Biology* (pp. 21–32). Cambridge: MIT Press.

Gissis S and Jablonka E (2011) *Transformations of Lamarckism: From Subtle Fluids to Molecular Biology*. Cambridge: MIT Press.

Glacken C (1967) *Traces on the Rhodian Shore: Nature and Culture in Western Thought from Ancient Times to the End of the Eighteenth Century*. Berkeley: University of California Press.

Glad J (2003) Hermann J. Muller's 1936 letter to Stalin. *Mankind Quarterly* 43(3): 305–319.

Glannon W (2002) Depression as a mind–body problem. *Philosophy, Psychiatry and Psychology* 9(3): 243–254.

Gluckman P and Hanson M (2005) *The Fetal Matrix*. Cambridge: Cambridge University.

Gluckman P, Hanson M, Beedle A et al. (2011) Epigenetics of human disease. In B Hallgrimsson and B Hall (eds.) *Epigenetics: Linking Genotype and Phenotype in Development and Evolution* (pp. 398–423). Berkeley: University of California Press.

Gluckman PD and Hanson MA (2012) *Fat, Fate and Disease: Why Exercise and Diet Are Not Enough*. New York: Oxford University Press.

Gluckman PD, Buklijas T and Hanson MA (2015) The developmental origins of health and disease (DOHaD) concept: Past, present, and future. In CS Rosenfeld (ed.) *The Epigenome and Developmental Origins of Health and Disease* (pp. 1–13). London: Academic Press.

Godfrey KM, Sheppard A, Gluckman PD et al. (2011) Epigenetic gene promoter methylation at birth is associated with child's later adiposity. *Diabetes* 60(5): 1528–1534.

Gokhman, D, Meshorer, E and Carmel, E (2016) Epigenetics: It's getting old. Past meets future in paleoepigenetics. *Trends in Ecology & Evolution* 31(4 (2016): 290–300.

Golden JL (2009) *Message in a Bottle: The Making of Fetal Alcohol Syndrome*. Cambridge: Harvard University Press.

Goldenberg DM (2003) *The Curse of Ham: Race and Slavery in Early Judaism, Christianity, and Islam*. Princeton: Princeton University Press.

Goldschmidt R (1937) Spontaneous chromatin rearrangements and the theory of the gene. *Proceedings of the National Academy of Sciences of the United States of America* 23(12): 621–623.

Goldschmidt R (1940) *The Material Basis of Evolution*. New Haven: Yale University Press.

Goldstein M (1943) *Demographic and Bodily Changes in Descendants of Mexican Immigrants: With Comparable Data on Parents and Children in Mexico*. Austin: Institute of Latin-American Studies, University of Texas.

Golinski J (2010) *British Weather and the Climate of Enlightenment*. Chicago: University of Chicago Press.

Gómez-Díaz E and Corces V (2014) Architectural proteins: Regulators of 3D genome organization in cell fate. *Trends in Cell Biology* 24(11): 703–711.

Gordin MD (2015). *Scientific Babel: How Science Was Done before and after Global English*. Chicago: University of Chicago Press.

Gould SJ (2002) *The Structure of Evolutionary Theory*. Cambridge: Harvard University Press.

Gowland R (2015) Entangled lives: Implications of the developmental origins of health and disease hypothesis for bioarchaeology and the life course. *American Journal of Physical Anthropology* 158(4): 530–540.

Graham DW (2015) Heraclitus. In EN Zalta (ed.) *The Stanford Encyclopedia of Philosophy*. Stanford: Stanford University.

Graham L (2014) A rise in nationalism in Putin's Russia threatens the country's science–again. *The Conversation*, 14. https://theconversation.com/a-rise-in-nationalism-in-putins-russia-threatens-the-countrys-science-again-41403

Graham L (2016) *Lysenko's Ghost*. Cambridge: Harvard University Press.

Grant M (2000) *Galen on Food and Diet*. New York: Routledge.

Grayson SE, Ponce de Leon FA and Muscoplat CC (2014) Epigenetics: Understanding how our choices lead to our diseases. *Journal of Clinical Case Reports* 4: 447.

Greco M (1998) *Illness as a Work of Thought: A Foucauldian Perspective on Psychosomatics*. London: Routledge.

Griesemer J (2002) What is "epi" about epigenetics? *Annals of the New York Academy of Sciences* 981(1): 97–110.

Griesemer J (2014) Reproduction and scaffolded developmental processes: An integrated evolutionary perspective. In A Minelli and T Pradeu (eds.) *Towards a Theory of Development* (pp. 183–202). Oxford: Oxford University Press.

Griesemer J (2018) Landscapes of developmental collectivity. In S Gissis, E Lamm and A Shavit (eds.) *Landscapes of Collectivity in the Life Sciences*. Cambridge, Mass: MIT Press.

Griffiths P and Stotz K (2006) Genes in the postgenomic era. *Theoretical Medicine and Bioethics* 27(6): 499.

Griffiths P and Stotz K (2013) *Genetics and Philosophy*. Cambridge: Cambridge University Press.

Grimsley DL and Windholz GL (2000) The neurophysiological aspects of Pavlov's theory of higher nervous activity: In honor of the 150th anniversary of Pavlov's birth. *Journal of the History of the Neurosciences* 9(2): 152–163.

Gudding G (1996) The phenotype/genotype distinction and the disappearance of the body. *Journal of the History of Ideas* 57(3): 525–545.

Günther H (1928) *Platon als hüter des lebens: Platons zucht-und erziehungsgedanken und deren bedeutung für die gegenwart*. Munich: JF Lehmann.

Guthman J and Mansfield B (2013) The implications of environmental epigenetics: A new direction for geographic inquiry on health, space, and nature-society relations. *Progress in Human Geography* 37(4): 486–504.

Guttinger S and Dupré J (2016) Genomics and postgenomics. In EN Zalta (ed.) *The Stanford Encyclopedia of Philosophy*. Stanford: Stanford University.

Hacking I (1996) The looping effects of human kinds. In D Sperber, D Premack and AJ Premack (eds.) *Causal Cognition*. Oxford: Oxford University Press.

Hacking I (2002) "Style" for historians and philosophers. In *Historical Ontology* (pp. 178–199). Cambridge: Harvard University Press.

Haig D (2004) The (dual) origin of epigenetics. *Cold Spring Harbor Symposia on Quantitative Biology* 69: 67–70.

Haig D (2011) Commentary: The epidemiology of epigenetics. *International Journal of Epidemiology* 41(1): 13–16.

Hales C and Barker D (1992) Type 2 (non-insulin-dependent) diabetes mellitus: The thrifty phenotype hypothesis. *Diabetologia* 35(7): 595–601.

Haller J (1971) *Outcasts from Evolution: Scientific Attitudes of Racial Inferiority, 1859–1900*. Urbana: University of Illinois Press.

Hallgrímsson B and Hall B (Eds.) (2011) *Epigenetics: Linking Genotype and Phenotype in Development and Evolution*. Berkeley: University of California Press.

Hallowell N (1999) Doing the right thing: Genetic risk and responsibility. *Sociology of Health & Illness* 21(5): 597–621.

Hallowell N, Arden-Jones A, Eeles R et al. (2006) Guilt, blame and responsibility: Men's understanding of their role in the transmission of BRCA1/2 mutations within their family. *Sociology of Health & Illness* 28(7): 969–988.

Hanghøj K and Orlando L (2018) Ancient epigenomics. In OP Rajora (ed.) *Population Genomics*. Cham: Springer.

Hannaford I (1996) *Race: The History of an Idea in the West*. Washington: Woodrow Wilson Center Press.

Hanson M, Low F and Gluckman P (2011) Epigenetic epidemiology: The rebirth of soft inheritance. *Annals of Nutrition and Metabolism* 58(Suppl. 2): 8–15.

Hanson MA and Skinner MK (2016) Developmental origins of epigenetic transgenerational inheritance. *Environmental Epigenetics* 2(1): 1–9.

Haraway D (1999) The biopolitics of postmodern bodies: Determinations of self in immune system discourse. In J Price and M Shildrick (eds.) *Feminist Theory and the Body: A Reader*. New York: Routledge.

Harrison M (1999) *Climates and Constitutions*. New York: Oxford University Press.

Harrison M (2000) From medical astrology to medical astronomy: Sol-lunar and planetary theories of disease in British medicine, c. 1700–1850. *The British Journal for the History of Science* 33(1): 25–48.

Harwood J (1993) *Styles of Scientific Thought: The German Genetics Community 1900–1933*. Chicago: University of Chicago Press.

Hasian MA Jr. (1996) *The Rhetoric of Eugenics in Anglo-American Thought*. Athens: University of Georgia Press.

Hasson O (2009) On sex-differences and science in Huarte de San Juan's "examination of men's wits". *Iberoamerica Global* 2(1): 195–212.

Hayles NK (1999) *How We Became Posthuman: Virtual Bodies in Cybernetics, Literature, and Informatics*. Chicago: Chicago University Press.

He XJ, Zhou LB, Pan QZ et al. (2017). Making a queen: An epigenetic analysis of the robustness of the honeybee (*Apis mellifera*) queen developmental pathway. *Molecular Ecology* 26(6): 1598–1607.

Healy M (2001) *Fictions of Disease in Early Modern England: Bodies, Plagues and Politics*. Basingstoke: Palgrave Macmillan.

Heard E and Martienssen R (2014) Transgenerational epigenetic inheritance: Myths and mechanisms. *Cell* 157(1): 95–109.

Heath D, Rapp R and Taussig KS (2004) Genetic citizenship. In D Nugent and J Vincent (eds.) *A Companion to the Anthropology of Politics* (pp.152–167). Hoboken: Wiley-Blackwell.

Heerboth S, Lapinska K, Snyder N, et al. (2014) Use of epigenetic drugs in disease: An overview. *Genetics & Epigenetics* 6: 9–19.

Helman CG (1984) *Culture, Health and Illness*. Boca Raton: CRC Press.

Herder JG (1778 [2002]) *Sculpture*. Chicago: University of Chicago Press.

Hertzman C and Boyce T (2010). How experience gets under the skin to create gradients in developmental health. *Annual Review of Public Health* 31: 329–347.

Hippocrates (1999) *On Head Wounds*. M Hanson (ed., trans.). Berlin: Akademie Verlag.

Hirai H (2005) *Le concept de semence dans les theories de la matiere a la Renaissance de Marsile Ficin ai Pierre Gassendi*. Turnhout: Brepols.

Hirai H (2007a) The invisible hand of god in seeds: Jacob Schegk's theory of plastic faculty. *Early Science and Medicine* 12(4): 377–404.

Hirai H (2007b) Semence, vertu formatrice et intellect agent chez Nicolò Leoniceno entre la tradition arabo-latine et la renaissance des commentateurs grecs. *Early Science and Medicine* 12(2): 134–165.

Hirai H (2016) Souls, formative power and animal generation in Renaissance medical debates. In A Blank (ed.) *Animals: New Essays*. Munich: Philosophia.

Hirai H (2017) Imagination, maternal desire and embryology in Thomas Fienus. In G Manning and C Klestinec (eds.) *Professors, Physicians and Practices in the History of Medicine*. Berlin: Springer.

Hobsbawm EJ (1995) *The Age of Empire, 1875–1914*. London: Weidenfeld & Nicolson.

Hodge J (2009) Darwin, the Galapagos and his changing thoughts about species origins: 1835–1837. *Proceedings of the California Academy of Sciences* Ser. 4, 61 (Supplement II): 89–106.

Hogben LT (1933) *Nature and Nurture*. New York: W.W. Norton Company.

Holliday R and Pugh JE (1975) DNA modification mechanisms and gene activity during development. *Science* 187(4173): 226–232.

Holliday R (2006) Epigenetics: A historical overview. *Epigenetics* 1(2): 76–80.

Holmes FL (1986) Claude Bernard, the" Milieu Intérieur", and regulatory physiology. *History and Philosophy of the Life Sciences* 8(1): 3–25.

Holquist M (1990) *Dialogism: Bakhtin and His World*. London: Routledge.

Hopwood N (2007) Artist versus anatomist, models against dissection: Paul Zeiller of Munich and the revolution of 1848. *Medical History* 51(3): 279–308.

Horden P and Hsu E (2013) *The Body in Balance: Humoral Medicine in Practice*. New York: Berghan.

Horstman J (2010) *Brave New Brain*. San Francisco: Jossey-Bass.

Horvath S (2013) DNA methylation age of human tissues and cell types. *Genome Biology* 14(10): 3156.

Horvath S, Gurven M, Levine ME et al. (2016) An epigenetic clock analysis of race/ethnicity, sex, and coronary heart disease. *Genome Biology* 17(1): 171.

Horvath S and Raj K (2018) DNA methylation-based biomarkers and the epigenetic clock theory of ageing. *Nature Reviews Genetics* 19(6): 371–384.

Huet M (1993) *Monstrous Imagination*. Cambridge: Harvard University Press.

Hughes V (2014) Epigenetics: The sins of the father. *Nature* 507: 22–24.

Hulse F (1981) Habits, habitats, and heredity: A brief history of studies in human plasticity. *American Journal of Physical Anthropology* 56(4): 495–501.

Hunter WB Jr (1950) The seventeenth century doctrine of plastic nature. *Harvard Theological Review* 43: 197–213.

Huxley J (1949) *Soviet Genetics and World Science.* London: Chatto & Windus.

Ingold T (1986) *Evolution and Social Life.* London: Routledge.

Ingold T and Palsson G (2013) *Biosocial Becomings: Integrating Social and Biological Anthropology.* Cambridge: Cambridge University Press.

Irby G (2016) Climate and courage. In RF Kennedy and M Jones-Lewis (eds.) *The Routledge Handbook of Identity and the Environment in the Classical and Medieval Worlds.* London: Routledge.

Isaac B (2006) *The Invention of Racism in Classical Antiquity.* Princeton: Princeton University Press.

Ishizuka H (2012) Fibre body: The concept of fibre in eighteenth-century medicine, c.1700–40. *Medical History* 56(4): 562–584.

Isrovich H (2015) New research discovery: Holocaust survivors "inherit" negative genetic changes. *Maariv,* 23 August.

Ivanovsky A (1923) Physical modifications of the population of Russia under famine. *American Journal of Physical Anthropology* 6(4): 331–353.

Iyengar S (2013) *Shades of Difference: Mythologies of Skin Color in Early Modern England.* Philadelphia: University of Pennsylvania Press.

Jablonka E and Lamb M (1989) The inheritance of acquired epigenetic characteristics. *Journal of Theoretical Biology* 139: 69–83.

Jablonka E and Lamb M (1995). *Epigenetic Inheritance and Evolution: The Lamarckian Dimension.* Oxford: Oxford University Press.

Jablonka E and Raz G (2009). Transgenerational epigenetic inheritance: Prevalence, mechanisms, and implications for the study of heredity and evolution. *Quarterly Review of Biology* 84: 131–176.

Jablonka E (2012) Behavioral epigenetics in ecological context. *Behavioral Ecology* 24(2): 325–326.

Jablonka E (2013) Epigenetic inheritance and plasticity: The responsive germline. *Progress in Biophysics and Molecular Biology* 111(2–3): 99–107.

Jablonka E and Lamb M (2014) *Evolution in Four Dimensions* (2nd ed.). Cambridge: MIT Press.

Jablonka E (2016) Cultural epigenetics. *The Sociological Review Monographs* 64: 42–60.

Jacob F and Monod J (1961) Genetic regulatory mechanisms in the synthesis of proteins. *Journal of Molecular Biology* 3(3): 318–356.

James W (1878) Remarks on Spencer's definition of mind as correspondence. *Journal of Speculative Philosophy* 12: 1–18.

James W (1880) Great men, great thoughts, and the environment. *Atlantic Monthly* 46: 441–459.

James W (1890) *The Principles of Psychology.* New York: H. Holt and Company.

James W (1988) *Manuscript Lectures.* Cambridge: Harvard University Press.

Jamieson M (2016) The politics of immunity: Reading Cohen through Canguilhem and new materialism. *Body & Society* 22(4): 106–129.

Jasanoff S (2009) *The Fifth Branch: Science Advisers as Policymakers*. Cambridge: Harvard University Press.

Jasienska G (2009) Low birth weight of contemporary African Americans: An intergenerational effect of slavery? *American Journal Human Biology* 21: 16–24.

Jenuwein T and Allis CD (2001) Translating the histone code. *Science* 293(5532): 1074–1080.

Johannsen W (1911) The genotype conception of heredity. *The American Naturalist* 45(531): 129–159.

Johnson C (2015) *Darwin's Dice: The Idea of Chance in the Thought of Charles Darwin*. Oxford: Oxford University Press.

Jones M (2008) *Skin Tight: An Anatomy of Cosmetic Surgery*. Oxford: Berg Publishers.

Jordanova L (1984) *Lamarck*. Oxford: Oxford University Press.

Jordanova L (1989) Nature's powers: A reading of Lamarck's distinction between creation and production. In JR Moore (ed.) *History, Humanity, and Evolution*. Cambridge: Cambridge University Press.

Jouanna J (1999) *Hippocrates*. Baltimore: Johns Hopkins University Press.

Joubert BR, Haberg SE, Nilsen RM et al. (2012). 450K epigenome-wide scan identifies differential DNA methylation in newborns related to maternal smoking during pregnancy. *Environmental Health Perspectives* 120: 1425–1431.

Kaati G, Bygren LO and Edvinsson S (2002) Cardiovascular and diabetes mortality determined by nutrition during parents' and grandparents' slow growth period. *European Journal of Human Genetics* 10: 682–688.

Kaiser J (2012) Genetic influences on disease remain hidden. *Science* 338(6110): 1016–1017.

Kalff S (2012) The body is a battlefield. In M Horstmanshoff, H King and C Zittel (eds). *Blood, Sweat and Tears – The Changing Concepts of Physiology from Antiquity* (pp. 171–194). Leiden: Brill.

Kant I (1784 [2013]) *An Answer to the Question: "What Is Enlightenment?"* UK: Penguin.

Kaplan B (1954) Environment and human plasticity. *American Anthropologist* 56(5): 780–800.

Kaplan P (2016) Location and dislocation in early Greek geography and ethnography. In RF Kennedy and M Jones-Lewis (eds.) *The Routledge Handbook of Identity and the Environment in the Classical and Medieval Worlds* (pp. 301–302). London: Routledge.

Kay LE (1993) *The Molecular Vision of Life*. Oxford: Oxford University Press.

Kay LE (2000) *Who Wrote the Book of Life?* Stanford: Stanford University Press.

Kay MA (1977) The Florilegio medicinal: Source of southwest ethnomedicine. *Ethnohistory* 24(3): 251–259.

Kazachenka, A., Bertozzi, T. M., Sjoberg-Herrera, M. K., Walker, N., Gardner, J., Gunning, R., ... & Ferguson-Smith, A. C. (2018). Identification, Characterization, and Heritability of Murine Metastable Epialleles: Implications for Non-genetic Inheritance. *Cell. 25 Oct*

Keller EF (1991) Genetics, reductionism, and the normative uses of biological information: Response to Kevles [comments]. *Southern California Law Review* 65(1): 285–292.

Keller EF (1992) Between language and science: The question of directed mutation in molecular genetics. *Perspectives in Biology and Medicine* 35(2): 292–306.

Keller EF (1996) *Refiguring Life: Metaphors of Twentieth Century Biology (The Wellek Library Lectures at the University of California, Irvine)*. New York: Columbia University Press.

Keller EF (2000) *The Century of the Gene*. Cambridge: Harvard University Press.

Keller EF (2011) Genes, genomes, and genomics. *Biological Theory* 6: 132–140.

Keller EF (2014) From gene action to reactive genomes. *Journal of Physiology* 592(11): 2423–2429.

Keller EF (2015) The postgenomic genome. In S Richardson and H Stevens (eds.) *Postgenomics: Perspectives on Biology after the Genome* (pp. 9–31). Durham: Duke University Press.

Kellermann NP (2013) Epigenetic transmission of Holocaust trauma: Can nightmares be inherited? *The Israel Journal of Psychiatry and Related Sciences* 50(1): 33.

Kelly A (1981) *The Descent of Darwin: The Popularization of Darwinism in Germany: 1860–1914*. Chapel Hill: University of North Carolina.

Kennedy RF (2016) Airs, waters, metals, earth: People and environment in archaic and classical Greek thought. In RF Kennedy and M Jones-Lewis (eds.) *The Routledge Handbook of Identity and the Environment in the Classical and Medieval Worlds* (pp. 23–42). London: Routledge.

Ker HJ (2017) *Epigenetics, Changing Understandings and Alternative Models of Heredity* (Master Thesis). Auckland: The University of Auckland.

Kern S (1975) *Anatomy and Destiny: A Cultural History of the Human Body*. New York: Bobbs-Merrill.

Kerr A and Cunningham-Burley S (2000) On ambivalence and risk: Reflexive modernity and the new human genetics. *Sociology* 34(2): 283–304.

Khlustova Y (2015) Holocaust and the Leningrad Siege are stuck in the genes. *Gazeta. Ru*, 24 August.

Kiberstis PA (2017) Cancer epigenetics in the driver's seat. *Science* 357(6348): 263–265.

Kimmel MS (2011) *Manhood in America*. Oxford: Oxford University Press.

King H (1998) *Hippocrates' Woman: Reading the Female Body in Ancient Greece*. New York: Routledge.

King H (2013) Female fluids in the Hippocratic corpus: How solid was the humoral body? In P Horden and E Hsu (eds.) *The Body in Balance: Humoral Medicine in Practice*. New York: Berghahn.

Kirmayer L (2006). Toward a medicine of the imagination. *New Literary History* 37(3): 583–605.

Kirmayer LJ, Gone JP and Moses J (2014) Rethinking historical trauma. *Transcultural Psychiatry* 51(3): 299–319.

Klein A (2016) Obese grandfathers pass on their susceptibility to junk food. *New Scientist*. Daily News, 18 July.

Klein-Franke F (1984) *Iatromathematics in Islam: A Study on Yūḥannā ibn al-Ṣalt's Book on Astrological Medicine*. Hildesheim: G. Olms.

Klibansky R, Panofsky E and Saxl F (1964) *Saturn and Melancholy. Studies in the History of Natural Philosophy, Religion, and Art*. New York: Basic Books.

Klitzman R (2009) "Am I my genes?": Questions of identity among individuals confronting genetic disease. *Genetics in Medicine* 11(12): 880.

Klosko G (1991) "Racism" in Plato's Republic. *History of Political Thought* 12(1): 1–14.

Kolchinsky EI, Kutschera U, Hossfeld U et al. (2017) Russia's new Lysenkoism. *Current Biology* 27(19): R1042–R1047.

Koller A (1918) *The Theory of Environment, an Outline of the History of the Idea of Milieu, and its Present Status*. Menasha: Banta.

Koonin E and Wolf Y (2009). Is evolution Darwinian or/and Lamarckian? *Biology Direct* 4: 42–57.

Koonin E (2012) *The Logic of Chance: The Nature and Origin of Biological Evolution*. Upper Saddle River: Pearson Education.

Koopman C (2013) *Genealogy as Critique: Foucault and the Problems of Modernity*. Bloomington: Indiana University Press.

Kowal E (2016) The promise of Indigenous epigenetics. *Discover Society* 4 October.

Kraft A and Rubin B (2016) Changing cells: An analysis of the concept of plasticity in the context of cellular differentiation. *Biosocieties* 11: 497–525.

Krishnaveni G and Yajnik C (2017) Developmental origins of diabetes – an Indian perspective. *European Journal of Clinical Nutrition* 71(7): 865–869.

Kroeber A (1916) The cause of the belief in use inheritance. *The American Naturalist* 50: 367–370.

Kroeber A (1917) The superorganic. *American Anthropologist* 19: 163–213.

Kroeber AL (1945) The ancient Oikoumene as an historic culture aggregate. *The Journal of the Royal Anthropological Institute of Great Britain and Ireland* 75(1/2): 9–20.

Kroeber A (1952) *The Nature of Culture*. Chicago: University of Chicago Press.

Kroenfeldner M (2007) Is cultural evolution Lamarckian? *Biology & Philosophy* 22(4): 493–512.

Kroenfeldner M (2009) "If there is nothing beyond the organic": Heredity and culture at the boundaries of anthropology in the work of Alfred L. Kroeber. *NTM Journal of the History of Science, Technology and Medicine* 17: 107–133.

Kroker A and Kroker M (1996) *Hacking the Future: Stories for the Flesh-eating 90s*. Montreal: New World Perspectives.

Kühn S and Hofmeyr J-HS (2014) Is the "histone code" an organic code? *Biosemiotics* 7(2): 203–222.

Kuhn TS (2012) *The Structure of Scientific Revolutions*. Chicago: University of Chicago Press.

Kukla R (2005) *Mass Hysteria: Medicine, Culture, and Mothers' Bodies*. Lanham: Rowman & Littlefield.

Kuklick H (1996) Islands in the Pacific: Darwinian biogeography and British anthropology. *American Ethnologist* 23: 611–638.

Kuriyama S (1999) *The Expressiveness of the Body and the Divergence of Greek and Chinese Medicine*. New York: Zone Books.

Kuriyama S (2008) The forgotten fear of excrement. *Journal of Medieval and Early Modern Studies* 38(3): 414–441.

Kuzawa C and Quinn E (2009) Developmental origins of adult function and health: Evolutionary hypotheses. *Annual Review of Anthropology* 38: 131–147.

Kuzawa C and Sweet E (2009) Epigenetics and the embodiment of race: Developmental origins of US racial disparities in cardiovascular health. *American Journal of Human Biology* 21(1): 2–15.

Kuzawa C and Bragg JM (2012) Plasticity in human life history strategy: Implications for contemporary human variation and the evolution of genus homo. *Current Anthropology* 53(6): 369–385.

Kuzawa CW (2005) Fetal origins of developmental plasticity: Are fetal cues reliable predictors of future nutritional environments? *American Journal of Human Biology* 17: 5–21.

LaCapra D (1996) *Representing the Holocaust: History, Theory, Trauma*. Ithaca: Cornell University Press.

Laderman C (1987) Destructive heat and cooling prayer: Malay humoralism in pregnancy, childbirth and the postpartum period. *Social Science & Medicine* 25(4): 357–365.

LaFreniere P and MacDonald K (2013) A post-genomic view of behavioural development and adaptation to the environment. *Developmental Review* 33(2): 89–109.

Laird ES (1990) Robert Grosseteste, Albumasar and medieval tidal theory. *Isis* 81: 684–694.

Lamm E and Jablonka E (2008) The nurture of nature: Hereditary plasticity in evolution. *Philosophical Psychology* 21(3): 305–319.

Lamoreaux J (2016) What if the environment is a person? Lineages of epigenetic science in a toxic China. *Cultural Anthropology* 31(2): 188–214.

Landecker H (2007) *Culturing Life*. Cambridge: Harvard University Press.

Landecker H (2011) Food as exposure: Nutritional epigenetics and the new metabolism. *BioSocieties* 6(2): 167–194.

Landecker H and Panofsky A (2013) From social structure to gene regulation, and back: A critical introduction to environmental epigenetics for sociology. *Annual Review of Sociology* 39: 333–357.

Landecker H (2016) The social as signal in the body of chromatin. In M Meloni, S Williams and P Martin (eds.) *Biosocial Matters: Rethinking Sociology–Biology Relations in the Twenty-First Century*. Oxford: Wiley Blackwell.

Langford J (2002) *Fluent bodies: Ayurvedic remedies for postcolonial imbalance*. Durham: Duke University Press.

Lappé M and Landecker H (2015) How the genome got a life span. *New Genetics and Society* 34(2): 152–176.

Lappé M (2016) The maternal body as environment in autism science. *Social Studies of Science* 46(5): 675–700.

Laqueur TW (1990) *Making Sex: Body and Gender from the Greeks to Freud*. Cambridge: Harvard University Press.

Las Casas B (1821 [1542]) *Breve relación de la destrucción de las Indias Occidentales*. Philadelphia: Juan J Hurtel.

Las Casas B (1992 [1552]) *Apologética historia sumaria*. Obras completas Madrid, Junta de Andalucía – Sociedad Estatal Quinto Centenario – Alianza Editorial.

Lasker GW (1952) Environmental growth factors and selective migration. *Human Biology* 24(4): 262–289.

Lasker GW (1954) The question of physical selection of Mexican migrants to the U. S. A. *Human Biology* 26 (1): 52–58.

Latour B (1993) *We Have Never Been Modern*. C Porter (trans.). Cambridge: Harvard University Press.

Laufer BI, Kapalanga J, Castellani CA et al. (2015) Associative DNA methylation changes in children with prenatal alcohol exposure. *Epigenomics* 7(8): 1259–1274.

Lawson GM, Duda JT, Avants BB et al. (2013) Associations between children's socioeconomic status and prefrontal cortical thickness. *Developmental Science* 16: 641–652.

Le Doux J (2015) *Anxious: Using the Brain to Understand and Treat Fear and Anxiety*. New York: Penguin.

Lederberg J and Mccray A (2001) 'Ome sweet 'omics – A genealogical treasury of words. *The Scientist* 17(7): 8.

Lee KW, Richmond R, Hu P et al. (2015) Prenatal exposure to maternal cigarette smoking and DNA methylation: Epigenome-wide association in a discovery sample of adolescents and replication in an independent cohort at birth through 17 years of age. *Environmental Health Perspectives* 123(2): 193.

Lennox J (2015) Darwinism. In EN Zalta (ed.) *The Stanford Encyclopedia of Philosophy*. http://plato.stanford.edu/archives/sum2015/entries/darwinism/.

Lewis AJ, Austin E and Galbally M (2016) Prenatal maternal mental health and fetal growth restriction: A systematic review. *Journal of Developmental Origins of Health and Disease* 7(4): 416–428.

Lewis HS (2001). Boas, Darwin, science, and anthropology. *Current Anthropology* 42(3): 381–406.

Lewontin, RC (1983) The organism as the subject and object of evolution. Reprinted in R Levins and RC Lewontin (eds.) (1985) *The Dialectical Biologist*. Cambridge: Harvard University Press.

Li L, Choi J-Y, Lee K-M, et al. (2012) DNA methylation in peripheral blood: A potential biomarker for cancer molecular epidemiology. *Journal of Epidemiology* 22(5): 384–394.

Liang C, Oest ME and Prater MR (2009) Intrauterine exposure to high saturated fat diet elevates risk of adult-onset chronic diseases in C57BL/6 mice. *Birth Defects Research B Developmental and Reproductive Toxicology* 86: 377–384.

Liebeskind C (2002) Arguing science: Unani tibb, hakims and biomedicine in India, 1900–50. In W Ernst (ed.) *Plural Medicine, Tradition and Modernity, 1800–2000*. London: Routledge.

Lightman B (2015) *Global Spencerism: The Communication and Appropriation of a British Evolutionist (Cultural Dynamics of Science)*. Leiden: Brill.

Lillycrop KA and Burdge GC (2015) Maternal diet as a modifier of offspring epigenetics. *Journal of Developmental Origins of Health and Disease* 6(2): 88–95.

Limoges C (1970) Darwinisme et adaptation. *Revue des Questions Scientifiques* 141: 353–374.

Lindee S (2005) *Moments of Truth in Genetic Medicine*. Baltimore: Johns Hopkins University Press.

Ling C and Groop L (2009) Epigenetics: A molecular link between environmental factors and type 2 diabetes. *Diabetes* 58(12): 2718–2725.

Lippman A (1991) Prenatal genetic testing and screening: Constructing needs and reinforcing inequities. *American Journal of Law and Medicine* 17: 15–50.

Liu Y (2008) A new perspective on Darwin's Pangenesis. *Biological Reviews* 83(2): 141–149.

Livingstone D (1987) Human acclimatization: Perspectives on a contested field of inquiry in science, medicine and geography. *History of Science* 25: 359–394.

Livingstone D (1991) The moral discourse of climate: Historical considerations on race, place and virtue. *Journal of Historical Geography* 17(4): 413–434.

Lloyd GER (Ed.) (1978) *Hippocratic Writings*. J Chadwick (trans.). Harmondsworth: Penguin.

Lloyd S (2018) Suicide and the epigenetic turn. In L Manderson and E Cartwright (eds.) *The Routledge Handbook of Medical Anthropology* (pp. 324–329). New York: Routledge.

Lloyd S and Raikhel E (2018) Epigenetics and the suicidal brain: Reconsidering context in an emergent style of reasoning. In M Meloni, J Cromby, D Fitzgerald et al. (eds) *The Palgrave Handbook of Biology and Society*. London: Palgrave Macmillan.

Lock M and Nguyen V (2010) *An Anthropology of Biomedicine*. Oxford: Wiley-Blackwell.

Lock M (2012) The epigenome and nature/nurture reunification: A challenge for anthropology. *Medical Anthropology* 32(4): 291–308.

Lock M (2015) Comprehending the body in the era of the epigenome. *Current Anthropology* 56(2): 151–177.

Locke J (1689/1967) *Two Treaties of Government*. P Laslett (ed.). Cambridge: Cambridge University Press.

Loke YJ, Hannan AJ and Craig JM (2015) The role of epigenetic change in autism spectrum disorders. *Frontiers in Neurology* 6: 107.

Loison L (2010) *Qu'est-ce que le néolamarckisme? Les biologistes français et la question de l'évolution des espèces, 1870–1940*. Paris: Vuibert.

Loison L (2016) Forms of presentism in the history of science. Rethinking the project of historical epistemology. *Studies in History and Philosophy of Science* 60: 29–37.

Longfellow HW (1886) *The Divine Comedy of Dante Alighieri, Translated by Henry Wadsworth Longfellow (Vol. 11).* Boston, Mass: Riverside Press.

Lonie IM (1981) *The Hippocratic Treatises "On Generation", "On the Nature of the Child", "Diseases IV": A Commentary.* Berlin: De Gruyter.

Löwy I (2014) How genetics came to the unborn: 1960–2000. *Studies in History and Philosophy of Science Part C: Studies in History and Philosophy of Biological and Biomedical Sciences* 47: 154–162.

Löwy I (2017) *Imperfect Pregnancies: A History of Birth Defects and Prenatal Diagnosis.* Baltimore: Johns Hopkins University Press.

Luke B and Johnson TRB (1991) Nutrition and pregnancy: A historical perspective and update. *Women's Health Issues* 1(4):177–186.

Lupton D (2012) "Precious cargo": Foetal subjects, risk and reproductive citizenship. *Critical Public Health* 22(3): 329–340.

Lutz P and Turecki G (2014) DNA methylation and childhood maltreatment: From animal models to human studies. *Neuroscience* 264: 142–156.

Lyons J (1977) *Semantics.* Cambridge: Cambridge University Press.

MacArthur B, Ma'ayan A and Lemischka I (2009) Systems biology of stem cell fate and cellular reprogramming. *Nature Reviews Molecular Cell Biology* 10(10): 672.

Macpherson CB (1962) *The Political Theory of Possessive Individualism (Hobbes to Locke).* Oxford: Oxford University Press.

Maerker A (2011) *Model Experts. Wax Anatomies and Enlightenment in Florence and Vienna, 1775–1815.* Manchester and New York: Manchester University Press.

Majnik AV and Lane RH (2015) The relationship between early-life environment, the epigenome and the microbiota. *Epigenomics* 7(7): 1173–1184.

Malabou C (2005) *The Future of Hegel: Plasticity, Temporality and Dialectic.* London: Routledge.

Malabou C (2008) *What Should We Do with Our Brain?* New York: Fordham University Press.

Malabou C (2009) *Ontologie de l'accident: Essai sur la plasticité destructrice.* Paris: Editions Léo Scheer.

Malabou C (2010) *Plasticity at the Dust of Writing.* New York: Columbia University Press.

Malpas J (2012) *Heidegger and the Thinking of Place.* Cambridge: MIT Press.

Manikkam M, Tracey R, Guerrero-Bosagna C et al. (2012) Dioxin (TCDD) induces epigenetic transgenerational inheritance of adult onset disease and sperm epimutations. *PLoS ONE* 7(9): e46249.

Mansfield B (2017) Folded futurity: Epigenetic plasticity, temporality, and new thresholds of fetal life. *Science as Culture* 26(3): 355–379.

Marcum J (2005) *Thomas Kuhn's Revolution.* London: Bloomsbury.

Margueron R and Reinberg D (2010) Chromatin structure and the inheritance of epigenetic information. *Nature Reviews Genetics* 11(4): 285.

Marsit CJ (2015) Influence of environmental exposure on human epigenetic regulation. *Journal of Experimental Biology* 218(1): 71–79.

Martin A (2007) The chimera of liberal individualism: How cells became selves in human clinical genetics. *Osiris* 22: 205–222.

Martin A (2010) Microchimerism in the mother(land): Blurring the borders of body and nation. *Body & Society* 16(3): 23–50.

Martin A (2011) "Your mother's always with you:" Material feminism and fetomaternal microchimerism. *Resources for Feminist Research / Documentation sur la Recherche Féministe* 33(3/4): 31–46.

Martin E (1991) The egg and the sperm: How science has constructed a romance based on stereotypical male–female roles. *Signs: Journal of Women in Culture and Society* 16(3): 485–501.

Martin E (1994) *Flexible Bodies: Tracking Immunity in American Culture from the Days of Polio to the Age of AIDS*. Boston: Beacon Press.

Marwick E (1995) Nature versus nurture: Patterns and trends in seventeenth century French child-rearing. In L Demause (ed.) *The History of Childhood*. Lanham: Jason Aronson.

Marx K (1978) *The Eighteenth Brumaire of Louis Bonaparte. Vol. 11*. Peking: Foreign Languages Press.

Mattern S (2008) *Galen and the Rhetoric of Healing*. Baltimore: Johns Hopkins University Press.

Mattern S (2013) *The Prince of Medicine: Galen in the Roman Empire*. Oxford: Oxford University Press.

Mattick J (2003) Challenging the dogma: The hidden layer of non-proteincoding RNAs in complex organisms. *Bioessays* 25(10): 930–939.

Mattick J (2004) Opinion: RNA regulation: A new genetics? *Nature Reviews Genetics* 5(4): 316–323.

Maubray J (1724) *The female physician, containing all the diseases incident to that sex, in virgins, wives, and widows*. London: James Holland.

Maynard Smith J (1990) Models of a dual inheritance system. *Journal of Theoretical Biology* 143: 41–53.

Mayr E (1972) Lamarck revisited. Reprinted in E Mayr (ed.) *Evolution and the Diversity of Life: Selected Essays* (pp. 222–250). Cambridge: Harvard University Press.

Mayr E (1982) *The Growth of Biological Thought: Diversity, Evolution, and Inheritance*. Cambridge: Belknap Press.

Mazzolini R (2004) Plastic anatomies and artifical dissections. In S De Chadarevian and N Hopwood (eds.) *Models: The Third Dimension of Science* (pp. 43–70). Stanford: Stanford University Press.

McGowan P, Suderman M, Sasaki A et al. (2011) Broad epigenetic signature of maternal care in the brain of adult rats. *PLoS ONE* 6: e14739.

McGranahan L (2011) William James's social evolutionism in focus. *The Pluralist* 6: 80–92.

McGranahan L (2012) *William James's evolutionary pragmatism: A study in physiology, psychology, and philosophy at the close of the nineteenth century*. Dissertation. University of California Santa Cruz.

McGuinness D, McGlynn LM, Johnson PC et al. (2012) Socio-economic status is associated with epigenetic differences in the pSoBid cohort. *International Journal of Epidemiology* 41(1): 151–160.

Mead R (1708) *Of the Power and Influence of the Sun and Moon on Humane Bodies*. London: R. Wellington.

Meaney M (2010) Epigenetics and the biological definition of gene X environment interactions. *Child Development* 81(1): 41–79.

Meaney MJ (2004) The nature of nurture: Maternal effects and chromatin remodeling. In JT Cacioppo and GG Berntson (eds.) *Essays in Social Neuroscience* (pp. 1–14). Cambridge: MIT Press.

Meloni M and Testa G (2014) Scrutinizing the epigenetics revolution. *BioSocieties* 9(4): 431–456.

Meloni M (2016a) *Political Biology: Science and Social Values in Human Heredity from Eugenics to Epigenetics*. London: Palgrave.

Meloni M (2016b) The transcendence of the social: Durkheim, Weismann, and the purification of sociology. *Frontiers in Sociology* 1: 11.

Meloni M, Williams S and Martin P (2016) *Biosocial Matters: Rethinking the Sociology–Biology Relations in the Twenty-first Century*. Oxford: Wiley Blackwell.

Meloni M (2017) Race in an epigenetic time: Thinking biology in the plural. *The British Journal of Sociology* 68(3): 389–409.

Meloni M, Cromby J, Fitzgerald D, and Lloyd S (2018) (eds) *The Palgrave Handbook of Biology and Society*. London: Palgrave Macmillan.

Menand L (2001) *The Metaphysical Club: A Story of Ideas in America*. New York: Farrar, Straus and Giroux.

Menestò E (1991) *Il processo di canonizzazione di Chiara da Montefalco*. Spoleto: Centro Italiano di Studi sull'Alto Medioevo.

Mennella J (2014) Ontogeny of taste preferences: Basic biology and implications for health. *American Journal of Clinical Nutrition* 99(3): 704–711.

Meredith B (1988) *A Change for the Better*. London: Grafton Books.

Meskimmon M (2002) Time is of the essence: Histories, bodies and art. *Art History* 25: 697–700.

Meyerhof M (1931) Alî at-Tabarî's paradise of wisdom, one of the oldest Arabic compendiums of medicine. *Isis* 16(1): 6–54.

Mignolo W (2000) *Local Histories/Global Designs: Coloniality, Subaltern Knowledges, and Border Thinking*. Princeton: Princeton University Press.

Moczek, AP (2015) Re-evaluating the environment in developmental evolution. *Frontiers in Ecology and Evolution* 3(7): 1–8.

Moller A (Ed.) (2006) *Reprogramming the Brain (Vol. 157)*. Amsterdam: Elsevier.

Montesquieu CS (1748/1914) *The Spirit of Laws*. T Nugent (trans.) and JV Prichard (revised). London: Bell & Sons.

Montserrat D (1998) *Changing Bodies, Changing Meanings: Studies on the Human Body in Antiquity.* London: Routledge.

Moore D (2015) *The Developing Genome: An Introduction to Behavioural Epigenetics.* Oxford: Oxford University Press.

Moore GE and Stanier P (2013) Fat dads must not be blamed for their children's health problems. *BMC Medicine* 11: 30.

Morange M (2009) How phenotypic plasticity made its way into molecular biology. *Journal of Biosciences* 34: 495–501.

Morange M (2013) What history tells us XXXII. The long and tortuous history of epigenetic marks. *Journal of Biosciences* 38(3): 451–454.

Moss L (2003) *What Genes Can't Do.* Cambridge, MA: MIT Press.

Mottier V (2010) Eugenics and the state: Policy-making in comparative perspective. In A Bashford and P Levine (eds.) *The Oxford Handbook of the History of Eugenics* (pp. 142–143). Oxford: Oxford University Press.

Mozersky J (2012) Who's to blame? Accounts of genetic responsibility and blame among Ashkenazi Jewish women at risk of BRCA breast cancer. *Sociology of Health & Illness* 34(5): 776–790.

Muller H (1963/2008) Genetic progress by voluntarily conducted germinal choice. In *Ciba Foundation Symposium – Hormonal Influences in Water Metabolism (Book II of Colloquia on Endocrinology).* Hoboken: John Wiley & Sons.

Müller R and Kenney M (2018) Restorative Justice and the Epigenetics of Early Life Adversity: New Approaches to the Biosocial Effects of Trauma. EASST conference, Lancaster, UK, 25–28 August.

Müller-Wille S (2007) Hybrids, pure cultures, and pure lines: From nineteenth-century biology to twentieth-century genetics. *Studies in History and Philosophy of the Biological and Biomedical Sciences* 38(4): 796–806.

Müller-Wille S and Rheinberger H (2012) *A Cultural History of Heredity.* Chicago: University of Chicago Press.

Muri A (2003) Of shit and the soul: Tropes of cybernetic disembodiment in contemporary culture. *Body & Society* 9(3): 73–92.

Murphy M (2006) *Sick Building Syndrome and the Problem of Uncertainty: Environmental Politics, Technoscience, and Women Workers.* Durham: Duke University Press.

Nanney D (1958) Epigenetic control systems. *Proceedings of the National Academy of Sciences of the United States of America* 44: 712–717.

Nash L (2006) *Inescapable Ecologies: A History of Environment, Disease, and Knowledge.* Berkeley: University of California Press.

Nature Editorial (2012) Life stresses. *Nature* 490(7419) (11 October).

Nedelsky J (1990) Law boundaries and the bounded self. *Representations* 30: 162–189.

Needham J (1959) *A History of Embryology* (2nd ed.). Cambridge: Cambridge University Press.

Needham J, Lu G-D and Sivin N (2000) *Science and Civilisation in China: Volume 6, Biology and Biological Technology.* Cambridge: Cambridge University Press.

Nelkin D and Lindee MS (1995). *The DNA Mystique: The Gene as a Cultural Icon.* New York: Freeman.

Nelson A (2012) Reconciliation projects: From kinship to justice. In K Wailoo, A Nelson and C Lee (eds.) *Genetics and the Unsettled Past: The Collision of DNA, Race, and History.* New Brunswick: Rutgers University Press.

Nelson A (2016) *The Social Life of DNA: Race, Reparations, and Reconciliation after the Genome.* New York: Beacon Press.

Ng S-F, Lin RCY, Laybutt DR et al. (2010) Chronic high-fat diet in fathers programs β-cell dysfunction in female rat offspring. *Nature* 467: 963–966.

Nicholson DJ (2014) The return of the organism as a fundamental explanatory concept in biology. *Philosophy Compass* 9(5): 347–359.

Nicoglou A (2015) The evolution of phenotypic plasticity: Genealogy of a debate in genetics. *Studies in History and Philosophy of Science Part C: Studies in History and Philosophy of Biological and Biomedical Sciences* 50: 67–76.

Nicoglou A (2018) The concept of plasticity in the history of the nature–nurture debate in the early twentieth century. In M Meloni, J Cromby, D Fitzgerald et al. (eds.) *The Palgrave Handbook of Biology and Society.* London: Palgrave Macmillan.

Niebyl PH (1970) The non-naturals. *Bulletin of the History of Medicine* 45(5): 486–492.

Nieratschker V, Grosshans M, Frank J et al. (2014) Epigenetic alteration of the dopamine transporter gene in alcohol-dependent patients is associated with age. *Addiction Biology* 19(2): 305–311.

Nietzsche F (1873 / 1997) *Untimely Meditations.* D Brezaele (ed.) Cambridge: Cambridge University Press.

Niewöhner J (2011). Epigenetics: Embedded bodies and the molecularisation of biography and milieu. *BioSocieties* 6(3): 279–298.

Niewöhner J and Lock M (2018) Situating local biologies: Anthropological perspectives on environment / human entanglements. *BioSocieties*: 1–17.

Non AL and Thayer ZM (2015) Epigenetics for anthropologists: An introduction to methods. *American Journal of Human Biology* 27(3): 295–303.

Norris S and Richter L (2016) The importance of developmental origins of health and disease research for Africa. *Journal of Developmental Origins of Health and Disease* 7(2): 121–122.

Novas C and Rose N (2000) Genetic risk and the birth of the somatic individual. *Economy and Society* 29(4): 485–513.

Nuriel-Ohayon M, Neuman H and Koren O (2016) Microbial changes during pregnancy, birth, and infancy. *Frontiers in Microbiology* 7: 10–31.

Nutton V (2004) *Ancient Medicine.* London: Routledge.

Oaks L (2001) *Smoking & Pregnancy: The Politics of Fetal Protection.* New Brunswick: Rutgers University Press.

Ojakangas M (2016a) *On the Greek Origins of Biopolitics: A Reinterpretation of the History of Biopower.* London: Routledge.

Ojakangas M (2016b) Biopolitics in the political thought of Classical Greece. *The Routledge Handbook of Biopolitics*. London: Routledge.

Olby R (1970) Francis Crick, DNA, and the Central Dogma. *Daedalus* 99: 938, 987.

Olby R (1974) *The Path to the Double Helix: The Discovery of DNA*. Seattle: University of Washington Press.

Olby R (2009) Variation and inheritance. In M Ruse and R Richards (eds.) *The Cambridge Companion to the "Origin of Species"* (pp. 30–46). Cambridge: Cambridge University Press.

Olden K, Lin YS, Gruber D et al. (2014) Epigenome: Biosensor of cumulative exposure to chemical and nonchemical stressors related to environmental justice. *American Journal of Public Health* 104(10): 1816–1821.

Olins DE and Olins AL (2003) Chromatin history: Our view from the bridge. *Nature Reviews Molecular Cell Biology* 4(10): 809.

Osborne MA (1996) Resurrecting Hippocrates: Hygienic sciences and the French scientific expeditions to Egypt, Morea and Algeria. In D Arnold (ed.) *Warm Climates and Western Medicine: The Emergence of Tropical*. Amsterdam: Rodopi.

Osborne MA (2000) Acclimatizing the world: A history of the paradigmatic colonial science. *Osiris* 5: 135–115.

Ospovat D (1995) *The Development of Darwin's Theory: Natural History, Natural Theology, and Natural Selection, 1838–1859*. Cambridge: Cambridge University Press.

Öst A, Lempradl A, Casas E et al (2014) Paternal diet defines offspring chromatin state and intergenerational obesity. *Cell* 159(6): 1352–1364.

Ouellet-Morin I , Wong CCY, Danese A et al. (2013) Increased serotonin transporter gene (SERT) DNA methylation is associated with bullying victimization and blunted cortisol response to stress in childhood: A longitudinal study of discordant monozygotic twins. *Psychological Medicine* 43(9): 1813–1823.

Overgaard M and Jensen M (2012) *Consciousness and Neural Plasticity*, Frontiers Research Topic, accessed at www.frontiersin.org/research-topics/77/consciousness-and-neural-plasticity

Padel R (1992) *In and Out of the Mind: Greek Images of the Tragic Self*. Princeton: Princeton University Press.

Pagel W (1982) *Paracelsus: An Introduction to Philosophical Medicine in the Era of the Renaissance*. Basel: Karger Medical and Scientific Publishers.

Paillard J (1976) Réflexions sur l'usage du concept de plasticité en neurobiologie. *Journal de Psychologie Normale et Pathologique* 1(1): 33–47.

Painter R, Osmond C, Gluckman P et al. (2008) Transgenerational effects of prenatal exposure to the Dutch famine on neonatal adiposity and health in later life. *BJOG: An International Journal of Obstetrics and Gynaecology* 115: 1243–1249.

Pallister JL (trans.) (1982) *Ambroise Paré, On Monsters and Marvels*. Chicago: University of Chicago Press.

Panofsky A (2014) *Misbehaving Science: Controversy and the Development of Behavior Genetics*. Chicago: University of Chicago Press.

Papadopoulos D (2011) The imaginary of plasticity: Neural embodiment, epigenetics and ecomorphs. *The Sociological Review* 59(3): 432–456.

Pappas G, Kiriaze IJ and Falagas ME (2008) Insights into infectious disease in the era of Hippocrates. *International Journal of Infectious Diseases* 12(4): 347–350.

Parel A (1992) *The Machiavellian Cosmos*. New Haven: Yale University Press.

Park DC and Huang C-M (2010) Culture wires the brain. A cognitive neuroscience perspective. *Perspectives on Psychological Science* 5(4): 391–400.

Park E, Kim Y, Ryu H et al. (2014) Epigenetic mechanisms of Rubinstein–Taybi syndrome. *Neuromolecular Medicine* 16(1): 16–24.

Park K (1998) Impressed images: Reproducing wonders. In CA Jones and P Galison (eds.) *Picturing Science, Producing Art* (pp. 254–271). New York: Routledge.

Park K (2002) Relics of a fertile heart: The "autopsy" of Clare of Montefalco. In AL McClanan and K Rosoff Encarnacion (eds.) *The Material Culture of Sex, Procreation, and Marriage in Premodern Europe* (pp.115–133). New York: Palgrave.

Paster GK (1993) *The Body Embarrassed: Drama and the Disciplines of Shame in Early Modern England*. Ithaca: Cornell University Press.

Paster GK (2004) *Humoring the Body: Emotions and the Shakespearean Stage*. Chicago: University of Chicago Press.

Pastore N (1949) *The Nature–Nurture Controversy*. New York: King's Crown Press.

Paul AM (2010) *Origins: How the Nine Months before Birth Shape the Rest of Our Lives*. New York: Simon and Schuster.

Paul D (2009) Darwin, social darwinism, and eugenics. In J Hodge and G Radick (eds.) *The Cambridge Companion to Darwin* (2nd ed.) (pp. 219–245). Cambridge: Cambridge University Press.

Paul D and Brosco J (2013) *The Paradox of PKU: A Short History of a Genetic Disease*. Baltimore: Johns Hopkins University Press.

Pearce T (2010) From "circumstances" to "environment". *Studies in History and Philosophy of Biological and Biomedical Sciences* 41: 241–252.

Peel J (1971) *Herbert Spencer: The Evolution of a Sociologist*. New York: Basic Books.

Peet R (1985) The social origins of environmental determinism. *Annals of the Association of American Geographers* 75(3): 309–333.

Pembrey M, Saffery R and Bygren LO (2014) Human transgenerational responses to early-life experience: Potential impact on development, health and biomedical research. *Journal of Medical Genetics* 51(9): 563–572.

Pembrey ME, Bygren LO, Kaati G et al. (2006) Sex-specific, male-line transgenerational responses in humans. *European Journal of Human Genetics* 14(2):159–166.

Pennisi E (2017) Watch the human genome fold itself in four dimensions. *Science Blogs*, 10 October 2017, accessed at www.sciencemag.org/news/2017/10/watch-human-genome-fold-itself-four-dimensions

Pentecost M (2018) The first thousand days. In M Meloni, J Cromby, D Fitzgerald et al (eds.) *The Handbook of Biology and Society*. London: Palgrave.

Perkins A (2016) *The Welfare Trait: How State Benefits Affect Personality*. London: Springer.

Pernick MS (1997) Eugenics and public health in American history. *American Journal of Public Health* 87(11): 1767–1772.

Perroud N, Rutembesa E and Paoloni-Giacobino A (2014) The Tutsi genocide and transgenerational transmission of maternal stress. *World Journal of Biological Psychiatry* 15: 334–345.

Petersen A (1998) The new genetics and the politics of public health. *Critical Public Health* 8(1): 59–71.

Petersen A and Bunton R (2002) *The New Genetics and the Public's Health*. London and New York: Psychology Press.

Peterson E (2017) *The Life Organic: The Theoretical Biology Club and the Roots of Epigenetics*. Pittsburgh: University of Pittsburgh Press.

Petit A (1997) L'héritage de Lamarck dans la philosophie positive d'Auguste Comte. In G. Laurent (ed.) *Jean-Baptiste Lamarck, 1744–1829* (pp. 543–556). Paris: CTHS.

Pickersgill M (2016) Epistemic modesty, ostentatiousness and the uncertainties of epigenetics: On the knowledge machinery of (social) science. *The Sociological Review* 64(1_suppl): 186–202.

Pigliucci M (2001) *Phenotypic Plasticity: Beyond Nature and Nurture*. Baltimore: The Johns Hopkins University Press.

Pigliucci M, Murren CJ and Schlichting CD (2006) Phenotypic plasticity and evolution by genetic assimilation. *Journal of Experimental Biology* 209: 2362–2367.

Pigliucci M and Müller G (eds.). (2010) *Evolution: The Extended Synthesis.* Cambridge: MIT Press.

Pinto-Correia C (1997) *The Ovary of Eve: Egg and Sperm and Preformation*. Chicago: University of Chicago Press.

Pitts-Taylor V (2010) The plastic brain: Neoliberalism and the neuronal self. *Health* 14(6): 635–652.

Pitts-Taylor V (2016) *The Brain's Body: Neuroscience and Corporeal Politics*. Durham: Duke University Press.

Plato (2004) *Theaetetus.* Newburyport: Focus Publishing/R Pullins & Co.

Pliny the Elder (1991) *Natural History: A Selection*. London: Penguin Books Ltd.

Plomin R and McGuffin P (2003) Psychopathology in the postgenomic era. *Annual Review of Psychology* 54(1): 205–228.

Plomin R, DeFries J, Craig I et al. (Eds.) (2003) *Behavioral Genetics in the Postgenomic Era*. Washington: American Psychological Association.

Pohodich AE and Zoghbi HY (2015) Rett syndrome: Disruption of epigenetic control of postnatal neurological functions. *Human Molecular Genetics* 24(R1): R10–R16.

Portela A and Esteller M (2010) Epigenetic modifications and human disease. *Nature Biotechnology* 28(10): 1057.

Prainsack B (2017) The "we" in the "me": Solidarity and health care in the era of personalized medicine. *Science, Technology, & Human Values* 43(1): 21–44.

Prescott SL and Logan AC (2016) Transforming life: A broad view of the developmental origins of health and disease concept from an ecological justice perspective. *International Journal of Environmental Research and Public Health* 13(11): 1075.

Preus A (2007) *Historical Dictionary of Ancient Greek Philosophy (Vol. 78).* New York: Scarecrow Press.

Proctor RN and Schiebinger L (Eds.) (2008) *Agnotology: The Making and Unmaking of Ignorance.* Stanford: Stanford University Press.

Profet M (1995) *Protecting Your Baby-to-Be: Preventing Birth Defects in the First Trimester.* New York: Perseus Books.

Prussing E (2014) Historical trauma: Politics of a conceptual framework. *Transcultural Psychiatry* 51(3): 436–458.

Rabelais F (1991) *The Complete Works of François Rabelais.* D Frame (trans.). Berkeley: University of California Press.

Radford EJ, Ito M, Shi H et al. (2014). In utero undernourishment perturbs the adult sperm methylome and intergenerational metabolism. *Science* 345(6198): 1255903.

Radick G (2016) Presidential address: Experimenting with the scientific past. *The British Journal for the History of Science* 49(2): 153–172.

Raj K (2013) Beyond postcolonialism … and postpositivism: Circulation and the global history of science. *Isis* 104(2): 337–347.

Rando O (2012) Daddy issues: Paternal effects on phenotype. *Cell* 151: 702–708.

Rando O and Simmons R (2015). I'm eating for two: Parental dietary effects on off-spring metabolism. *Cell* 161(1): 93–105.

Rando O (2016) Intergenerational transfer of epigenetic information in sperm. *Cold Spring Harbor Perspectives in Medicine* 6(5): a022988.

Rapp R (2000) *Testing Women, Testing the Fetus: The Social Impact of Amniocentesis in America.* London: Routledge.

Rather LJ (1968) The six things non-natural: A note on the origin and fate of a doctrine and a phrase. *Clio Medical* 13: 337–347.

Reardon, J (2017) *The Postgenomic Condition.* Chicago: Chicago UP.

Redinger S, Norris SA, Pearson RM, et al. (2017) First trimester antenatal depression and anxiety: Prevalence and associated factors in an urban population in Soweto, South Africa. *Journal of Developmental Origins of Health and Disease* 9(1): 30–40.

Rees T (2016) *Plastic Reason: An Anthropology of Brain Science in Embryogenetic Terms.* Berkeley: University of California Press.

Reichard JF and Puga A (2010) Effects of arsenic exposure on DNA methylation and epigenetic gene regulation. *Epigenomics* 2(1): 87–104.

Reiss TJ (2003) *Mirages of the Selfe: Patterns of Personhood in Ancient and Early Modern Europe.* Stanford: Stanford University Press.

Relton CL, Hartwig FP and Smith GD (2015) From stem cells to the law courts: DNA methylation, the forensic epigenome and the possibility of a biosocial archive. *International Journal of Epidemiology* 44(4): 1083–1093.

Resnick I and Albertus Magnus (2010) *On the Causes of the Properties of the Elements.* Milwaukee: Marquette University Press.

Reynolds G (2014) How exercise changes our DNA. *New York Times,* 17 December.

Rheinberger H-J (2003) Gene Concepts. Fragments from the perspective of molecular biology. In P. Beurton, R. Falk and HJ Rheinberger (eds.) *The Concept of the Gene in Development and Evolution. Historical and Epistemological Perspectives* (pp. 219–239). Cambridge: Cambridge University Press.

Rheinberger H-J (2010) *On Historicizing Epistemology.* Stanford: Stanford University Press.

Rheinberger H-J and Müller-Wille S (2017) *The Gene: From Genetics to Postgenomics.* Chicago: University of Chicago Press.

Richards E (2006) Inherited epigenetic variation: Revisiting soft inheritance. *Nature Reviews Genetics* 7: 395–401.

Richards R (1987) *Darwin and the Emergence of Evolutionary Theories of Mind and Behavior.* Chicago: University of Chicago Press.

Richardson R (2006) *William James: In the Maelstrom of American Modernism.* Boston: Houghton Mifflin.

Richardson S, Daniels CR, Gillman MW et al. (2014) Society: Don't blame the mothers. *Nature* 512: 131–132.

Richardson S (2015) Maternal bodies in the postgenomic order. In S Richardson and H Stevens (eds.) *Postgenomics* (pp. 201–231). Durham: Duke University Press.

Richardson S and Stevens H (eds.) (2015) *Postgenomics.* Durham: Duke University Press.

Richardson W (1974) *Heidegger: Through Phenomenology to Thought.* The Hague: Martinus Nijhof.

Ridley M and Matthews P (1999) *Genome: The Autobiography of a Species in 23 Chapters* (p. 12). London: Fourth Estate.

Risse G (1997) La synthese entre la anatomie et la chirurgie. In M Grmek (ed.) *Histoire de la Pensee Medical Occidentale Vol. 2* (pp. 177–197). Paris: Seuil.

Roberts EF (2017) WHAT GETS INSIDE: Violent entanglements and toxic boundaries in Mexico City. *Cultural Anthropology* 32(4): 592–619.

Roberts EF and Sanz C (2018) Bioethnography: A how-to guide for the twenty-first century. In Meloni et al. (Eds) *The Palgrave Handbook of Biology and Society* (pp. 749–775). London: Palgrave Macmillan.

Roberts M (2013) Ways of seeing: Whakapapa. *Sites* 10(1): 93–120.

Rodgers AB, Morgan CP, Bronson SL et al. (2013) Paternal stress exposure alters sperm microRNA content and reprograms offspring HPA stress axis regulation. *Journal of Neuroscience* 33(21): 9003–9012.

Rodríguez-Paredes M and Esteller M (2011) Cancer epigenetics reaches mainstream oncology. *Nature Medicine* 17(3): 330.

Romanes G (1899) *An Examination of Weismannism* (2nd ed.). Chicago: Open Court.

Romm JS (1994) *The Edges of the Earth in Ancient Thought: Geography, Exploration, and Fiction.* Princeton: Princeton University Press.

Roodenburg H (1988) The maternal imagination. The fears of pregnant women in seventeenth-century Holland. *Journal of Social History* 21(4): 701–716.

Roos AM (2000) Luminaries in medicine: Richard Mead, James Gibbs, and solar and lunar effects on the human body in early modern England. *Bulletin of the History of Medicine* 74: 433–457.

Roper AG (1913) *Ancient Eugenics: The Arnold Prize Essay for 1913*. Oxford: Blackwell.

Rose N (1996) *Inventing Our Selves: Psychology, Power and Personhood*. Cambridge: Cambridge University Press.

Rose N (2007) *The Politics of Life Itself: Biomedicine, Power, and Subjectivity in the Twenty-First Century*. Princeton, NJ: Princeton University Press.

Rose N and Abi-Rached J (2013) *Neuro: The New Brain Sciences and the Management of the Mind*. Princeton: Princeton University Press.

Rosen C (2004) *Preaching Eugenics: Religious Leaders and the American Eugenics Movement*. Oxford: Oxford University Press.

Rosenberg C (1985) The therapeutic revolution. In JW Leavitt and RL Numbers (eds.) *Sickness and Health in America*. Madison: University of Wisconsin Press.

Rosenberg C (2012) Epilogue: Airs Waters Places. *Bulletin of the History of Medicine* 86(4): 661–670.

Rosenberg E, Sharon G and Zilber-Rosenberg I (2009) The hologenome theory of evolution contains Lamarckian aspects within a Darwinian framework. *Environmental Microbiology* 11: 2959–2962.

Rosenberg E and Zilber-Rosenberg I (2014) *The Hologenome Concept: Human, Animal and Plant Microbiota*. Dordrecht: Springer Science & Business Media.

Rosenthal C and Vanderbeke D (2015) *Probing the Skin: Cultural Representations of Our Contact Zone*. Newcastle upon Tyne: Cambridge Scholars Publishing.

Rosivach VJ (1987) Autochthony and the Athenians. *Classical Quarterly* 37: 294–306.

Rothstein M, Cai Y and Marchant G (2009) The ghost in our genes: Legal and ethical implications of epigenetics. *Health Matrix* 19: 1–62.

Rothstein M, Harrell H and Marchant G (2017) Transgenerational epigenetics and environmental justice. *Environmental Epigenetics* 3(3): dvx011.

Rubin B (2009) Changing brains: The emergence of the field of adult neurogenesis. *BioSocieties* 4: 407–424.

Rugg-Gunn PJ, Ogbogu U, Rossant J et al. (2009) The challenge of regulating rapidly changing science: Stem cell legislation in Canada. *Cell Stem Cell* 4(4): 285–288.

Saavedra-Rodríguez L and Feig LA (2013) Chronic social instability induces anxiety and defective social interactions across generations. *Biological Psychiatry* 73: 44–53.

Saif L (2017) Between medicine and magic: Spiritual aetiology and therapeutics in medieval Islam. In S Bhayro and C Rider (eds.) *Demons and Illness from Antiquity to the Early-Modern Period* (pp. 313–338). Leiden: Brill.

Saleeby C (1914) *The Progress of Eugenics*. London: Cassell and Company, Ltd.

Sanchez-Mut JV and Gräff J (2015) Epigenetic alterations in Alzheimer's disease. *Frontiers in Behavioral Neuroscience* 9: 347.

Sanderson S (2007) *Evolutionism and its Critics: Deconstructing and Reconstructing an Evolutionary Interpretation of Human Society*. Boulder: Paradigm Publisher Press.

Sapolsky R (2014) Sperm contains dad's lifestyle information alongside basic genetic material. *Wall Street Journal* 11 September.

Sapp J (1983) The struggle for authority in the field of heredity, 1900-1932: New perspectives on the rise of genetics. *The Journal of the History of Biology* 16; 311–342.

Sapp J (1987) *Beyond the Gene: Cytoplasmic Inheritance and the Struggle for Authority in Genetics*. New York: Oxford University Press.

Sargent F (1982) *Hippocratic Heritage. A History of Ideas about Weather and Human Health*. New York and Oxford: Pergamon Press.

Schabas M (1990) Ricardo naturalized: Lyell and Darwin on the economy of nature. In DE Moggridge (ed.) *Perspectives on the History of Economic Thought, Vol. III, Classicals, Marxians and Neo-Classicals*. Hants: Edward Elgar Publishing Limited.

Schaffer S (2010) The astrological roots of mesmerism. *Studies in History and Philosophy of Biological and Biomedical Sciences* 41(2): 158–168.

Schmidt A (2013) *The Concept of Nature in Marx*. London: Verso.

Schoenfeldt M (1997) Fables of the belly in early modern England. In D Hillman and C Mazzio (eds.) *The Body in Parts: Fantasies of Corporeality in Early Modern Europe* (pp. 243–262). London: Routledge.

Schoenfeldt M (1999) *Bodies and Selves in Early Modern England*. Cambridge: Cambridge University Press.

Schweber S (1977) The origin of the "Origin" revisited. *Journal of the History of Biology* 10(2): 229–316.

Schweber S (1980) Darwin and the political economists: Divergence of character. *Journal of the History of Biology* 13(2): 195–289.

Shackel P (2018). Structural violence and the industrial landscape. *International Journal of Heritage Studies*, 1–13.

Shapiro HL and Hulse F (1939) *Migration and Environment; a Study of the Physical Characteristics of the Japanese Immigrants to Hawaii and the Effects of Environment on Their Descendants*. London; New York: Oxford University Press.

Sharkey P (2014) *Stuck in Place: Urban Neighborhoods and the End of Progress toward Racial Equality*. Chicago: University of Chicago Press.

Sharma S, Kelly T and Jones P (2010) Epigenetics in cancer. *Carcinogenesis* 31(1): 27–36.

Sharp J (1671) *The Midwives Book, or, The Whole Art of Midwifry Discovered: Directing Childbearing Women how to Behave Themselves in Their Conception, Breeding, Bearing, and Nursing of Children in Six Books*. London: Simon Miller.

Shenk D (2010) *The Genius in All of Us: The New Science of Genes, Talent and Human Potential*. London: Icon.

Shiffman M (2011) *Aristotle's On the Soul*. Bemidji: Focus Publishing.

Shildrick M (2001) *Embodying the Monster: Encounters with the Vulnerable Self*. Thousand Oaks: Sage Publications.

Shostak S and Moinester M (2015) The missing piece of the puzzle? Measuring the environment in the postgenomic moment. In S Richardson and H Stevens (eds.) *Postgenomics: Perspectives on Biology after the Genome*. London: Duke University Press.

Siddiqui MZ (Ed.) (1996). *Firdausu'l HHikmat: Or paradise of wisdom*. Frankfurt am Main: Institute for the History of Arabic-Islamic Science at Johann Wolfgang Goethe University.

Simcock G, Kildea S, Elgbeili G et al. (2017) Prenatal maternal stress shapes children's theory of mind: The QF2011 Queensland Flood Study. *Journal of Developmental Origins of Health and Disease* 8(4): 483–492.

Siraisi N (1990) *Medieval and Early Renaissance Medicine: An Introduction to Knowledge and Practice.* Chicago: University of Chicago Press.

Siraisi NG (2015) *The Clock and the Mirror: Girolamo Cardano and Renaissance Medicine.* Princeton: Princeton University Press.

Skinner MK (2007) Endocrine disruptors and epigenetic transgenerational disease etiology. *Pediatric Research* 61(5 Part 2): 48R.

Skinner MK, Manikkam M, Tracey R et al. (2013) Ancestral dichlorodiphenyltrichloroethane (DDT) exposure promotes epigenetic transgenerational inheritance of obesity. *BMC Medicine* 11(1): 228.

Skinner MK (2015) Environmental epigenetics. *Environmental Epigenetics* 1(1): dvv002.

Sloan PR (1973) The idea of racial degeneracy in Buffon's *Histoire Naturelle.* In HE Pagliaro (ed.) *Racism in the Eighteenth Century (Vol. 3)* (pp. 293–321). Cleveland: Case Western Reserve University.

Small JP (1997) *Wax Tablets of the Mind: Cognitive Studies of Memory and Literacy in Classical Antiquity.* London: Routledge.

Smith J (2006) *The Problem of Animal Generation in Early Modern Philosophy* (Cambridge Studies in Philosophy and Biology). Cambridge: Cambridge University Press.

Smith J and Phemister P (2007) Leibniz and the Cambridge Platonist in the debate over plastic natures. In P. Phemister and S. Brown (eds.) *Leibniz and the English-Speaking World* (pp. 95–110). Dordrecht: Springer.

Smith J (2013) *Divine Machines: Leibniz and the Sciences of Life.* Princeton: Princeton University Press.

Smith PJ (2014) Landscape and body in Rabelais's Gargantua and Pantagruel. In W Melion, B Rothstein and M Weeman (eds.) *The Anthropomorphic Lens: Anthropomorphism, Microcosmism and Analogy in Early Modern Thought and Visual Arts* (pp. 67–92). Leiden: Brill.

Smith RW, Monroe C and Bolnick DA (2015) Detection of cytosine methylation in ancient DNA from five Native American populations using bisulfite sequencing. *PLoS ONE* 10(5): e0125344.

Snowden FM (1983) *Before Color Prejudice. The Ancient View of Blacks.* Cambridge: Harvard University Press.

Solomon H (2016) *Metabolic Living: Food, Fat, and the Absorption of Illness in India.* Durham: Duke University Press.

Soubry A, Schildkraut JM, Murtha A et al. (2013) Paternal obesity is associated with IGF2 hypomethylation in newborns: Results from a Newborn Epigenetics Study (NEST) cohort. *BMC Medicine* 11(1): 29.

Soubry A (2015) Epigenetic inheritance and evolution: A paternal perspective on dietary influences. *Progress in Biophysics and Molecular Biology* 118(1–2): 79–85.

Sparks CS and Jantz RL (2003) Changing times, changing faces: Franz Boas's Immigrant study in modern perspective. *American Anthropologist* 105(2): 333–337.

Spencer H (1851/1883). *Social Statics: Or, the Conditions essential to Happiness specified, and the First of Them Developed.* New York: Appleton and Co.

Spencer H (1855) *The Principles of Psychology.* London: Longman, Brown, Green, and Longmans.

Spencer H (1857) Progress: Its law and causes. *Westminster Review* 67(April): 445–447.

Spencer H (1876) The comparative psychology of man. *The Journal of the Anthropological Institute of Great Britain and Ireland* 5: 301–316.

Spencer H (1877) *The Principles of Sociology (Vol. 1)*. London: Williams and Norgate.

Spencer H (1886) *The Principles of Biology (Vol. 1)*. New York: Appleton and Co.

Spencer H (1891) *Essays: Scientific, Political, and Speculative*. London: Williams and Norgate.

Spiller E (2011) *Reading and the History of Race in the Renaissance*. Cambridge: Cambridge University Press.

Spitzer L (1942) Society milieu and ambiance: An essay in historical semantics. *Philosophy and Phenomenological Research* 3(2): 169–218.

Squier SM (2017) *Epigenetic Landscapes: Drawings as Metaphor*. Durham: Duke University Press.

Stahnisch FW (2003) Making the brain plastic: Early neuroanatomical staining techniques and the pursuit of structural plasticity, 1910–1970. *Journal of the History of the Neurosciences* 12(4): 413–435.

Stallins JA, Law D, Strosberg S and Rossi JJ (2016) Geography and postgenomics: How space and place are the new DNA. *GeoJournal* 83(1): 153–168.

Staum M (2011) *Nature and Nurture in French Social Sciences, 1859–1914 and beyond*. Montreal: McGill-Queens University Press.

Stepan N (1982) *The Idea of Race in Science: Great Britain, 1800–1960*. Hamden: Archon Books.

Stepan N (1991) *The Hour of Eugenics: Race, Gender, and Nation in Latin America*. Ithaca: Cornell University Press.

Stevens H (2016) *Biotechnology and Society: An Introduction*. Chicago: University of Chicago Press.

Stolberg M (2012) Sweat. Learned concepts and popular perceptions, 1500–1800. In H Horstmanshoff, H King and C Zittel (eds.) *Blood, Sweat and Tears: The Changing Concepts of Physiology from Antiquity into Early Modern Europe* (pp. 503–521). Leiden: Brill.

Stoler AL (1995) *Race and the Education of Desire: Foucault's History of Sexuality and the Colonial Order of Things*. Durham: Duke University Press.

Stotz K (2006) With genes like that, who needs an environment? Postgenomics' argument for the ontology of information. *Philosophy of Science* 73: 905–917.

Stotz K (2008) The ingredients for a postgenomic synthesis of nature and nurture. *Philosophical Psychology* 21: 359–381.

Strahl BD and Allis CD (2000). The language of covalent histone modifications. *Nature* 403(6765): 41.

Strasser B (2006) A world in one dimension: Linus Pauling, Francis Crick and the Central Dogma of Molecular Biology. *History and Philosophy of the Life Sciences* 28: 491–512.

Stringhini S, Polidoro S, Sacerdote C et al. (2015) Life-course socioeconomic status and DNA methylation of genes regulating inflammation. *International Journal of Epidemiology* 44(4): 1320–1330.

Stringhini S and Vineis P (2018) Epigenetic signatures of socioeconomic status across the lifecourse. In M Meloni, J Cromby, D Fitzgerald and S Lloyd (eds.) *The Palgrave Handbook of Biology and Society*. London: Palgrave Macmillan.

Sunder Rajan K (2006). *Biocapital: The Constitution of Postgenomic Life*. Durham: Duke University Press.

Szyf M (2001) Towards a pharmacology of DNA methylation. *Trends in Pharmacological Sciences* 22(7): 350–354.

Tabery J (2014) *Beyond versus: The Struggle to Understand the Interaction of Nature and Nurture*. Cambridge: MIT Press.

Takahashi K (2012) Cellular reprogramming – lowering gravity on Waddington's epigenetic landscape. *Journal of Cell Science* jcs-084822.

Takahashi K and Yamanaka S (2006) Induction of pluripotent stem cells from mouse embryonic and adult fibroblast cultures by defined factors. *Cell* 126(4): 663–676.

Takeshita C (2018) From mother/fetus to holobiont(s): A material feminist ontology of the pregnant body. *Catalyst: Feminism, Theory, Technoscience* 3(1): 128.

Tark-Dame M, van Driel R and Heermann D (2011) Chromatin folding – from biology to polymer models and back. *Journal of Cell Science* 124(6): 839–845.

Taschwer K (2016) *Der Fall Paul Kammerer: Das abenteurliche Leben des umstrittensten Biologen seiner Zeit*. Munich: Carl Hanser Verlag.

Taussig KS (1997) Calvinism and chromosomes: Religion, the geographical imaginary, and medical genetics in the Netherlands. *Science as Culture* 6(4): 495–524.

Taylor C (1989) *Sources of the Self: The Making of the Modern Identity*. Cambridge: Harvard University Press.

Temkin O (Ed.) (1956) *Soranus' Gynecology*. Baltimore: Johns Hopkins University.

Temkin O (1973) *Galenism: Rise and Decline of a Medical Philosophy*. Ithaca: Cornell University Press.

Thayer Z and Kuzawa C (2011) Biological memories of past environments: Epigenetic pathways to health disparities. *Epigenetics* 6(7): 798–803.

Thayer Z and Non AL (2015) Anthropology meets epigenetics: Current and future directions. *American Anthropologist* 117(4): 722–735.

Thayer Z, Barbosa-Leiker C, McDonell M et al. (2016) Early life trauma, post-traumatic stress disorder, and allostatic load in a sample of American Indian adults. *American Journal of Human Biology* 29(3): e22943.

Therborn G (2003) Entangled modernities. *European Journal of Social Theory* 6(3): 293–305.

The Economist (2013) Poisoned inheritance, 14 December. www.economist.com/news/science-and-technology/21591547-lack-folate-diet-male-micereprograms-their-sperm-ways

Thomas F (1925) *The Environmental Basis of Society*. New York and London: The Century Company.

Thomas R (2000) *Herodotus in Context: Ethnography, Science and the Art of Persuasion*. Cambridge: Cambridge University Press.

Thomson AJ (1911) *Darwinism and Human Life: The South African Lectures for 1909*. New York: Andrew Melrose.

Tilmann JP (1971) *An Appraisal of the Geographical Works of Albertus Magnus and His Contributions to Geographical Thought.* Ann Arbor: University of Michigan.

Todes DP (1989) *Darwin without Malthus: The Struggle for Existence in Russian Evolutionary Thought.* New York: Oxford University Press.

Todes DP (2014) *Ivan Pavlov: A Russian Life in Science.* Oxford: Oxford University Press.

Tollefsbol T (Ed.). (2017) *Handbook of Epigenetics: The New Molecular and Medical Genetics.* London: Academic Press.

Tolwinski K (2013) A new genetics or an epiphenomenon? Variations in the discourse of epigenetics researchers. *New Genetics and Society* 32(4): 366–384.

Tomes N (1999) *The Gospel of Germs: Men, Women, and the Microbe in American Life.* Cambridge: Harvard University Press.

Totelin L (2015) When foods become remedies in ancient Greece: The curious case of garlic and other substances. *Journal of Ethnopharmacology* 167: 30–37.

Toynbee A (1934) *A Study of History.* New York: Oxford University.

Trawick M (1992) Death and nurturance in Indian systems of healing. In C Leslie and A Young (eds.) *Paths to Asian Medical Knowledge* (pp. 129–159). Berkeley: University of California Press.

Tresch J (2012) *The Romantic Machine: Utopian Science and Technology after Napoleon.* Chicago: University of Chicago Press.

Tuana N (1988) Aristotle and the politics of reproduction. In B-A Bar On (ed.) *Engendering Origins: Critical Feminist Readings in Plato and Aristotle.* Albany: State University of New York Press.

Tuana N (2007) Viscous porosity: Witnessing Katrina. In S Alaimo and S Heikman (eds.) *Material Feminisms* (pp. 188–212). Bloomington: Indiana University Press.

Turner BS (1993) *Max Weber: From History to Modernity.* London: Routledge.

Ungerer M, Knezovich J and Ramsay M (2013) In utero alcohol exposure, epigenetic changes, and their consequences. *Alcohol Research: Current Reviews* 35(1): 37.

Urdinguio RG, Sanchez-Mut JV and Esteller M (2009) Epigenetic mechanisms in neurological diseases: Genes, syndromes, and therapies. *The Lancet Neurology* 8(11): 1056–1072.

van Dijck J (1998) *Imagenation, Popular Images of Genetics.* New York: New York University Press.

van Sertima I (1992) *The Golden Age of the Moor.* Piscataway: Transaction Publishers.

Vassoler FM, White SL, Schmidt HD et al. (2013) Epigenetic inheritance of a cocaine-resistance phenotype. *Nature Neuroscience* 16: 42–47.

Vineis P, Chatziioannou A, Cunliffe VT et al. (2017) Epigenetic memory in response to environmental stressors. *The FASEB Journal* 31(6): 2241–2251.

Waddington C (1940) *Organisers and Genes.* Cambridge: Cambridge University Press.

Waddington C (1957) *The Strategy of the Genes. A Discussion of Some Aspects of Theoretical Biology.* London: Allen & Unwin.

Waddington C (ed.) (1968) *Towards a Theoretical Biology.* Edinburgh: Edinburgh University Press.

Waddington C (2012, reprinted) The epigenotype. *International Journal of Epidemiology* 41: 10–13.

Waggoner M (2017) *The Zero Trimester: Pre-pregnancy Care and the Politics of Reproductive Risk*. Berkeley: University of California Press.

Wailoo K, Nelson A and Lee C (Eds.) (2012) *Genetics and the Unsettled Past: The Collision of DNA, Race, and History*. New Brunswick, NJ: Rutgers University Press.

Walters KL, Mohammed SA, Evans-Campbell T et al. (2011) Bodies don't just tell stories, they tell histories: Embodiment of historical trauma among American Indians and Alaska Natives. *Du Bois Review: Social Science Research on Race* 8(1): 179–189.

Walzer M (1984) I. Liberalism and the art of separation. *Political Theory* 12(3): 315–330.

Warbrick I, Dickson A, Prince R et al. (2016) The biopolitics of Māori biomass: Towards a new epistemology for Māori health in Aotearoa/New Zealand. *Critical Public Health* 26(4): 394–404.

Ward L (1891) *Neo-Darwinism and Neo-Lamarckism*. Washington: Press of Gedney & Roberts.

Warin M, Moore V, Zivkovic T et al. (2011) Telescoping the origins of obesity to women's bodies: How gender inequalities are being squeezed out of Barker's hypothesis. *Annals of Human Biology* 38(4): 453–460.

Warin M, Zivkovic Moore V and Davies M (2012) Mothers as smoking guns: Fetal overnutrition and the reproduction of obesity. *Feminism & Psychology* 2(3): 360–375.

Warin M, Moore V, Davies M et al. (2015) Epigenetics and obesity: The reproduction of habitus through intracellular and social environments. *Body & Society* 22(4): 53–78.

Warin M, Kowal E and Meloni M (2018) Indigenous knowledge in a postgenomic landscape: The politics of epigenetic hope and reparation in Australia. *Manuscript submitted for publication*.

Washbrook D (1997) From comparative sociology to global history: Britain and India in the pre-history of modernity. *Journal of the Economic and Social History of the Orient* 40(4): 410–443.

Wastell D and White S (2017) *Blinded by Science. The Social Implications of Epigenetics and Neuroscience*. London: Policy Press.

Watanabe A, Yamada Y and Yamanaka S (2013) Epigenetic regulation in pluripotent stem cells: A key to breaking the epigenetic barrier. *Philosophical Transactions of the Royal Society of London. Series B, Biological Sciences* 368(1609): 20120292.

Waterland RA and Jirtle RL (2003) Transposable elements: Targets for early nutritional effects on epigenetic gene regulation. *Molecular Cell Biology* 23: 5293–5300.

Watson E, Philippe J, Estelle DW et al. (2017) The effect of lifestyle interventions on maternal body composition during pregnancy in developing countries: A systematic review. *Cardiovascular Journal of Africa* 28: 1–7.

Watson S (1998) The neurobiology of sorcery: Deleuze and Guattari's brain. *Body and Society* 4(4): 23–45.

Weaver IC, Cervoni N, Champagne FA et al. (2004). Epigenetic programming by maternal behavior. *Nature Neuroscience* 7(8): 847.

Weber M (1930/2001) *The Protestant Ethic and the Spirit of Capitalism.* London: Routledge.

Weber B and Depew D (eds.) (2003) *Evolution and Learning: The Baldwin Effect Reconsidered.* Cambridge: MIT Press.

Webster C (1977) *The Great Instauration: Science, Medicine and Reform 1626–1660.* London: Duckworth.

Webster, E W (1923) Works of Aristotle, translated into English: Meteorologica. Oxford: Clarendon Press. Available at: http://classics.mit.edu/Aristotle/meteorology.html

Weidman NM (2006). *Constructing Scientific Psychology: Karl Lashley's Mind–Brain Debates.* Cambridge: Cambridge University Press.

Weingart P (2011) Struggle for existence: Selection, retention and extinction of a metaphor. In A Fasolo (ed.) *The Theory of Evolution and Its Impact* (pp. 69–82). Berlin: Springer.

Weismann A (1891) *Essays upon Heredity and Kindred Problems,* vol. 1. E Poulton (ed.). Oxford: Clarendon Press.

Weismann A (1892) Thoughts upon the musical sense in animals and man. In EB Poulton and AE Shipley (eds.) *Essays upon Heredity and Kindred Biological Problems.* Oxford: Clarendon Press.

Weiss SF (2010) *The Nazi Symbiosis: Human Genetics and Politics in the Third Reich.* Chicago: The University of Chicago Press.

Wells J (2010) Maternal capital and the metabolic ghetto: An evolutionary perspective on the transgenerational basis of health inequalities. *American Journal of Human Biology* 22(1): 1–17.

Wells JC (2012) The capital economy in hominin evolution: How adipose tissue and social relationships confer phenotypic flexibility and resilience in stochastic environments. *Current Anthropology* 53(S6): S466–S478.

Welshman J (2013) *Underclass: A History of the Excluded since 1880.* London: Bloomsbury.

West-Eberhard M (2003) *Developmental Plasticity and Evolution.* Oxford: Oxford University Press.

West-Eberhard MJ (2005) Developmental plasticity and the origin of species differences. *Proceedings of the National Academy of Sciences* 102(suppl 1): 6543–6549.

Wey Gómez N (2008) *The Tropics of Empire. Why Columbus Sailed South to the Indies.* Cambridge: MIT Press.

Wild CP (2005) Complementing the genome with an "exposome": The outstanding challenge of environmental exposure measurement in molecular epidemiology. *Cancer Epidemiology, Biomarkers & Prevention* 14 (8): 1847–1850.

Wild CP (2012) The exposome: From concept to utility. *International Journal of Epidemiology* 41(1): 24–32.

Will B, Dalrymple-Alford J, Wolff M et al. (2008) Reflections on the use of the concept of plasticity in neurobiology. *Behavioural Brain Research* 192(1): 7–11. Translation and adaptation by B Will, J Dalrymple-Alford, M Wolff et al. from J Paillard (1976) *Journal of Psychology* 1: 33–47.

Williams GC (1966) *Adaptation and Natural Selection: A Critique of Some Current Evolutionary Thought.* Princeton: Princeton University Press.

Wilson PK (1999) *Surgery, Skin and Syphilis: Daniel Turner's London.* Amsterdam: Rodopi.

Winther R (2000) Darwin on variation and heredity. *Journal of the History of Biology* 33(3): 425–455.

Worster D (1985) *Nature's Economy: A History of Ecological Ideas.* Cambridge: Cambridge University Press.

Wujastyk D (2003) *The Roots of Ayurveda: Selections from Sanskrit Medical Writings.* London: Penguin.

Wynne B (2005) Reflexing complexity: Post-genomic knowledge and reductionist returns in public science. *Theory, Culture & Society* 22(5): 67–94.

Yadav SP (2007) The wholeness in suffix-omics,-omes, and the word om. *Journal of Biomolecular Techniques: JBT* 18(5): 277.

Yajnik C (2001) Fetal origins of cardiovascular risk in developing countries. Paper presented at the First Congress on Fetal Origins of Adult Disease (Mumbai, India) February 2001.

Yajnik C (2004) Obesity epidemic in India: Intrauterine origins? *Proceedings of the Nutrition Society* 63(3): 387–396.

Yehuda R, Engel SM, Brand SR et al. (2005) Transgenerational effects of posttraumatic stress disorder in babies of mothers exposed to the World Trade Center attacks during pregnancy. *Journal of Clinical Endocrinology and Metabolism* 90(7): 4115–4118.

Yehuda R and Bierer LM (2008) Transgenerational transmission of cortisol and PTSD risk. *Progress in Brain Research* 167: 121–135.

Yehuda R, Golier JA, Bierer LM et al. (2010). Hydrocortisone responsiveness in Gulf War veterans with PTSD: Effects on ACTH, declarative memory hippocampal [(18)F]FDG uptake on PET. *Psychiatry Research* 184(2): 117–127.

Yehuda R, Daskalakis NP, Lehrner A et al. (2014) Influences of maternal and paternal PTSD on epigenetic regulation of the glucocorticoid-receptor gene in Holocaust survivor offspring. *American Journal of Psychiatry* 171(8): 872–880.

Yoshizawa RS (2016). Fetal–maternal intra-action: politics of new placental biologies. *Body & Society,* 22(4), 79–105.

Youdell D (2018) Genetics, Epigenetics and Social Justice in Education: Learning as a Complex Biosocial Phenomenon. In Meloni et al. (Eds.) *The Palgrave Handbook of Biology and Society* (pp. 275–316). London: Palgrave Macmillan.

Young RM (1969) Malthus and the evolutionists: The common context of biological and social theory. *Past & Present* 43: 109–145.

Zambelli P (1992) *The Spéculum Astronomiae and its Enigma: Astrology, Theology and Science in Albertus Magnus and his Contemporaries.* Berlin: Springer.

Zambelli P (2012) *Astrology and Magic from the Medieval Latin and Islamic World to Renaissance Europe: Theories and Approaches* (Variorum Collected Studies Series). Farnham: Ashgate.

Zammito JH (2006) Policing polygeneticism in Germany, 1775: (Kames,) Kant, and Blumenbach. In S Eigen and M Larrimore (eds.) *The German Invention of Race.* Albany: State University of New York Press.

Zimmermann F (1988) The jungle and the aroma of meats. *Social Science and Medicine* 27(3): 197–206.

Zirkle C (1946). The early history of the idea of the inheritance of acquired characters and of pangenesis. *Transactions of the American Philosophical Society* 35: 91–151.

Index

End of chapter notes are denoted by a letter n between page number and note number.